Sustainable Performance and Tourism

Sustainable Performance and Tourism:

A Collection of Tools and Best Practices

Edited by

José Mondéjar-Jiménez
Guido Ferrari
María-del-Val Segarra-Oña
and
Angel Peiró-Signes

CHARTRIDGE
BOOKS OXFORD

Chartridge Books Oxford
5 & 6 Steadys Lane
Stanton Harcourt
Witney
Oxford OX29 5RL, UK
Tel: +44 (0) 1865 882191
Email: editorial@chartridgebooksoxford.com
Website: www.chartridgebooksoxford.com

First published in 2014 by Chartridge Books Oxford

ISBN print: 978-1-909287-94-5
ISBN ebook: 978-1-909287-95-2

© The editors and the contributors, 2014

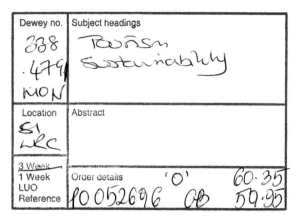

The right of the editors and the contributors to be identified as author of this work has been asserted by them in accordance with sections 77 and 78 of the Copyright, Designs and Patents Act 1988.

British Library Cataloguing-in-Publication Data: a catalogue record for this book is available from the British Library.

Chartridge Books Oxford is an imprint of Biohealthcare Publishing (Oxford) Ltd.

Produced from camera-ready copy supplied by the editors/contributors
Printed in the UK and USA

***To Dr. Paul P. Ting,
our particular surgeon in Shanghai,
with gratitude***

Preface

This book contains some of the contributions made at the V International Conference on Tourism and Environment that took place on Shanghai, China, on April 2013.

The editors present a collection of case studies and best practices linking sustainability to tourism. Taking a general view with chapters exploring ancient Mediterranean theatres or equestrian routes, slow tourism strategies, innovative marketing strategies based on murals, trade shows, social networks on protected areas or even GIS and new opportunities for ecotourism.

Especially interesting is the international approach that looks at the latest trends in a reach eco-environment like Latin America.

There are also ethical approaches and energy related analysis to respect the environment as the photovoltaic plants study, a regulatory analysis on competences on tourism and environment, a singular approach to the pensions´ systems and also to improve its measurements and metrics, as the USALI convention.

The role of corporations and their practices are addressed as well as the case study based on the reposition of the Neptuno terrace and the co-management of sustainable fisheries. The analysis of the touristic firms on an economic crisis environment adds the topically ingredient to this book. To sum up, the book gives a vast set of visions and innovations that link the growing and necessary sustainability movement in the sustainable tourism industry, with hands-on examples that show a wide range of examples.

We cannot conclude this preface without mentioning those great memories from our particular "China Adventure". We all greatly appreciate the assistance received from the Consul General of Spain in Shanghai, D. Gonzalo Ortiz and also the professional support given by Dr. Maite Calderon and the entire team of the Shanghai United Family Hospital, especially from Dr. Paul P. Ting, Chairman of Surgery.

Of course, nothing would have been possible without the guidance and leadership of Prof. Dr. Guido Ferrari, true "soul" of the Conference, and Prof. Dr. Zhao Yanyun´s motivation and enthusiasm. Our sincere thanks from the whole "G&T" team.

CONTENTS

Recreational carrying capacity as a tool for managing visitor experience and heritage protection of the ancient Mediterranean theatres

M. J. VIÑALS
Universitat Politècnica de València, Cartographic Engineering, Geodesy and Photogrammetry Department, Spain
M. MORANT
Universitat Politècnica de València, Cartographic Engineering, Geodesy and Photogrammetry Department, Spain
P. ALONSO-MONASTERIO
Universitat Politècnica de València, Cartographic Engineering, Geodesy and Photogrammetry Department, Spain
M. D. TERUEL
Universitat Politècnica de València, Economy and Social Sciences Departament, Spain

ABSTRACT

Tourism in Ancient Theatres demands specific tools to guarantee both the heritage protection and visitor satisfaction. This paper focuses on the elements of the Recreational Carrying Capacity Assessment, on its standards, especially those relating to perceptual components. As a result, a touring pattern for managing visitors in the Ancient Theatres is suggested to avoid negative impacts and congestion, as well as to provide quality experiences to visitors.

Six Mediterranean Roman Theatres were studied to test this procedure: The Theatres of Sagunto and Cartagena (both in Spain); the Theatre of Carthage (Tunis); and the Jordanian Theatres of Jerash, Amman and Petra.

1. INTRODUCTION

Ancient Theatres represent some of the most significant cultural heritage remains of the Greco-Roman Mediterranean civilizations. The diffusion of this architectural type throughout the whole Mediterranean Basin is extraordinary. These theatres are considered physical witnesses of the past. Thus, reconstructing and understanding the past allows local people to reinforce their identity links, and permits the general public access to history.

A large number of Ancient Theatres are still used for various activities; they serve as cultural venues, especially for performances and staging activities, but they are also important tourism attractions that can contribute to increasing public awareness and to local socio-economic development if they are managed adequately. Ancient Theatres, being outdoor heritage sites, are fragile and subject to physical degradation from natural hazards and weathering conditions, as well as from visitors and spectators. For these reasons, there is a need for technical management tools for tourism that avoid the degradation of these sites and contribute to appropriately conserving them.

This research is part of the Euromed Heritage Program[1] entitled, "Athena project. Ancient Theatres Enhancement for New Actualities". This paper focuses on tourism activities that take place in Ancient Theatres, and particularly on the planning and management tools that can contribute to heritage conservation and also those that can help provide a satisfactory experience to the visitors, as the Verona Charter[2] suggests. One of these tools, the Recreational Carrying Capacity Assessment (RCCA) procedure is analysed by this paper. RCCA has scientifically proven its value as an instrument that sets the limits of established and desired site conditions according to both the proposed recreational use level and conservation goals. RCCA addresses the question of how many people can be permitted into an area without risk of degrading it and the visitors' experience [1].

Previous studies on Ancient Theatres' management have dealt with theatres in the Mediterranean area. For example, the ERATO Project was devoted to the "Identification, evaluation and revival of the acoustical heritage of Ancient Theatres and Odea"[3]. Moreover, Haddad [2] studied, in the framework of this project, criteria for the modern uses assessment of these monuments. These criteria considered several parameters related to human comfort, in addition to architectural and acoustic qualities. Moreover, studies relating to the Seating Capacity of the theatres have also been performed. These studies consider the number of spectators that an Ancient Theatre can accommodate in staging and performing activities. However, no previous research has been identified that deals particularly with the Recreational Carrying Capacity Assessment for these sites. Coccossis and Mexa [3] broadly studied the limits related to the build-cultural environment aspects for cultural sites (ancient theatres, museums, etc.) and indicated the need to establish the cultural sites' capacity in terms of an acceptable level of congestion or density. Rose [4] also studied factors relating to spectators' comfort in Roman entertainment buildings, and Morant and Viñals [5], Viñals *et al.* [6] and Viñals *et al.* [7] have presented results regarding the recreational carrying capacity assessment of archaeological sites and other outdoor heritage sites.

Our research is based on literature review and field studies (direct and participative observation; space measurement, building design analysis, etc.) in several Ancient Theatres of the Mediterranean Basin: Sagunto (Valencia) and Cartagena (Murcia), both in Spain; Carthage in Tunis; and Amman, Jerash (Southern Theatre) and Petra in Jordan. These monuments were built between the 1st century BC (Cartagena) and the 2nd century

---

[1] EUROMED HERITAGE IV. European Neighbourhood and Partnership (ENP) financial co-operation with Mediterranean countries. EuropeAid/126266/C/ACT/Multi.

[2] The Verona Charter on the use of performance (1997) is the result of co-operation between the Council of Europe, the European Union and Unesco (Accessed 10 June 2012).

[3] This research project was implemented within the Fifth Framework INCOMED Program of the European Commission, under the thematic title 'Preserving and Using Cultural Heritage'.

AD (Carthage and Amman). This research applies the Recreational Carrying Capacity Assessment procedures to these Roman settings. General data regarding each theatre were obtained, but specific tourism information was not available for every site. Nevertheless, the similarities among the sites have allowed us to outline some relevant findings. In the study of Recreational Carrying Capacity, the modern setting of the theatres after their respective restoration projects is more important to the analysis than the original theatres' features. This is because the current spaces are the monuments' real available areas that can be visited. Therefore, the analysis has been performed on the basis of the monuments' current states.

2. APPLYING THE RECREATIONAL CARRYING CAPACITY ASSESSMENT (RCCA) PROCEDURE TO ANCIENT THEATRES

Although RCCA appears to be a simplistic and easy-to-implement tool, it is quite complex and operates based on a systematic approach, examining the areal issues from different perspectives and studying specific site conditions and limiting factors. It also must be considered within the framework of a large planning process for tourism development. The key components of the analysis are the following: the space where the activity takes place (size and features of the theatres); the resources involved; the recreational activities planned (interpretative and cultural visits); and the visitors' profiles, behaviours and expectations. In addition, conservation standards and aspects of visitors' physical and psychological comfort are considered. The results from the different analyses are then integrated, and finally, the relationships between the components, standards and limiting factors are highlighted.

The process to establish all of the aforementioned components and data follows the classical consecutive level approach: Physical Carrying Capacity (PCC), Real Carrying Capacity (RCC), and Effective Carrying Capacity (ECC). The analysed Mediterranean theatres follow, as do other Roman Theatres, a similar Vitrubian architectural structure. According to Segal [8], they can be considered as large theatres because all of them present a diameter exceeding 60 m (Sagunto: 90 m; Cartagena: 87.20 m; Carthage: 105 m; Jerash: 70.50 m; Amman: 102 m; Petra: 69 m). The theatres are semi-circular shaped and open air historical buildings consisting of different spaces: the auditorium or *cavea* (seating area), which is made up of several concentric rows of steps; the auditorium is radially split into sectors by stairs converging at the orchestra pit, which is a circular or semi-circular platform for musicians and dancers; a raised narrow platform called stage or scene (*scaena*) is situated within this circle; the scene building (*scaenae frons*) encloses the stage. Numerous and spacious entrances exist in the Ancient Theatres in order to safely handle the number of spectators in attendance. The most important entrances are the two *aditus maximum*, one on each *scaena* side, located between the orchestra and the scene (fig.1).

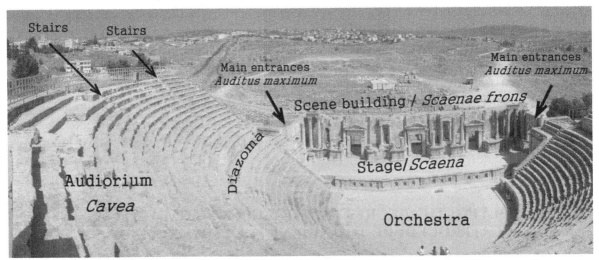

Figure 1. Different parts of an Ancient Theatre (Ancient Southern Theatre of Jerash, Jordan).

These ancient archaeological monuments are 2,000 years old or more. They were solidly constructed and have stood the test of time. The raw materials basically consist of hard stones such as limestone, sandstone or even marble rocks. The resources involved in the Recreational Carrying Capacity are the monuments themselves; in other words, the architectural structure is simultaneously both the main attraction and the physical support for the activities. This means that Ancient Theatres are subject to the natural damage caused by weathering and natural hazards (earthquakes, floods, fires, etc.), the damaging effects caused by humans throughout history (theft, vandalism, abandonment, war damage, etc.), and also the most recent damaging effects caused by staging and visitation activities. The impacts on the monuments can be multiple and represent a great threat to the conservation of this heritage.

Tourism activities, in particular visitation actions, are the focus of this RCCA study. These actions can fall within the category of leisure and entertainment activities or within the category of educational and interpretative ones. In the case of Ancient Theatres, interpretative activities have been identified as the best activities for providing historical knowledge and awareness to the public. Current types of visits to the analysed theatres that are commonly registered include extraordinary pre-arranged visits composed of special groups of experts, and ordinary visits (individual guided visits, individual self-guided visits, and domestic or international packaged guided tour groups).

2.1. Physical Carrying Capacity
The first stage in the RCCA is to determine the Physical Carrying Capacity (PCC), which is a rough estimation of the maximum number of visitors that an Ancient Theatre is actually able to support. In the case of individual attractions, as in our case, PCC will be the maximum number of people who can fit into the site at any given time and still allow people to be able to move.

PCC essentially addresses spatial considerations and is easier to determine in limited well-defined areas. Space limiting factors such as the existence of restricted areas must be taken into account because archaeological resources are unique and fragile[4] and must be preserved, and also for safety reasons. A clear exponent of this situation is the Theatre of Petra, where the Petra Archaeological Park authorities have recently prohibited entry by cordoning off the entire monument [9]. This site has suffered serious and constant deterioration over time due to its fragile sandstone rock structure, the earthquakes and floods of nearby Wadi Mousa (seasonal watercourse), and more recently the increasing foot tread associated with tourism visits. Consequently, the front of the theatre, including most of the stage building, has been seriously damaged. Regarding the impacts of tourism, Paradise [10] stated that in 1990, 15-20% of the theatre displayed original stonemason dressing marks, whereas in 1999, only 5-10% of the theatre exhibited the same stone dressing.

Spatial limitations can also result from the incompatibility of visitation activities with archaeological works in operation, and also with other staging and performance activities. This is the current situation in the Theatre of Carthage, where restoration and re-building works that have been carried out since the 1960s have arranged this space for theatrical performances, musical shows, and similar events. Currently, this theatre hosts the Carthage International Festival, but during the summer time, when this festival takes place, other visitation activities are not fully compatible with it due to the light, sound and audiovisual equipment, and stage sets and decor that are permanently installed during the entire performance season. The Theatre of Jerash is a similar case because in the summer time, the Festival of Arts takes place there, and the *cavea,* orchestra and stage are occupied by staging equipment, which makes access to the theatre difficult and also damages the aesthetics of the theatre.

In Ancient Theatres, the *cavea*, the orchestra pit, and partially and occasionally the stage can all be considered as suitable spaces for visitation activities. Nevertheless, some restoration works have restricted access to these areas, especially to some parts of the *summa cavea*. In the case of the Theatre of Sagunto, some areas of the *cavea* have not been restored, and now access to those areas has been barred by the use of fences and handrails, restricting in this way the available visiting area (fig.2). In the Theatre of Jerash, the *summa cavea* also cannot be used for visitation purposes due to its critical conservation condition and safety considerations.

---

[4] The Verona Charter suggests building "attractive paths that steer the public away from fragile areas. In some cases, access to sensitive or dangerous areas will have to be prohibited".

Figure 2. Restoration works in the *cavea* of the Theatre of Sagunto (Spain).

Once a zoning system is established that describes the Available Visiting Surface, the PCC can be easily calculated by following Boullon's formula [11]: the area used by visitors divided by the average individual standard. Using this method, peak capacity is obtained. The total number of daily visits is obtained by applying a rotation coefficient (number of daily hours available for the visit divided by average duration of the visit).

The standard of individual space requirements is directly linked to Visitors' Psychological Comfort. Proxemic studies developed by Hall [12] state that the need for inter-personal space in a social context is 120 cm^2 greater than the area used for seating capacity calculations, which is estimated at 0.5 m^2 per person following the Spanish National Regulation.

2.2. Real Carrying Capacity
The second stage in the RCCA is evaluation of the Real Carrying Capacity (RCC). This stage basically incorporates the limiting factors that reduce the maximum amount of visitors obtained from the previous PCC calculation. This stage includes the analysis of site conditions, as well as physical and social factors. This is the most complex stage to address because there are many variables influencing the analysis. The results of this stage of evaluation can vary according to the different settings, activities, resources or visitors' profiles considered. Thus, the limiting factors are not necessarily the same for each theatre; they are particular to each site.

Identification of the physical and social limiting factors is based upon the application of performance criteria. These are the standards that define the desirable site conditions. The method to use is the following: outperform an Inventory of Resources that records the current *status quo* of the ancient theatre elements, and then consider the minimal acceptable condition level needed to conserve the site while also expecting to improve the site as much as possible through management techniques and strategies. Furthermore, a direct and indirect, short-term and long-term impacts study must be performed in order to discern the different levels of archaeological elements degradation or even destruction, as well as the preventive and contingency measures necessary in order to prepare the site for presentation to the public. Results of this stage of the evaluation allow us to do the following: refine the zoning system previously established and determine the most appropriate areas for visitation (i.e., where materials, fabrics and pavements are inherently more resistant and where delicate floors are to be avoided); set the visitors' touring pattern inside the site, identifying areas that need particular physical protection through ropes, fences, handrails, etc.; and avoid improper uses.

Regarding tourism activities, it is necessary to undertake a detailed study of the features of and actions occurring during these activities. Consequently, information concerning activity schedules in terms of availability (explanations such as whether the activity is held on a daily, weekly, or monthly basis, and the reason for this schedule) and duration (the estimated time required to carry out the activity) is needed. Additionally, whether these activities are programmed or are sporadic or specific must be taken into account. Additionally, a detailed study evaluating the potential damage that public access may cause must be carried out. With regard to this issue, the most relevant degradations detected of archaeological sites are, as aforementioned, mechanical and occasionally voluntarily inflicted degradations that exist in various forms. Individually, a visitor does not cause significant damage, but many small acts of degradation are cumulative. Therefore, it may be argued that the risks to archaeological sites are to a certain extent related to the number of visitors. Another impact is the destruction of the archaeological setting (the falling of blocks and fabric degradation), which is closely related to the action of stepping on the archaeological structures. Littering is an action that often occurs and causes visual and olfactory impacts. Other voluntary damaging actions are related to plundering and looting, painting graffiti, carving on fabrics and committing vandalism.

On the other hand, limiting social factors are related to the Visitors' Psychological Comfort, as well as to their needs, motivations and expectations. Several variables must be taken into account in determining these social standards, including the following: features of the setting where the activity is held; thermo-hygrometric features that determine human bio-climatic comfort (weather limiting factors); visitors' motivations and behaviour; visitors' expectations; existing facilities (facilities limiting factor); and safety conditions (safety limiting factor). Several other social standards are usually considered as well, especially for highly frequented sites, such as visitors' perception of crowding and the number of visitor encounters with other groups at the site.

The configuration, shape and characteristics of the space where tourism activity takes place are important to the design and implementation of the optimal touring pattern for avoiding impacts and congestion and to provide a sound interpretation program and a quality experience to the visitors. The Ancient Theatres' configuration imposes a complicated touring pattern because they are open-air spaces with a high visual fragility due to the existence of many viewing locations, many available viewpoints (at the foreground, middle ground and background planes), and panoramic views. Nothing, including the presence of visitors, can be hidden in these sites. Visitors themselves also constitute an acoustic intrusion that reduces the quality of the experience.

The entrances to Ancient Theatres are the *aditus maximum*, but due to the ongoing restoration works and the overlapping of other structures, currently the entrances into the sites are different depending on the particular theatre. Only Sagunto and Jerash maintain the same access doors as the Roman theatres. The most striking example of an unconventional entry is that of the Theatre of Cartagena. Several historical building structures had overlapped the theatre over past centuries, the most significant of these structures being the Old Cathedral of the city, which was erected during the 13th century and laid over the *summa* (fig.3). Currently, the main entrance for visitors to this theatre is a zigzagging tunnel under the ruins of this medieval cathedral.

Figure 3. Old Cathedral door leading to the media cavea of the Theatre of Cartagena (Spain).

No matter which form the entrance access may take, the *orchestra* appears to be the best meeting point for visitors, and the first station on their tour. Moreover, walking the *cavea* implies going up steps and stairs. For these reasons, the logical touring pattern to guarantee minimum visual impact and the most physical and psychological comfort for visitors is a pie-shaped pathway, with the *orchestra* being the apex of the triangle and the side staircase providing access to the upper part of the *cavea* (*summa cavea*). Additionally, an access to the large passage or corridor (*diazoma*) between the *summa cavea* and *media cavea* must be facilitated for people with a lower physical fitness level.

Once in the upper or medium levels of rows, some spontaneous visitor diversions to the *media cavea* and *ima cavea* (lower part) can be permitted. Nevertheless, it is expected that visitors will not do much climbing or descending on the steps because it is exhausting (especially in the Theatre of Amman). Afterwards, the pathway leads visitors to come back down to the orchestra by descending the opposite side staircase (fig.4). Other pathways could be established from the orchestra to the stage when not in the staging season. In any case, it is important to emphasize that the orchestra is the core element from which groups must be organized and distributed to avoid congestion. The approximate length of this pathway should be between 90 m and 450 m, depending on the dimensions of the theatre; this means that visitors spend 30 min. to 50 min visiting the theatre.

Additionally, Ancient Theatres provide a unique sensory landscape due to their particular acoustic features. To enjoy this experience, one must be aware that a large number of visitors all talking at once can affect the theatre's acoustic performance and limit visitors' opportunity to benefit from the uniqueness of this special soundscape.

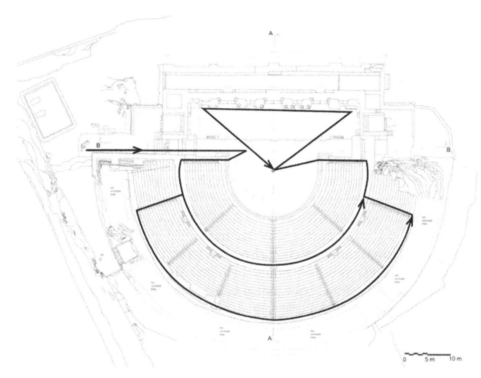

Figure 4. Suggested Touring Pattern for visiting the Southern Theatre of Jerash (Jordan).

Regarding weather limiting factors that determine the physical comfort of visitors, the thermo-hygrometric features of the Mediterranean climate allow the development of open-air activities throughout almost the entire year; therefore, the weather limiting factors are negligible. Nevertheless, summer time is the peak season for tourism and the higher temperatures occur in the early afternoon; therefore, visitation activities must be restricted during this time period to prevent the risk of heat strokes and heat exhaustion.

Visitors are another key component of the RCCA analysis. The crucial data in this stage of the study is the number of visitors. Accordingly, the total number of visitors per year must be registered, and the peak season and low season noted. Other useful data include the following: the maximum number of visitors recorded in one day (especially for theatres in those cities that are cruise ship destinations); the daily and monthly average number of visitors; and the types of visitors in terms of socio-demographic traits (national, international, age, gender, level of education, occupation, individuals or scholar groups, tourist package groups, others).

Unfortunately, there do not exist many socio-demographic studies concerning tourism in Ancient Theatres. The most accessible visitors' data are from the Theatre of Jerash, where the Jordan Ministry of Tourism and Antiquities has periodically performed survey campaigns over the last fifteen years. The results of these surveys show that the number of visitors to Jerash fluctuates between 100,000 to 300,000 per year. This oscillation in the annual visitation is attributable to international visitor flows that change due to the ongoing political conflicts in the surrounding countries and to the recent world economic crisis. Of this total amount of visitors, nearly 50,000 are always domestic visitors and the rest are foreign visitors, primarily Europeans and secondly Americans. This makes the archaeological site economically dependent solely on international tourism.

The peak visiting season for this theatre varies depending on visitor type: Jordanian visitors prefer to visit in July, whereas foreign visitors visit Jerash in the spring (March and April) and also in October [13]. International visitors come to Jerash as part of a one-day tour from Amman.

Abu Ali and Howaidee [14] described the demographic variables of Jerash visitors, stating that senior tourists (34.1%) were the most highly represented tourist group vacationing in Jerash during the spring season. The sample of respondents was very uniformly divided in terms of gender, with 56.9% males and 43.1% females. The majority (78%) of the surveyed tourists were visiting Jerash for the first time. There were more visits by group tour (54.5%) than visits by free individual groups (45.5%). Tourists who visited Jerash for leisure purposes comprised the largest proportion (65%). It can be concluded based on these results that International tourists are basically general or accidental cultural tourists that are not too specialized and have limited expectations for the visit. The highly motivated cultural tourist commonly prefers an individual visit and his/her expectations for the visit are high.

Different tour-operators as Kuoni, TuI or Kirunna dedicate the second day in Jordan to going to Jerash. All of the visitors reach Jerash in the morning and stay there until midday. The time spent in the ancient city of Jerash is just three hours, and because many tour-operators follow the same trip schedule, a concentration of visitors and buses is observed. Furthermore, not too much time on these tours can be devoted to visiting the Southern Theatre.

Although it is true that the volume of tourist flows is an important variable, McCool [15] and Pedersen [1] suggest that rather than the number of users, it is the behaviour of those users what creates the problematic impacts of recreational use.

Furthermore, it is important to guarantee psychological comfort for the visitors in order to provide a satisfactory experience for them. Therefore, understanding the needs and expectations of the visitors and designing activities to meet them is a relatively straightforward commitment. In addition to personal factors (age, gender, etc.), it is also crucial to consider the cultural backgrounds (beliefs, rituals, values, ways of thinking, etc.) and social influences (references groups, lifestyle, etc.) of visitors.

Visiting Mediterranean Ancient Theatres is an increasing trend among tourists, but when tourists choose a destination in which to spend their holiday, they look for vital experiences beyond just gaining knowledge regarding the heritage; thus, managers should not only strive to conserve and accurately present the site but also seek to evoke visitors' emotions and provide them with valuable experiences. This approach has already been adopted by the Verona Charter as a principle strongly recommended to ensure a satisfying and enjoyable experience for visitors. The authors of this research have not found examples of these practices, as the interpretation programs are not substantially developed.

The social limiting factors regarding the psychological comfort of users also incorporate other issues such as the perception of crowding, group size, and the number of encounters with other groups. Congestion or overcrowding of the main iconic attractions produces a psychological constraint to visitors. Other elements related to unsatisfactory experiences include the presence of large queues for some iconic attractions, and also for restrooms, entrances and ticket offices.

For interpretative and educational activities and to appreciate the theatre's visual and acoustical features, the suggested number of encounters with other groups must be low. This means that few groups can visit the theatre at the same time because visitors feel uncomfortable meeting many other people who do not belong to their group. Stankey and McCool [16] note that this experience greatly influences visitor attitudes towards encounters with others, and it is an indicator of satisfaction. Field observations show that most visitors prefer visiting these unique sites in the context of a quiet atmosphere and an acceptable solitude level; thus, no more than four or five groups should visit the site at the same time.

The American Educational Research Association [17], the National Gallery Management authorities (UK)[5] and the Alhambra (Granada, Spain) managers[6] have recommended groups of less than 30 people, and the appropriate group-size was established to be 20 people or less. Regarding the Ancient Theatres, it is reasonable to propose a group size limited to 10 people. This figure is justified by reasons of heritage conservation, safety measures, as well as educational and interpretative effectiveness.

The safety limiting factors are also strongly linked to visitors' physical and psychological comfort, and consequently to the quality of their experience. Safety issues concern the risks encountered by visitors during the course of their activity (i.e., places with stairs or slopes, irregular floor surface, holes, etc.) and must be taken into consideration, especially with regard to children and elderly visitors. Emergency and evacuation measures (ways of escape, entry/exit access, etc.) must be planned to reinforce visitors' perception of safety and, of course, to handle any contingency.

The facilities limiting factor the theatres' existing facilities and services. The study of facilities addresses their design and location, as these factors could have negative impacts on the settlement, aesthetics, visitors, etc. Recreational facilities in Ancient Theatres provide the physical support to handle various activities such as the Visitors' Welcome

---

[5] http://www.nationalgallery.org.uk/visiting/organise-a-group-visit/ (Accessed 3 September 2011)
[6] http://www.alhambra.org/esp/index.asp?secc=/alhambra/visitas (Accessed 3 September 2011)

services, the Information and Interpretation programs, the Awareness and Public Participation programs, the Visitors Management program, the Safety Measures program and the Promotion of the Institutional Public Image, among others.

There are several categories of recreational facilities in Ancient Theatres: basics (restrooms, paths and trails, first aid, parking area, entry/exit access, management offices, others); impaired facilities (adapted trails, disabled restrooms, handicap parking stalls, others); information facilities (reception and information points, information signage, directional signage); and interpretive facilities (interpretation centre, museum, cultural park, interpretative routes, interpretative signage). In general, the analysed theatres have the basic facilities, but impaired facilities are not evident when they exist; moreover, their information facilities are scarce and poor, and their interpretative ones are not located *in situ* but rather in the museums. Almost all of the theatres have a museum, but following old fashioned conceptions, these museums closer to archaeological remains collections.

In essence, social limiting factors, which basically involve visitor comfort, reduce the maximum number of visitors. In any case, many types of visitors exist, and it is necessary to have a solid knowledge of the target audience in order to implement the best measures for providing them with a quality experience. This finding implies that the level of reduction in the number of visitors due to limiting factors could vary depending on the visitors' profiles, needs, motivations and expectations.

2.3. Effective Carrying Capacity

Finally, the third analytical stage is the Effective Carrying Capacity (ECC) that evaluates the management capacity of the site administrators (managerial limiting factor). Managing capacity is defined as the sum of conditions that the site administrators require in order to carry out their functions and objectives [18]. Measuring managing capacity is not an easy task because many variables (several of which are quite subjective) are involved, such as policy measures, legislation, infrastructure, facilities and equipment, staff, funding, and motivation for heritage conservation.

Establishing appropriate prevention and protection policies is absolutely essential in order to avoid negative impacts on Ancient Theatres from recreational activities. Planning tools, such as zoning, and management techniques, such as visitor flow management as mentioned previously, can mitigate the recreation impacts. Moreover, alternative plans of action must be evaluated, and strategies for tourist development formulated. Additionally, the utilization of adequate information, interpretation, education, and involvement of visitors in the preservation process can help the management to achieve their conservation goals. Then, raising visitors' awareness and integrating them into the protection process not only contributes to site preservation but also provides visitors with a better quality experience.

Furthermore, an effective legal framework (mandatory permits, regulations, rules, restrictions, etc.) can help to reduce/mitigate the negative impacts of recreation in order to preserve the Ancient Theatres' valuable resources. Nevertheless, regulations by themselves are insufficient to conserve the sites, and the administrators also need to have the managing capacity to apply these legal measures.

Apparently, an effective legal framework exists to protect all of these theatres, but further developments are necessary in the field of tourism management. The aforementioned project ATHENA has developed guidelines to help the Ancient Theatres' managers implement a Management Plan that adequately addresses heritage conservation issues and public use activities. The Southern Theatre of Jerash was the pilot experience in applying these guidelines. According to these guidelines, a diagnostic analysis of the current situation was performed, highlighting its strengths and weaknesses, and several recommendations were consequently made.

It has been already stated that facilities definitively determine the maximum allowable number of visitors, independently of the available space. Regarding this point, excessive facilities is equally as harmful to conservation and recreation purposes as a lack of them. Therefore, an excessive number of facilities may provoke site damage by disguising the Real Carrying Capacity of the resources themselves. In addition, visitation facilities are scarce in comparison to the staging facilities that are quite bulky and heavy and cause a noticeable visual impact on the theatre. The only exception to this phenomenon is the Theatre of Cartagena, where no staging activities take place.

Regarding the theatres' staff members, a sufficient number of staff members are needed to carry out the managerial and monitoring conservation and tourism tasks. Moreover, staff members must have appropriate qualifications obtained through regular training programs. The presence of wardens to take care of the site and/or interpreters capable of explaining the site and its conservation issues is a helpful tool in safeguarding these sites and preventing damage to them. In all of the theatres we studied, the number of staff members appeared insufficient, especially in relation to the number of people devoted to interpretation and guiding tasks. These professionals are key workers in dealing with recreational carrying capacity management and in providing quality experiences to visitors.

Financial support is always necessary to maintain heritage conservation, at least in the first stages of the enhancement process. Later, a portion of the necessary funds can be raised from visitors through ticketing policies, fees, merchandising, etc., and also from donors. In any event, funding is an important limiting factor in framing the effectiveness of the management plan. The analysed theatres have different policies on entrance fees. The Sagunto theatre permits free entrance to the monument, but the rest of the theatres charge admittance fees. Petra, Amman, Jerash, and Cartagena sell tickets that provide access to the entire archaeological site; meanwhile, in Carthage the different settings can be visited separately, and the separate visits can be paid for separately. Nevertheless, the prices are very attractive and convenient to visitors, even to foreign visitors. The final amount from these entrance fees does not come close to covering the theatres' maintenance expenses, and even the operating costs must be assumed by the authorities in charge.

3. DISCUSSION AND CONCLUSIONS

The Recreational Carrying Capacity Assessment on its own is unable to address all of the relevant managerial issues and cannot work independently of other tools. It must be part of an integrated management plan in which all of the theatres' activities (staging and performance, tourism, scientific and research, cultural, etc.) are considered from a comprehensive and long-term perspective, taking into account the intrinsic value and the iconic attraction value that these sites have at the local, national and international levels. It is desirable to implement all of the necessary management tools and measures because an Ancient Theatre is a valuable cultural resource that deserves this type of consideration and presentation.

Furthermore, it is important to recall that performance criteria in relation to spatial standards and perceptual components only adequately address the peak use level of the site at a given moment. This analysis is insufficient to guarantee site conservation because the impacts from recreation are cumulative, and it is necessary to know the weekly, monthly and yearly use levels as well.

The limiting factors working in the RCCA analysis are multiple and vary depending on the theatre. In archaeological sites such as the Ancient Theatres, space and cultural resources are the most restrictive factors that set the conditions for all of the others because of their intrinsic historical value.

With regard to the analysed Ancient Theatres, additional data are necessary in order to gain a full picture of their situations, and no visitors' management tools, including Recreational Carrying Capacity, have currently been implemented. Nevertheless, the same strengths and weaknesses have been detected in all of the theatres.

In addition, Ancient Theatres are not saturated spaces, and congestion is negligible. However, the managerial limiting factors at this moment constitute a constraint in the process of managing recreational carrying capacity. In other words, these theatres can accommodate a larger number of visitors than the administration is effectively able to manage.

Finally, theatres have all undergone significant restorations, mostly following the criteria for staging functionality. After the restoration works were completed, the theatres lost part of their available visitation surface. Additionally, staging activities make difficult the compatible utilization of a theatre for visitation activities because both take place at the same place and have their peak season at the same time. Thus, during the peak season, visiting activities can be seriously affected, and due to the intrusive presence of these staging elements, the aesthetics and image of the site may be overlooked. In all the theatres except Cartagena, authorities devote more attention to the staging activities than to tourism ones.

REFERENCE LIST

[1] Pedersen, A. (2002). *Managing Tourism at World Heritage Sites: a Practical Manual for World Heritage Sites Managers.* UNESCO Word Heritage Manuals. 1, 96 pp.
[2] Haddad, N. (2007). Criteria for the Assessment of the Modern Use of Ancient Theatres and Odea. *International Journal of Heritage Studies.* 13 (3), 265-280.
[3] Coccossis, H. and Mexa, A. (eds). (2004). *The challenge of Tourism Carrying Capacity Assessment. Theory and Practice.* Ed. Ashgate Publishing Limited, UK. 310pp.
[4] Rose, P. (2005). Spectators and Spectator Comfort in Roman Entertainment Buildings: A Study in Functional Design. *Papers of the British School at Rome.* 73, 99-130.

[5] Morant, M. and Viñals, M.J. (2010). *Modelo para evaluar la capacidad de carga recreativa en áreas de uso intensivo de espacios protegidos. Casos de estudio de la Comunidad Valenciana (España)*. In López Olivares (ed.): Turismo y gestión de espacios protegidos. Ed. Tirant lo Blanch. 618-636.

[6] Viñals, M.J., Alonso-Monasterio, P. and Alonso-Monasterio, M. (2013a). *Analysis of the spatial standards and perceptual components of the Recreational Carrying Capacity applied to the Archaeological sites. Case Study of the Castellet de Bernabé (Llíria, Spain)*. In Mondéjar, Vargas, Ortega y Pérez Calderón (eds.): Methods and Analysis on Tourism and Environment. Ed. Nova Publisher. 109-120.

[7] Viñals, M.J., Morant, M., and Alonso-Monasterio, P. (2013b). *Key issues in the Ancient Theatres Recreational Carrying Capacity Assessment Studies.* En Juan (coord.): Prototype of Management Plan for Enhancement of New Actualities. Edit. Instituto Universitario de Restauración del Patrimonio Arquitectónico (UPV). 89-96.

[8] Segal, A. (1995). *Theatres in Roman Palestine and Provincia Arabia.* Ed. E.J. Brill. 117pp.

[9] Farajat, S. (2011). *Analysis of the Tourism Activities in the Petra Archaeological Park (Jordan)*. Unpublished Doctoral Thesis, Universitat Politècnica de València. 387 pp.

[10] Paradise, T.R. (2005). Petra revisited: An examination of sandstone weathering research in Petra, Jordan. In Turkington (ed.): Stone decay in the architectural environment. *Geological Society of America, Special Paper.* 390, 39-49.

[11] Boullon, R. (1985). *Planificación del espacio turístico.* Ed.Trillas. México. 245pp.

[12] Hall, T. (1966). *The Hidden Dimension.* Anchor Books, New York. 201pp.

[13] Ministry of Tourism and Antiquities of Jordan (2012). Tourism Statistical data 2011. *Tourism Statistical Newsletter.* 7 (4).

[14] Abu Ali, J., and Howaidee, M. (2012). The impact of service quality on tourism satisfaction in Jerash. *Interdisciplinary Journal of Contemporary Research in Bussiness.* 3 (12), 164-187.

[15] McCool, S.F. (1996). *Limits of Acceptable Change: A Framework for Managing National Protected Areas: Experiences from the United States.* Unpublished paper. Missoula, MT: School of Forestry, University of Montana.15pp.

[16] Stankey, G.H. and McCool, S.F. (1984). Carrying Capacity in recreational settings: Evolution, appraisal and application. *Leisure Sciences.* 6 (4), 453-473.

[17] American Educational Research Association (2003). Class size: counting students can count. *Essential Information for Education Policy.* v.1 (2), 4pp.

[18] Tran Nghi, Nguyen Thanh Lan, Nguyen Dinh Thai, Dang Mai, and Dinh Xuan Thanh (2007). Tourism carrying capacity assessment for Phong Nha-Ke Bang and Dong Hoi, Quang Binh Province. *VNU Journal of Science, Earth Sciences.* 23, 80-87.

Sustainable performance and tourism: a collection of tools and best practices

Slow tourism: an alternative model for local and tourist development

E. DI-CLEMENTE
University of Extremadura, Department of Business Management and Sociology, Spain.
J. M. HERNÁNDEZ-MOGOLLÓN
University of Extremadura, Department of Business Management and Sociology, Spain.
P. DE SALVO
University of Perugia, Department of Institutions and Society, Italy.
A. M. CAMPÓN- CERRO
University of Extremadura, Department of Business Management and Sociology, Spain.

1   ABSTRACT

In this chapter, we focus on the determination of the slow tourism concept based on the study of the scientific literature published on this topic. Literature review lets us identify the main approaches from which slow tourism has been addressed. Despite the fact that scientific production on this issue must be considered still in its infancy, it is worth noting that there are already worthwhile contributions and research aimed at conceptualizing the feasibility of the slow philosophy in the tourism sector. The aim of this chapter is to clarify the concept of slow tourism and identify its antecedents.

2   1 INTRODUCTION

The economic models of developed modern economies are based on neoclassical theories of economic growth, according to which the utility increases monotonically with consumption [1, 2]. These systems correlate socioeconomic wellbeing with the increase of consumption of goods and services which, in turn, is associated with an increase in the volume of domestic production, with greater use of available resources and monetary wealth. In more recent times, the neoclassical growth theories have found criticism in ecological economics [3-6] and the economy of happiness [7] that begin to call into question the convenience and the efficacy of an economic model which equates higher consumption levels with higher levels of welfare, using resources in an uncontrolled manner, without considering the impact caused on the environment and societies [8]. From these early criticisms of neoclassical theory, growth concept has evolved to acquire meanings consistent with the context and the needs of economic and social systems of the particular historical moment.

In recent years, the global economy has developed profound imbalances which impose the need to re-evaluate the way in which we use available resources, the development objectives we pursue and the type of growth that is sought. The recent economic and financial crisis suffered worldwide caused a deep malaise among the people of various regions of the world, especially those of Mediterranean Europe. This has led to conventional economic models losing their credibility. The discrepancy between intensive use of resources and the effects on the real welfare of the population, has led academics and researchers to consider the feasibility of new models of development and of a different concept of growth, more comprehensive and complex, capable of overcoming the myth of the exponential growth of material goods available and to consider the importance of social and qualitative aspects of wealth as essential elements of economic sustainability.

The welfare of society cannot be measured solely by the product per capita tool, as it provides partial information of the wealth of a country. It becomes necessary to look at other indicators of social wealth as the quality of the workplace, the environment in which a person develops their quality of life, diet, level of happiness, etc. [9-11]. The Gross Domestic Product (GDP), as a reference measure of the level of a country's development, it is an inadequate indicator of the welfare and wealth of a nation. Following this, a new stream of thought called "degrowth", also known as "Décroissance" has been developed. This posits that a change in the rhythms of consumption and life is the only way to avoid the collapse of actual productive systems [12-18]. The international financial crisis has led to an investigation into possible ways of pursuing a change in the economic growth paradigm traditionally applied, in favor of the de-growing principles which start to be considered as an acceptable option, especially for some specific economic sectors.

The recent increase in scientific publications related to this topic demonstrates the interest this issue is generating within the academic community and confirms the general interest in the theme. However, it is worth noting that the necessity of slowing the pace of growth and consumption is not new, but dates back to the seventies, when the economist Nicholas Georgescu-Roegen [19] published a book entitled *The Entropy Law and the economic Process* in which he questions neoclassical economic theories and explicitly states the need of downshifting the use of available resources. Later, in the 80s, sustainability was assumed to be the right response to self-destructive consumption systems. Nevertheless, despite the plethora of publications, conferences, international meeting, plans and agendas that have been dedicated to sustainability, the reality has not changed and the world is experiencing increasing levels of unsustainability [20].

At present, degrowth has created a new perspective on economic welfare, being considered the right tool to solve some of the most critical aspects which concern modern society: i) the urgency of adopting lifestyles, production and consumption patterns which will protect the environment and stop climate change, ii) the need to factor into development plans the social and psychological costs of current economic growth models [16]. Under this perspective, people and territories have been placed back at the center of a "re-humanization" of the production processes and of the physical spaces [21]. This understanding of the concept of degrowth carries a comprehensive application of the same in all aspects of life and human activities.

The various efforts to implement economic and social models of degrowth into a real context, share one common feature: a new attitude toward time and the importance of the qualitative aspects of welfare. Thus, the temporal component and the slowing down in the pace of life, consumption and production represent the differential element and the discriminant matrix of degrowth with respect to traditional approaches.

We can identify in the experiences of Slowfood and Cittaslow, the first examples of degrowth applied to reality, limitedly to two specific sectors: the agri-food and the urban-social [22-24]. Slow food is an international movement which stresses the urgent need to respect the rhythms of nature and the quality of typical products in relation to agriculture. Its main purpose is to defend traditional production processes, foodstuffs and small producers from food standardization. As a result, Slowfood aims to strengthen fragile farming economies and their local communities for whom this industry is their livelihood and that, nowadays, run the risk of succumbing under the pressure of intensive production and the globalization of cultures [22]. On the other hand, Cittaslow, which in italian means slow cities, is considered to be the bulwark of the "good lifestyle" and of the need to preserve cities and places that are distinguished by having architectural, social and touristic features and infrastructure that promote a healthy lifestyle for their inhabitants [23-25].

The tourism industry has at least two major reasons for considering the influences of the slow philosophy on the sector and to concentrate on the potential it offers for adopting a new approach for destination development, consistent with the theories of degrowth:

Tourism is one of the major industries worldwide.
Environmental impacts generated by tourism are recognized on a global scale and affect global warming, especially after the intensification of international movements and of long distance air travel [20, 26-28].

Thus, the growth of tourism and the increasing number of tourists who can afford to have a holiday and to travel long distances imposed a reflection on the need of operating a slowing down in the tourism sector. The degrowth philosophy applied to tourism has given rise to a new way of understanding the journey known as "Slow Tourism". This term identifies an alternative mindset adopted by both the travelers and the tourist planners and tour operators. Calzati and De Salvo [29] argue that slow tourism is not a passing trend or a fad, but rather should be understood as a new cultural model. Slow tourism proposes an alternative mentality, a new way to live tourist activities, responsibility towards territories and local communities and focused on exalting the human component and relational aspects of the journey. From these considerations, the main objective of this chapter is to carry out a review of the scientific literature which addresses the issue of slowness in relation to tourism development.

3   2 SLOW TOURISM: DEFINITIONS AND CONCEPTS

Slow tourism has not yet been defined unanimously in scientific literature. However, there are noteworthy contributions on the subject which attempt to explain and define this new tourism trend. Dickinson and Lumsdon [30] state that the term of slow tourism is accompanied by other expressions that refer to the same concept such as slow travel, slow mobility, soft mobility, etc. All of them pinpoint a new attitude towards the journey, whose key features are marked environmental sensitivity and responsibility of tourist behaviour, in particular in relation to the means of transport, recognizing that the faster the means the higher the attributable CO_2 emissions. Car and air travel, with their large carbon footprint, are therefore incompatible with slow travel. Within a slow approach, the preferred means of transport are "green ones", with low environmental impact, including walking, cycling, horse riding, etc... [31]. Thus, the means used for the trip is one of the determinants of slow tourism model. However, being aware that the terms slow travel, slow mobility, soft mobility and the concept of slow tourism are currently used synonymously, we wish to emphasize a differentiating nuance especially between the concepts of slow travel and slow tourism. The latter covers a broader notion and considers the slowness as a cross-cutting factor of the whole tourist experience. On the other hand, the concept of slow travel (and similar ones), while considering slowness to be an integral element of the trip, places special emphasis on the environmental responsibility of the tourist and on the choice of clean transportation means as a key feature for a slow journey.

On the basis of this differentiation, it is possible to order the current scientific production on this topic according to two different approaches: the first focuses on the slowness-transport dichotomy and the second considers slowness as a structural element of the journey [32]. Dickinson *et al.* [33] define *"slow travel as an emerging conceptual framework which offers an alternative to air and car travel where people travel to destinations more slowly overland, stay longer and travel less[...]"*.

The investigations that extend the concept of slow tourism and overcome the limitations set by slow travel, continue to stress the importance of the dichotomy slowness-transport, but begin to explore other tourist areas where trends favourable to slowing down can be detected, or rather, where downshifting is necessary in order to preserve architectural, environmental and social heritage [29,30,34-39]. Lumsdon and McGrath [34] even if referring to slow travel, propose a definition with a broad conceptual content, closer to what we have identified here as slow tourism.

> *Slow travel is a sociocultural phenomenon, focusing on holidaymaking but also on day leisure visit, where use of personal time is appreciated differently. Slowness is valued, and journey is integral to the whole experience. The mode of transport and the activities undertaken at the destination enhance the richness of the experience of locality counts for much, as does reduced duration of distance of travel [...][34].*

Calzati and De Salvo [29] refer to slow tourism as an active experience, where slowness, in addition to encouraging more environmentally friendly tourist behavior, leads the traveler into a cultural, spiritual and relational experience which characterizes the journey in all its phases and stages. Thus, slow travelers' choices not only affect the transport field, but cover all the elements that make up vacation time and are embodied in the pursuit of a deep approach, authentic and open towards territories and people, favored by adopting more relaxed rhythms [40]. In table 1 we collect the main literature of reference explicitly dealing with the relationship between slowness and tourism. We differentiate between the two approaches outlined above: the slowness-transport dichotomy and the one that considers the slowness as integral, structural element for a new tourist and territorial system.

Table 1: Main literature of reference

	Author	Title	Journal/Editorial
Slowness as structural change	Blanco[35]	Una aproximación al turismo Slow. El turismo Slow en las Cittàslow de España	Investigaciones Turísticas
	Heitmann *et al.* [39]	Slow food, Slow Cities, slow tourism,	Cabi International Willingford
	CST [37]	Sviluppo turistico e territori lenti	Franco Angeli Milano
	Calzati and De Salvo [29]	Le strategie per una valorizzazione sostenibile del territorio. Il valore della lentezza, della qualità dell'identità per il turismo del futuro	Franco Angeli Milano
	Dickinson and Lumsdon [30]	Slow Travel and Tourism: Tourism, Environment and Development Series	Earthscan, London, Washington, DC
	Lumsdon and McGrath [34]	Developing a conceptual framework for slow travel: a grounded theory approach	Journal of Sustainable Tourism
	Matos [38]	Can "slow tourism" bring new life to Alpine Regions?	Haworth New York, NY
	Nocifora *et al.*[36]	Territori lenti e turismo di qualità, prospettive innovative per lo sviluppo di un turismo sostenibile	Franco Angeli Milano
	Fullagar *et al.*[41]	Slow tourism. Experience and Mobility.	Channel view publication Bristol
Slowness-transport dichotomy	Buckley [42]	Tourism Under Climate Change: Will Slow Travel Supersede Short Breaks?	Ambio
	Dickinson *et al.* [33]	Holiday travel discourses and climate change	Journal of Transport Geography
	Dickinson *et al.* [31]	Slow travel: issues for tourism and climate change	Journal of Sustainable Tourism
	Fosgerau [43]	Investigating the distribution of the value of travel time savings	Transportation Research Part B
	Nijkamp and Baaijens [44]	Time pioneers and travel behaviour: an investigation into de viability of "Slow motion".	Growth and Change

Source: Own elaboration

It is worth noting that the slowness in tourism is not associated with a psychosocial fad [29, 44], but that it identifies the beginning of a new attitude and approach which brings structural changes in social, economic and anthropological fields [34]. Slow tourism needs a specific attitude towards both a certain style of holiday and means of transport used for travelling. Therefore, Dickinson *et al.* [31] specify that slow tourism should be the result of a combination of slow travel and slow holiday.

Lumsdon and McGrath [34], in their review of the literature on the subject of slow tourism, propose an initial conceptual framework that consists of four key pillars: "slowness and the value of time, locality and activities in the destination, mode of transport and travel experience and environmental consciousness". In this conceptualization of slow tourism, transport accounts for only one of the determinants and not the primary or sole component (see Figure 1).

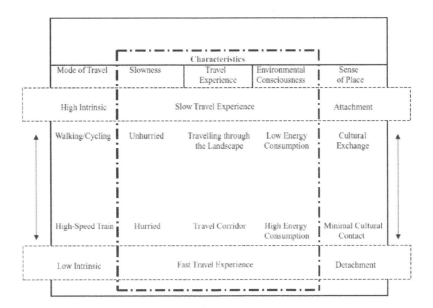

Figure 1: Slow travel conceptual framework
Source: Lumsdon and McGrath [34]

However, we should recognize that this conceptual approach analyzes and determines slow tourism mainly from the perspective of traveller and tourist demand. In fact, the elements that comprise the framework are identified in a set of attitudes and choices assumed by the tourist: choosing green transportation, preferring local activities instead of visiting several places around the main locality of the stay, choosing to stay longer in one destination, travelling at a slow pace, etc ...

In order for the slow approach to have a consistent and credible application in reality, it is essential to effect a change to the supply system too. A positive attitude among tourists towards the adoption of a set of slow behaviors should be promoted by tourist and territorial systems designed and organized under the slow philosophy, sustainable criteria and degrowth theories [29,36]. Otherwise, slow practices will remain the preserve of elite consumers, those willing to accept many important limitations to their range of tourism opportunities in terms of "where" and "how" to travel, as the destinations and locations that enable them to comply with the plurality of constrictions imposed by slow tourism are few, little known or too close to the place of habitual residence in order to be considered as tourist destinations. For this reason, we propose an integrated approach to slow tourism, developed from the perspective of management and territorial marketing which facilitates the identification of the crucial aspects defining a slow destination.

The key determinants of a slow territorial approach have been identified in the following concepts: degrowth, quality, sustainability and slow territories [45]. We propose a graphical explanation of them in Figure 2.

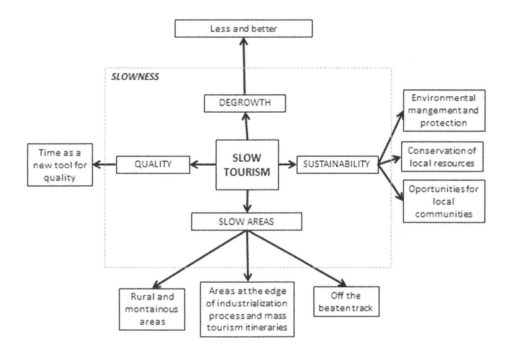

Figure 2: Determining elements for a slow tourism development approach
Source: Own elaboration

3.1 Slow territories

"Slow territories" is a term coined by researcher Emanuel Lancerini [46] to identify those areas that combine rural features with new urban and landscape elements, thus giving rise to environments that require different and innovative development paths. Therefore, it is noteworthy that these territories should not be identified with depressed areas or with regions in decline, marked by degenerative processes in its development, but rather as places that are able to value endogenous characteristics of places combining them with some exogenous impulses [46, 47]. Thus, slow territories are defined as rural, mountainous or peripheral areas, far away from massive urban and industrial systems and presenting new features as a special quality, strong tradition and local identity [48].

These territories have remained, voluntarily or not, outside of development systems based on an intensive use of land and local resources. Their economies are not monosectoral, being characterized by multiple activities that give life to rich, hybrid environments difficult to identify with a specific productive sector. Here, landscape and local identities become the protagonists of a territory-oriented development that respects natural rhythms. In these areas, slowness is therefore a strategic and distinctive tool, able to place the development beyond the typical quantitative logic which rules over the current economic systems. Lancerini [46] notes that these territories pursue qualitative growth that focuses on values such as the availability of a greater amount of leisure time, higher levels of happiness, quality and freedom, rather than an increase in income.

These aspects make slow territories ideal candidates for the application of alternative, flexible models of growth, valuing their identities and local peculiarities which allow them to remain robust against economic instability [49].

A study carried out by the CST, Center for Advanced Studies in Tourism, based in Assisi, Italy [37], describes slow territories using the following concepts: shady area, quality landscapes, depopulation, networks of small hotels, agriculture and biological agriculture, agri-food economy, lower tourism development [45]. Lanzani [47], meanwhile, states that such peculiar territorial districts need to adopt development policies capable of reinventing local tradition, integrating technological innovation, enhancing landscapes and ensuring tourism models that are light, slow and fully integrated with the existing social and economic background.

3.2 Sustainability

From the 80s onwards, principles of sustainability have represented a real opportunity to make development profitable to three different levels: economic, environmental and social [50, 51]. The roll-out of sustainable plans has been a real priority, especially for those rural and peripheral territories whose socio-economic and geographical environments impose the need for *ad hoc* growth patterns, due to the constant threat of depopulation, economic depression, abandonment of tangible and intangible assets to which they are exposed. For slow territories, the increasing attention to the specificities unique to these areas imposes the need for a model of economic development which is compatible with their slowness. As pointed out by Capuano [52], in recent years, the economic literature has recognized the inefficiency of traditional economic models for these types of environments and has focused on the study of new opportunities and synergies for local economic development.

Tourism has been regarded as a sector capable of promoting sustainable growth in rural areas, as long as tourist development is planned in a different way than traditional "mass" tourism model. Thus, the concepts of tourism development and sustainable development have been converging, recognizing tourism as an industry capable of achieving the sustainable goals set out by the Bruntland Report [53]. However, nowadays, tourism is identified as one of the most polluting industries worldwide, causing increasingly negative impacts in terms of the uncontrolled use of resources, transformation of land use and loss of biodiversity [28]. Thus, while the literature defends and asserts the direct relationship between tourism development and sustainability in theory, the actual data belies it. In order to talk about sustainability in a credible and consistent way, within the current socio-economic context, and to present it as a key element in the definition of slow tourism, we must adopt a new critical perspective in order to avoid becoming bogged down by the vagueness of the concept.

Hall [20] suggests a reconceptualization of sustainability proposing a new definition of it which includes the territorial and spatial extent of impacts, while stressing the balance between social, economic and environmental development. Along the same lines, Gössling [26], emphasizes the current incoherence of the concept of environmental sustainability beyond a strictly local dimension, noting that many tourist activities trigger environmental care activities that provide positive results on a very limited territory. Furthermore, this is completely nullified by pollution caused by air transport in international tourism [28].

Slow Tourism, considered as a type of tourism which excludes the use of highly polluting means of transport such as planes or cars, attributes absolute priority to the concern about the environmental impacts caused by tourism, not only locally, but at an international level. It is considered to be an alternative tourism, in line with a new meaning of sustainability by which the territorial scope of impacts play a crucial role. Slow tourism, promoting a new culture of more local trips, imposes a territorial delimitation of tourist travel which is embodied in an invitation to spend more time doing activities at the destination which help to establish more genuine relationships with residents and local operators and accrues the benefits that directly affect the indigenous communities and economy [25, 36, 45].

3.3 Degrowth

The same re-conceptualization of sustainability highlights the need to consider a concept of development in which quality is the core and principal value [36, 54]. Hall [28], in an attempt to mold this new approach to sustainability in a real context, proposes a circular system of production and consumption based on the concepts of efficiency and sufficiency. The former provides better use of raw materials and energy, which implies a change in the behavior of producers; the second refers to a change in consumer attitudes towards forms of slow consumption, aimed to slowing down in rhythm of use of resources. This approach would reduce the consumption of energy and raw materials used for production to levels compatible with regeneration and absorption of impacts caused by the same system [28]. Latouche [54], one of the leading theorists of degrowth, stresses that this expression should not be conflated with a concept antithetical to growth, but rather, it highlights the inconsistency of economic development goals exclusively set on a quantitative logic whose consequences are devastating from a social and environmental perspective. This understanding of degrowing criticizes the purely economic and quantitative tools of measurement of wealth, such as GDP, due to the fact that these indicators exclude all other forms of social wealth, environmental quality, quality of life, quality of human relationships, the democratic nature of the institutions and all those qualitative components that affect the welfare of populations [48]. In the tourism sector, the adoption of a development philosophy based degrowth involves the application of tourist territorial systems in which the positive impacts generated by tourism activities, compensate for the negative ones caused by this activity on natural and social heritage [20].

Daly [55] maintains that consumption of both natural and artificial capital must be subtracted in calculating the benefit, recognizing the importance of this type of cost, usually ignored, in the growth mechanism. The application of the degrowing philosophy in tourism does not suggest the immobilization of quantitative economic and monetary growth, but rather proposes the possibility of reaching a steady-state for tourism, beyond which environmental and social costs become unsustainable and adversely affect the balance of the system [20]. The achievement of steady-state tourism involves the admission of an optimal size of production systems, which can only be achieved by choosing a growth model that focuses on qualitative development and rejects cumulative mechanisms of growth in favor of a slow and sufficient consumption of resources [45]. Degrowing in the travel industry means the acceptance of a more localized and limited mobility at territorial level. This will lead to the achievement of economic and environmental benefits [30]. The first, as many regions will get advantage from a more dynamic tourism created by an increased number of trips next to places of residence, and the latter because localized mobility involves reducing the major environmental impacts of travel generated by fast or ultrafast means of transport [20, 26, 28, 56].

3.4 Quality

In the tourism sector quality is a differentiator and a strategic factor to stand out against competitors [57]. Quality is currently a complex concept, and it is difficult to find a universally valid and comprehensive definition for its different meanings and scope. In general, we can say that quality should be considered as a dynamic concept, either because of the rapid technological improvements that define it, or because of societal change and the appearance of new needs and different perceptions of the concept. Over the years, there have been various interpretations and definitions of the concept of quality. Above all, the scope of the concept has changed. Nowadays quality does solely relate to the intrinsic characteristics of a product, but covers the entire production chain of an industry: business organization, business ethics, happiness of employees, business creativity, etc.

De Masi [58] defines quality as a particular halo that turns a good or an object into something unique and irreplaceable. Calzati [48], on the other hand, equates quality with "what is well done" and "what is beautiful" and, particularly, with the luxury of enjoying scarce goods such as time, autonomy, tranquillity, silence, safety and a healthy environment. For what concerns a tourism model focused on slowness, quality is determined by a set of tangible and intangible elements. Within the latter, time is a prerequisite for a quality experience, offered and lived. Thus, from a slow perspective, quality is rooted in respect for unhurried rhythms that can care for the small details of the trip and allow enjoying the social and cultural content of tourism activities.

Following this understanding, the quality of a slow tourist experience has to be understood beyond the material and physical connotations of the product/service, focusing on its intangible elements, which are those that can affect the emotional responses of the tourist to their stay. In this sense a quality slow trip is such as provides experiences that can improve mental and physical wellbeing of the tourist and affects their quality of life and contributes to increase their levels of happiness [11, 59]. Thus, in the theoretical framework of slow tourism, quality is identified as a new attitude toward the value of time by both tour operators and travellers. Paused rhythms are considered to be a tool that facilitates respect for local identities, the authenticity of the destination and the opportunity to spend time creating enriching relationships with people and territories throughout the stay. Quality is so considered as a fundamental and constitutive element in the model of slow tourism, since it is essential for the creation of alternative models in which slowness is a value and a tool for "good work" and "good living"[36].

4 CONCLUSIONS

From the urgent need for a change in our production systems, emerge the reflections on the role of the slowness in the frenetic rhythms of modern society. The difficulty of ensuring continuity and stability within current economic systems, has led to the consideration of policies for development and growth, both economic and social, which have slow philosophy at their heart and need to decrease the pace of life and consumption (degrowth). In the tourism sector slowing pace takes on a special meaning as it is not only a way to defend and preserve finite resources, but above all, it offers a new opportunities for the diversification and legitimization of tourism in certain fragile environments, such as rural or mountain areas. The adoption of lower rates of consumption and of a simpler life represents a potential tool for destination management, and the chance to conceive, create and promote a tourism system in line with the expectations of the modern tourist. The latter, in fact, is no longer identified with a consumer indifferent to the physical and social environments in which he travels, and has begun to demonstrate his desire to experience authentic relationships and territories [37].

After studying the scientific literature on the topic of slow tourism produced so far, we can conclude that it is still an incipient typology. On an academic level, a precise definition of slow tourism hasn't been reached, although attempts have been made in order to achieve an early conceptualization [30, 31, 34]. It is noteworthy that the first contributions in the field of slow tourism come from the perspective of the demand, defining slow tourism practices as a set of behaviors and attitudes adopted by an emerging segment of consumers, motivated by the need to live deeper and more authentic tourist experiences, and to behave responsibly towards local societies and environments. We must recognize that, in the field of international literature [30, 31, 33, 34], a certain centrality has been recognized to choices concerning means of transport used for tourist travel, as a determinant element in the definition of slow tourism. From this perspective, slowness is conceived in its dichotomous relationship with the means of transport. Walking, cycling and horse riding are assumed to be slow choices, so tourists who travel this way are considered to be slow traveller, developing slow practices. On the contrary, the most popular transport means, as car and plane, are labelled as fast and highly polluting choices [20, 26, 28], so they are usually rejected by those who wish to follow slow patterns during their holidays.

On the other hand, we have to acknowledge the presence of an abundant Italian literature that addresses the issue of slow tourism from a supply perspective and from the point of view of tourism destination management [30, 37, 38]. Under this approach slowness is considered as the structural element of a new tourist philosophy which, in addition to affecting the transport sector, covers more varied and complex fields as urban planning, sociology, agro-food, heritage conservation, economics and psychophysical welfare of local communities. These contributions are essential to the conception of slow philosophy as a new opportunity for the development of new, innovative, efficient and sustainable tourism systems. From this approach has been outlined a first conceptual framework that could be considered as a reference for slow tourism and whose constituent pillars have been identified in the concepts of sustainability, degrowth, quality and slow territories (see Figure 2).

To conclude, note that the knowledge gained so far in the conceptualization of slow tourism represents an initial approach to the issue which suggests the potential of the beneficial impact possibly generated by a slow development of the tourism sector. It is necessary to persist with this research line, as many questions remain open regarding the actual feasibility of a slow tourism model [30]. It will be important to investigate the real possibility of applying the paradigm of slow tourism to specific destinations and to figure out how to combine environmental precepts imposed by the slowness philosophy with the current reality of international mobility, with its huge tourist flows, and the ones economically more beneficial to tourist destinations, are used to travel with highly polluting means such as aircraft, high speed trains and cars.

Beyond foreseeable difficulties, adopting a slow tourism model would represent the ideal answer for many of the current requirements of the tourism market. From the supply perspective, tourism would develop a system able to enhance and protect local identities and heritages. On the other hand, in relation to tourist demand, slow tourism is proposed as a model in line with current expectations of tourists, able to meet the current needs of the modern traveller, more interested in living responsible tourism experiences, both from an environmental and social perspective, and rich in its cultural and human content.

5   REFERENCE LIST

[1] Ramsey, F. (1928). A mathematical theory of savings. *Economic Journal.* 38, 543–559.

[2] Cass, D. (1965). Optimum growth in an aggregative model of capital accumulation. *Review of Economic Studies.* 32, 233–240.

[3] Arrow, K., Bolin, B., Costanza, R., Dasgupta, P., Folke, C., Holling, C.S., Jansson, B., Levin, S., Mäler, K., Perrings, C. & Pimentel, P. (1995). Economic growth, carrying capacity, and the environment. *Tourism Management.* 15, 91-95.

[4] Max Neef, M. (1995). Economic growth and quality of life: a threshold hypothesis. *Ecological Economics.* 15(2), 115–118.

[5] Van Den Bergh, J.C.J.M., Ferrer-I-Carbonell, A. & Munda, G. (2000). Alternative models of individual behaviour and implications for environmental policy. *Ecological Economics.* 32(1), 43–61.

[6] Siebenhüner, B. (2000). Homo sustinens-towards a new conception of humans for the science of sustainability. *Ecological Economics.* 32(1), 15–25.

[7] Kahneman, D., Krueger, A. B., Schkade, D. A., Schwarz, N. & Stone, A. A. (2004). A survey method for characterizing daily life experience: the day reconstruction method. *Science.* 306, 1776–1780.

[8] Ayres, R.U. (1996). Limits to the growth paradigm. *Ecological Economics.* 19(2), 117-134.

[9] Nordhaus W. D. & Tobin J. (1972). Is Growth Obsolete? in Nordhaus, W.D. & Tobin J. *Economic Research: Retrospect and Prospect,* 5, *Economic Growth,* Cambridge: National Bureau of Economic Research, 1-80.

[10] Daly, H. & Cobb, J. (1989). *For the Common Good: Redirecting the Economy towards Community, the Environment and a Sustainable Future.* Boston: Beacon Press.

[11] Bimonte, S. & Faralla, V. (2012). Tourist types and happiness a comparative study in Maremma, Italy. *Annals of Tourism Research.* 39(4), 1929–1950.

[12] Griethuysen, P. (2010). Why are we growth-addicted? The hard way towards degrowth in the involutionary western development path. *Journal of Cleaner Production.* 18, 590–595.

[13] Schneider, F., Kallis, G. & Martinez-Alier, J. (2010). Crisis or opportunity? Economic degrowth for social equity and ecological sustainability. Introduction to this special issue. *Journal of Cleaner Production.* 18, 511–518.

[14] Kallis, G. (2011). In defence of degrowth. *Ecological Economics.* 70, 873–880.

[15] Kerschner, C. (2010). Economic de-growth vs. steady-state economy. *Journal of Cleaner Production.* 18, 544–551.

[16] Whitehead, M. (2013). Degrowth or Regrowth?. *Environmental Values*. 22, (2), 141-145.

[17] Demaria, F., Schneider, F., Sekulova, F. & Martinez-Alier, J. (2013). What is Degrowth? From an Activist Slogan to a Social Movement. *Environmental Values*. 22, 191–215.

[18] Trainer, T. (2012). De-growth: Do you realise what it means?. *Futures*. 44(6), 590–599.

[19] Georgescu-Roegen, N. (1971). *The Entropy Law and the Economic Process*. Cambridge, Massachusetts: Harvard University Press.

[20] Hall, C.M. (2010). Changing paradigms and global change: from sustainable to steady- state tourism. *Tourism Recreation Research*. 35(2), 131-145.

[21] Bonomi, A. & Rullani, E. (2005). *Il capitalismo personale. Vite al lavoro*. Torino: Einaudi.

[22] Petrini, C. (2001). *Slow Food: The case for taste*. New York: Columbia University Press.

[23] Pink, S. (2007). Sensing CittaSlow: Slow Living and The Constitution of The Sensory City. *The Senses and Society*. 2(1), 59–77.

[24] Knox, P.L. (2005). Creating ordinary places: slow cities in a fast world. *Journal of Urban Design*. 10(1), 1-11.

[25] Dietz, A. (2006). *Cittaslow - das gute Leben Kulturelles Erbe, Nachhaltigkeit und Lebensqualität in Kleinstädte*. Saarbrücken: VDM Verlag Dr. Müller.

[26] Gössling, S. (2002). Global environmental consequences of tourism. *Global Environmental Change*. 12, 283-302.

[27] Gössling, S., Borgström-Hansson, C., Hörstmeier, O. & Saggel, S. (2002). Ecological footprint analysis as a tool to assess tourism sustainability. *Ecological Economics*. 43(2-3), 199-211.

[28] Hall, C.M. (2009). Degrowing Tourism: Décroissance, Sustainable Consumption and Steady-State Tourism. *Anatolia*. 20(1), 46-61.

[29] Calzati, V. & De Salvo, P. (coord.) (2012). *Le strategie per una valorizzazione sostenibile del territorio. Il valore della lentezza, della qualità e dell'identità per il turismo del futuro*. Milano: Franco Angeli.

[30] Dickinson, J. & Lumsdon, L.M. (2010). *Slow Travel and Tourism*. Environment and Development Series, London, Washington: Earthscan.

[31] Dickinson, J., Lumsdon, L.M. & Robbins, D. (2011). Slow travel: issues for tourism and climate change. *Journal of Sustainable Tourism*. 19(3), 281-300.

[32] Hernández-Mogollón, De Salvo, P. & Di-Clemente, E. (2012). Una aproximación al concepto de slow tourism: el caso del territorio del Valle de Jerte. *Turismo&Desenvolvimiento*. 3(17-18), 1681-1693.

[33] Dickinson, J., Robbins, D. & Lumsdon, L.M. (2010). Holiday travel discourses and climate change. *Journal of Transport Geography*. 18, 482–489.

[34] Lumsdon, L.M. & Mcgrath, P. (2011). Developing a conceptual framework for slow travel: a grounded theory approach. *Journal of Sustainable Tourism*. 19(3), 265-279.

[35] Blanco, A. (2011). Una aproximación al turismo slow. El turismo slow en las Cittáslow de España. *Investigaciones Turísticas*. 1, 122-133.

[36] Nocifora, E., De Salvo, P. & Calzati, V. (2011). *Territori lenti e turismo di qualità, prospettive innovative per lo sviluppo di un turismo sostenibile*. Milano: Franco Angeli.

[37] CST. (2009). *Sviluppo turistico e territori lenti*. Milano: Franco Angeli.

[38] Matos, W. (2004). Can slow travel bring new life to the Alpine regions? In K.Weiermair & C.Mathies, *The tourism and leisure industry*. New York, NY: Haworth, 93–103.

[39] Heitmann, S., Robinson, P. & Povey, G. (2011). Slow food, slow cities and slow tourism. In Robinson, P. Heitmann, S., & Dieke, P. *Research themes for tourism*, Willingford: Cabi International, 114-127.

[40] Yurtseven, H.R. & Kaya, O. (2011). Slow Tourists: A Comparative Research Based on Cittaslow Principles. *American International Journal of Contemporary Research.* 1(2), 91-98.

[41] Fullagar, S., Markwell, K. & Wilson, E. (2012). *Slow tourism. Experience and Mobility*. Bristol: Channel view publication.

[42] Buckley, R. (2011). Tourism Under Climate Change: Will Slow Travel Supersede short Breaks?. *AMBIO*. 40, 328–331.

[43] Fosgerau, M. (2006). Investigating the distribution of the value of travel time savings. *Transportation Research Part B: Methodological*. 40, 8, 688–707.

[44] Nijkamp, P. & Baaijens, S. (1999). Time pioneers and travel behavior: an investigation into de viability of "Slow motion". *Growth and Change*. 30(2), 237-263.

[45] Di-Clemente, E., De-Salvo, P. & Hernández-Mogollón, J.M. (2011). Slow tourism o turismo de la lentitud: un nuevo enfoque al desarrollo de territorios lentos. *Tourism & Management Studies*. 1, 883-893.

[46] Lancerini, E. (2005). Territori Lenti: Contributi per una nuova geografia dei paesaggi abitati italiani. *Territorio*. 34, 9-15.

[47] Lanzani, A. (2005). Geografie, paesaggi, pratiche dell'abitare e progetti di sviluppo. *Territorio*. 34, 19-37.

[48] Calzati, V. (2009). I territori lenti: definizione e caratteri, In CST, *Sviluppo turistico e territori lenti*. Milano: Franco Angeli, 15-30.

[49] Bonomi, A. (2009). La piattaforma alpina nell'ipermodernità, In Borghi, E.,(eds) *La sfida dei territori nella green economy*. Roma: Il Mulino, 131-147.

[50] Giaoutzi, M. & Nijkamp, P. (1993). *Decision support model for sustainable development*. Aldershot: Avebury.

[51] Camagni, R., Capello, R. & Nijkamp, P. (2001). Managing sustainable urban environments, In Paddison, R. *Handbook of urban studies*. London: Sage, 124-139.

[52] Capuano, G. (2007). *Mesoeconomia. Teorie ed evidenze empiriche di economia regionale*. Milano: Franco Angeli.

[53] Wced (1987). *Our common future*. Nairobi: UNEP.

[54] Latouche, S. (2010). *La scommessa della decrescita*. Milano: Feltrinelli.

[55] Daly, H.E. (2008). *A Steady-State Economy*. London: Sustainable Development Commission.

[56] Holden, E. (2007). *Achieving sustainable mobility: every day and leisure-time travel in the EU*. Aldershot: Ashgate.

[57] Witt, C.A. & Muhlemann, A.P. (1994). The implementation of total quality management in tourism: some guidelines. *Tourism management*. 15(6), 416-424.

[58] De Masi, D. (2006). *Cos'è la qualità. Come evolverà nel prossimo quinquennio*, Symbola: Fondazione per le qualità italiane: Roma.

[59] McCabe, S. & Johnson, S. (2013). The happiness factor in tourism: subjective well-being and social tourism. *Annals of Tourism Research*. 41, 42–65.

Marketing places: highlighting the key elements for attracting mural-based tourism

M. DE-MIGUEL-MOLINA
Universitat Politècnica de València, Management Department, Spain
V. SANTAMARINA-CAMPOS
Universitat Politècnica de València, Conservation and Restoration of Cultural Heritage Department, Spain
M. SEGARRA-OÑA
Universitat Politècnica de València, Management Department, Spain
B. DE-MIGUEL-MOLINA
Universitat Politècnica de València, Management Department, Spain

ABSTRACT

Strategic place marketing is an approach adopted to attract tourism, industry and investment. Among the possible attractions of a place, cultural features can attract not only tourists but also residents and a creative industry. Some locations have successfully developed their place image based on having an important set of mural artworks. The goal of this paper is to highlight the key elements in attracting mural-based tourism. Based on case study analysis, we find that attractions alone cannot attract tourism; amenities, hotels and restaurants are also needed to create a comparative advantage.

1 INTRODUCTION

Strategic place marketing is an approach adopted to attract tourism, industry and investment. It is based on four main strategies: image marketing, attractions marketing, infrastructure marketing and people marketing [1]. Among the possible attractions of a place, cultural features can attract not only tourists but also residents and a creative industry.

Culture has a direct impact on the value of urban real estate and is a key element of culture-led urban regeneration strategies. This impact can come from major flagship developments – an art gallery, concert hall or museum – as well as from micro-activities associated with small-scale cultural entrepreneurs and urban activists. However, the urbanity of city life is also a crucial resource for all kinds of cultural activities which move between the commercial and the non-commercial, the subsidized and the entrepreneurial with great fluidity [2]. This is the link between culture and creative industries.

Moreover, creative cities can establish two types of strategy [3]: a culture-centric orientation or an econo-centric orientation. The former sees the creative city as a place with strong flourishing arts and culture, creative and diverse expressions, and inclusivity, artistry and imagination in which creativity is related to identity, rights, beliefs and social well-being. The latter sees the creative city as a place that is driven by strong, innovative, creative, competitive, cultural and creative industries, and economically sustainable artists and arts organizations. Creativity is a means by which to achieve the main goal of local economic development. Whereas the first approach involves building from the inside out, the second focuses on helping a place enhance its competitiveness [1].

Several approaches can be applied from a strategic marketing point of view. That is, it could be conceived as a strategy to reach a sustainable tourism which, according to the United Nations World Tourism Organization, is tourism that achieves an effective balance between the environmental, economic and socio-cultural aspects of tourism to guarantee long-term benefits to communities [4]. In this case, mural-based tourism, as a form of cultural or historic tourism, has the potential to combine the creative work of different professions, including restoration experts, artists, heritage developers and architects, with a strategic marketing focus.

2 LITERATURE FRAMEWORK

Some locations have successfully developed their place image based on having an important set of mural artworks. We have analysed some related literature focused on industry development around murals, although this was scarce [5] (See table 1).

Table 1. Selected literature related to creative cities and murals.

Authors	Country/objective
[6] Koster, 2008	Canada (beautification, tourism)
[7] Mohd Fabian et al., 2012	Malaysia (beautification)
[8] Rolston, 2012	Northern Ireland (politics)
[9] Coffey, 2012	Mexico (tourism)

As is apparent from Table 1, the focus of mural development can be totally different depending on location. In countries such as Northern Ireland, the approach is clearly based on community development, trying to promote a peaceful environment. Canada combines community development with an economic development approach, as in the famous case of Chemainus. However, perhaps Mexico is the country with a stronger image of mural-based tourism.

Murals can be broadly conceived as a form of art that is readily and freely accessible to the public at large. However, the tourism "business model" proposed (Figure 1) clearly requires a conscious effort to encourage its implementation as it does not occur naturally [6]. Koster [6] also defined four categories of murals according to the functions they serve and the reasons for which they were developed:

1. Murals for public art include those painted on city walls for a variety of reasons unrelated to tourism. These include the development and promotion of art and

business advertising. Nonetheless, they could serve to provide a location for tourism purposes.

2. Murals for youth development include the creation of a mural project specifically to address the needs of a particular age group. Participation in the programme develops job skills training, a sense of community and an understanding of history. These murals tend to be eclectic in nature, but are often historically based. This category also includes murals developed as anti-graffiti projects.

3. Murals as community beautification are undertaken to enhance a building or neighbourhood. Although there is no tourism motivation, tourism may result by default. The content of these murals varies from wildlife and community events to abstract images and historical occurrences.

4. Murals as a tourist attraction are developed and marketed to draw people into the community. The focus is on developing murals to distinguish the community as a unique destination. These murals generally follow a heritage-based theme. They represent what a group within the local community believes to comprise local heritage alongside what they believe people want to see. As more communities are choosing mural development to pull in tourists, this leads to the question of how many more mural-based attractions can exist, as these communities can develop an almost homogeneous appearance, especially when one considers that the pool of professional mural artists is relatively small.

Based on the above approaches, communities need to consider carefully the extent to which particular strategies have been utilized elsewhere.

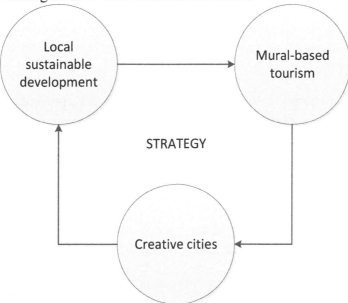

Figure 1. A mural-based tourism strategy [5].

3 CASE STUDY

3.1 Data

We have taken as a case study the country of Uruguay and specifically two of their locations: the city of Montevideo and the town of Colonia de Sacramento. The first is the capital of the country and the second was declared a World Heritage site, that is, it has the infrastructure and previous image to support this particular tourism attraction.

We collected primary data from a research project conducted by Professor Santamarina as well as secondary data from government websites.

In the case of Uruguay, muralism has great potential. The project team has catalogued approximately 600 mural artworks throughout the country and specifically 278 in Montevideo and 60 in the department of Colonia (55 in Rosario and five in Colonia de Sacramento). Uruguayan mural painting in the 20th century constitutes an unknown chapter in the history of art, in both national and international circles. During this period, which was the most prolific in terms of Uruguayan art, there were two completely different active trends:

- The constructivist trend, represented by Joaquín Torres García, was taken as a national symbol from the 1940s. From the middle of the 20th century, the Uruguayan government promoted the inclusion of murals at the entrances of new buildings or in community spaces.

- Social realist art was centred on Berdía and Seade as the major figures. Social realism inspired the Mexican figurative muralism of the beginning of the 20th century. It represents social and politic topics related to social levels, workers or historic events. These murals are normally located in public buildings and schools.

There are many works on Torres García, but literature on other Uruguayan mural artists is particularly scarce [10]. Broadly speaking, we have historical murals that could serve for tourism purposes although they face some conservation problems. The issues concerning the preservation and conservation of contemporary Uruguayan muralist production primarily centre on their deactivation, absence of planning, lack of economic resources and professional intrusion. These factors are related to certain conservation and restoration problems:

1. Integral mimetic retouching treatments as well as inappropriate treatments due to non-professional interventions.

2. The detachment of mural paintings as the only means of ensuring their survival because of heritage deactivation processes in those situations where murals represent a secondary interest in relation to the property where they are located.

3. The defective condition of murals located in schools resulting from cultural deactivation processes and the absence of guidelines for their management.

4. The accelerated degradation of materials used by contemporary mural artists during the experimentation period that resulted in challenging problems.

5. Artists' lack of technical knowledge concerning adapting traditional techniques to outdoor murals, which has resulted in their rapid degradation because of the environmental agents.
6. The lack of private and public investment as a consequence of heritage deactivation

processes, which is precipitating the degradation of mural paintings and even their complete loss because of urban reorganization processes.

Murals appear in several Uruguayan locations. The type of tourism available in the districts to which they belong may influence the potential of mural art as a tourist attraction (Table 2). At present, and with the exception of the towns of Rosario and San Gregorio Polanco which have a mural-based tourism strategy, the remaining locations do not take advantage of this opportunity. Rosario and San Gregorio have used murals as an identity factor and to enhance their heritage, developing participative projects between artists and residents, seeking to aggregate value at their locations.

Montevideo and Colonia could develop mural-based tourism, being two of the locations in the country more frequently visited (with the exception of the summer destinations of Punta del Este and the Litoral Termal) and both having a cultural focus that could easily incorporate a mural artworks itinerary. In the case of Colonia de Sacramento, this tourism could be generated by developing a form of co-branding with Rosario (52 km away), which belongs to the same territorial department. The principal targets of both locations, Montevideo and Colonia, are people between 30 and 64 years old.

Table 2. Uruguayan districts and types of tourism offered [5].

Districts (locations) with mural art	Type of tourism
Montevideo (Montevideo)	Cultural
Maldonado (Maldonado, Punta del Este, Pan de Azúcar, Punta Ballena)	Sun and sand
Colonia (Colonia del Sacramento, Rosario)	Cultural
Tacuarembó (San Gregorio Polanco)	Rural
Canelones	Rural
Salto	Rural
Lavalleja	Rural
Florida	Rural

In 2012, Montevideo was the main place visited (27.4%), the primary purposes being visiting and recreation (66.5%) [11]. There are 87 hotels in the city and most of the hotels in the country are 3 and 4 stars. Feedback from visitors reports that they like the kindness of Uruguayan people, but they think the city is expensive and not clean. Thus, visitors consider it necessary to improve the infrastructure in relation to hygiene and reduce prices. The department of Colonia received 9.8% of the country's visits in 2012. It has the advantage of being the main entrance to the country. The number of hotels is 38. The town which is most oriented towards cultural tourism is Colonia de Sacramento as it was declared a World Heritage site in 1995 by the United Nations Organization for Education, Science and Culture (UNESCO). The Old Town began to be restored in the 1970s and it attracts many visitors each year. The town of Colonia has developed a hospitality industry, which mainly comprises restaurants and hotels. The major investments were made from the 1970s onwards by Argentinean businesses. While the first tourists were Argentines and Brazilians, the number of European tourists has grown in the last 10 years.

3.2 Method

In a previous study [5], we gained an appreciation of the potential of mural-based tourism strategies in Uruguay. To achieve this, we developed a qualitative analysis. In March and April 2011, a team led by Professor Santamarina undertook 42 in-depth, face-to-face interviews as part of a project on the social implications of Uruguayan muralism, supported by the Spanish Agency for International Development Cooperation (AECID).

The sample consisted of people involved in the conservation of Uruguayan muralism in the city of Montevideo and the town of Colonia del Sacramento. All the interviews were conducted using the same scripted set of questions, which included minor changes depending on the particular town and respondent and were based on a semi-structured format. This format was chosen to allow respondents to express themselves freely and provide as much information as possible [12]. The interviews were used to identify tourism opportunities through content analysis [10, 13, 14], but also enabled us to analyse the content in greater depth. With this data, we analyse the key factors in developing a mural-based place tourism strategy following the methodology proposed by Kotlet et al. [1].

4 RESULTS

Regarding the infrastructure, both locations have developed a hospitality sector to support tourists and visitors, but they also need sufficient infrastructure to conserve and provide access to the mural artworks that could be included in a special itinerary. The lack of resources and professional training in heritage restoration has led to a loss of the symbolic dimension of the murals, forgetting their social function and accelerating their damage. Furthermore, mural artworks are difficult to conserve and the lack of a legal framework for governing restoration professionals has resulted in improper interventions.

Moreover in some places, for example in Colonia, residents consider that certain traditions that differentiate their location from others have been lost: "...*we do not have typical places to eat any more*". In addition, they report that the tourism strategy is poor:
> "*There is no tourism policy, unfortunately. Uruguay could become a tourist destination, but it has not been able to exploit its potential. To make matters worse, cultural and artistic attractions are not being developed as they should be.*"

Whilst the World Heritage designation has contributed to the promotion of tourism, there is still a long way to go:

> "*About 15 years ago, after 1995, when the town was named as a World Heritage site, a series of guidelines were established. However, many of these have not been implemented. I think this is partly because the state has not enforced their implementation. ... I think ... the state has not had a well-defined strategy in terms of urban planning and certain historical and cultural issues. Recently, they seem to be more focused on these points. However, in my opinion, many things that were done before were done haphazardly and there was never a clear strategy...*"

That is, when Colonia gained the World Heritage designation, no management programme had been developed, causing damage to the original values of the historic town. In 2012, a management plan was approved with the participation of several actors, but no reference to muralism was included.

This lack of planning is also perceived in Montevideo. Thus, the lack of a defined strategy may be a threat to sustainable development of these towns:

"We are immersed in the process of creating a plan and that is going to be very difficult. However, if it is successful, it could give us tools to manage the city based on the idea of a more integrated landscape, where the environment is integrated, where all eras of our historical narrative are integrated."

However, some participants think mural-based tourism is possible:

"I think there's an organizational problem, there is a definite lack of organization. I think there are isolated cases, e.g. here in San Gregorio Polanco [in Tacuarembó district], which are using murals as a tourist attraction and as a distinctive feature, which make the murals a place for people to go and visit."

However, this initiative has been promoted by a neighbourhood committee, not by a public initiative. Another comment was that:

"...in the 90s, work was done to use walls as a form of expression. This sought to generate resort towns from the use of mural painting. That was in the 90s in San Gregorio Polanco. There was also another experience in Rosario ... and another one in Pan de Azúcar, in Maldonado, which was based on a social standpoint, creating a tourist village from the mural as an element to attract people and generate tourism."

In short, the participants identified clear opportunities for Uruguay to develop mural-based tourism, although this would initially need the introduction of a plan to restore all its muralism:

"I think if we improve the tourism on offer, we will improve the tourist profile. Personally I am not optimistic; we have no cultural tourism to offer. I think that what we have, if there is any at all, is very ... poor and small scale."

A mural artwork attraction can be created in both locations if a strategy is defined. This could be based on a place marketing strategy [1], which should first analyse the following (see Figure 2):

1. Possible target markets. In this case, actual visitors and tourists could be the target initially, but also residents and other types of industry apart from hospitality, such as creative industries. It would also be advantageous to try to attract investors. In the town of Colonia, Argentinian investors are the most important group.

2. Marketing features of the location. The image of the locations could be improved by providing cleaner surroundings and also accessible prices. With regard to pricing, mural artworks need to be restored but an advantage is that many of them are outdoors, so they can be promoted as a free attraction. However, in attracting mural-based tourism related businesses, such as hospitality, amenities, restaurants

and creative industries, should also be developed. Moreover, accessible transportation will be needed to reach all the mural artworks that could be included in a special itinerary. Hence, a mural-based place image could be promoted if the locations have all these things to offer. In the case of Colonia, there could be the opportunity to develop a co-itinerary with Rosario.

3. The establishment of a planning group. From our primary data, we can see that there is no strategic plan around mural artworks, not only from a tourism point of view but also from a restoration perspective. For this reason, a planning group should be formed, integrating all the public and private actors interested in the promotion of mural artworks.

Market Targets: residents, visitors, tourists, investors

Marketing factors: mural-based image, infrastructure, mural artworks, Uruguayan people

Planning group: public and private actors involved

Figure 2. Levels of place marketing applied to mural-based tourism. Own elaboration based on [1].

5 DISCUSSION AND CONCLUSION

Uruguay has great potential as a mural-based tourism destination, but it needs a strategic plan to supervise the permanent restoration of its murals and also to involve the local community in this task, an opportunity illustrated by the following comments:

"I speak of a deeper appreciation [of muralism], of how important it really has been for society ... I don't think this has been investigated."
"...we are proud to have a city like this."

In relation to this, Koster's [6] study could be a good starting point. Moreover, it could be useful to define the type of mural each location wants to develop according to the four mural categories defined by Koster, based on the functions they serve and the reasons underpinning their development. It would also be necessary to combine the two types of strategy proposed by Smith and Warfield [3], i.e. a culture-centric orientation and an econo-centric orientation, supported by creative governance that connects different vertical levels of government and horizontal ministries, as well as public–private partnerships.

To start with, a good methodology to follow could be the place marketing strategy [1] to analyse first the possible targets, the key marketing factors (image, infrastructure, attractions and people) and to create a planning group which would represent all the public and private actors involved. When designing this strategy, it should be borne in mind that muralism, as a cultural resource, is related not only to economic development (the tourism and creative industry) but also to community development (identity). If used only as an economic resource, the impact of industries on the environment can be forgotten and the social values of muralism can be lost. Murals, by their very nature, cannot be removed from their environment.

On the other hand, using muralism as a resource for tourism can enhance heritage conservation if the community is involved in the process. Among other artworks, murals are seen as "social art" because in many cases they represent the community's history or values, being a component of identity. While other artworks are seen as "high culture", muralism has a social focus, a direct communication with the community. It is thus like an "open book" that everybody can understand.

AKNOWLEDGEMENTS

This work has been carried out thanks to the support of different research projects: Creative Industries (PAID2012-487-UPV), conducted by Blanca de Miguel Molina; Participative decision-making for sustainable management (ECO2011-27369-MEyC), conducted by Concepción Maroto; Impacto de las prácticas innovadoras en el "performance" medioambiental de la empresa: identificación de factores moderadores (PAID2011-1879-UPV), conducted by María del Val Segarra Oña; and Design and implementation of inclusive cultural policies: contemporary Uruguayan muralism as a tool of a sustainable heritage activity and Uruguayan 20th century muralism as a tool and model for cultural local sustainable development (HAR2012-32060 and PAID2011-2035-UPV), conducted by Virginia Santamarina Campos.

REFERENCE LIST

[1] Kotler, Ph. Haider, D.H. & Rein, I. (1993) *Marketing places. Attracting investment, industry, and tourism to cities, states, and nations.* The Free Press: New York.
[2] O'Connor, J. (2007) *The cultural and creative industries: a review of the literature.* Creative Partnerships Series. Arts Council England.
[3] Smith, R. & Warfield, K. (2008) The creative city: a matter of values, In: Cooke, P. & Lazzeretti, L. (2008). *Creative cities, cultural clusters and Local Economic Development.* Edward Elgar Publishing Limited: Cheltenham, 287-312.
[4] UNWTO (2004) *Sustainable Development of Tourism, Mission statement, Conceptual Definition.* Available at http://www.unwto.org/sdt/mission/en/mission.php?op=1 (accessed November 2013).
[5] De Miguel-Molina, M., Santamarina-Campos, V., de Miguel-Molina, B. & Segarra-Oña, M. (2013). Creative cities and sustainable development: mural-based tourism as a local public strategy. *Dirección y Organización.* 50, 31-36.

[6] Koster, R.L.P. (2008). Mural-based tourism as a strategy for rural community economic development, In Arch G. Woodside (ed.): *Advances in Culture, Tourism and Hospitality Research*, 2, 153- 292.

[7] Mohd Fabian, H., Osman, M.T. & Mohd Nasir, B. (2012). Towards integrating public art in Malaysian urban landscape. *Pertanika Journal of Social Science and Humanities*, 20, 251-263.

[8] Rolston, B. (2012) Re-imaging: Mural painting and the state in Northern Ireland. *International Journal of Cultural Studies*, 15, 447-466.

[9] Coffey, M. K. (2012) *How a Revolutionary Art Became Official Culture: Murals, Museums, and the Mexican State*. Duke University Press Books.

[10] Santiago Kern, L. & Santamarina Campos, V. (2010) *Aproximación a la Función Social del Muralismo Uruguayo del Siglo XX*. Master Thesis. Universitat Politècnica de València.

[11] Uruguayan Ministry of Tourism and Sports (2013). *Uruguayan Tourism statistics Report 2013*. Available at http://turismo.gub.uy/es-ES/estadisticas/itemlist/category/430-2013 (accessed November 2013).

[12] Bernard, H. (2000) *Social research methods: Qualitative and quantitative approaches*. London:Sage.

[13] Weber, R.P. (1990) *Basic Content Analysis*, 2nd edition, Series: Quantitative Applications in the Social Sciences, number 49. Sage University Paper: Newbury Park, California.

[14] Sierra Bravo, R. (2001). *Técnicas de Investigación Social*, 14th edition. Thomson: Madrid.

Tourist local destination, trust and business opportunities: the role of ethical business management certification

P. RUIZ-PALOMINO
University of Castilla-La Mancha, Department of Business Management, Spain
R. DEL POZO-RUBIO
University of Castilla-La Mancha, Department of Economic & Financial Analysis, Spain
J. RODRIGO-ALARCÓN
University of Castilla-La Mancha, Department of Business Management, Spain

ABSTRACT

Business people are increasingly recognizing that a good reputation in business ethics confers many business opportunities, especially in local markets such as the tourist local destination sector. The purpose of this chapter is to analyse the mechanisms through which an ethical business management certification can help local tourist companies to obtain high value-added business possibilities. The chapter concludes by exploring how gaining a reputation on this issue can confer tourist firms with trustworthiness, relational social capital, and greater opportunities to cooperate with others in creating more and superior business.

1 INTRODUCTION

During the past decades, ethics have become a major issue in the everyday activities of business managers and professionals [1]. That is, the level of implementation of ethics practices is increasingly higher in business contexts [2,3,4], with at least some ethics practices (e.g. code of ethics) implemented in most companies [5]. Notwithstanding the importance of ethical management for both academic and professional entities, ethical lapses continue to occur in the business world. The number of employees who observe misconduct at work continues to be relatively high [6,7], as are the number of ethical lapses continuously publicized in the media (e.g. Health South Corp., Lehman Brothers, Fannie Mae, AIG, Tyco International, Barclays Libor manipulation). Considering this negative scenario in which even firms implementing useful ethics practices (i.e. code of ethics) [8] suffer from a "rotten apples" corporate reputation [9], business people can be inferred not to be truly viewing ethics as something positive in running their firms.

Most likely, the increased managerial interest in business ethics in the past decades might have been raised as a response to the need to comply with external stakeholder demands. Such interest could have responded to that both business ethics and corporate social responsibility requirements have, over time, come to the fore of society's general conscience [10]. As a result, businesses might have been increasingly implementing ethics practices (e.g. code of ethics, training) and creating social corporate reports (e.g. sustainability memos) in order to exclusively provide an image of ethical and good corporate citizenship. In effect, firms could have been extending a great amount of effort to instill ethical practices while believing that ethics leads really to competitive disadvantages, and failing to appreciate the value that might come from being ethical.

However, while business ethics is not firmly internalized and integrated into daily business activities, the efforts extended in implementing such ethics initiatives are likely in vain, without visible ethical outcomes in decisions, behaviors, and interrelationships with stakeholders. This is especially true in the tourist local destination context because daily contacts between different agents involved in tourism are expected to be really frequent. While the Tourism Productive Structure is a group of organizations geared toward the creation of a global tourist product, the tourism product is usually structured as a multidimensional network of horizontal, vertical, and diagonal connections between different business tourism firms [11], which tend to occur more often in tourist local destinations. As such, it appears mandatory to engage in real ethical practices to reflect good citizenship to stakeholders in such concentrated business contexts. These are ideal scenarios where the good ethical reputation attained can more easily enhance business operations and strengthen relationships with other tourist partners.

Therefore, the focus of this chapter is on advancing knowledge on the important role of ethical business management certifications in enhancing local tourist firms' ethical reputations to stakeholders. Ethical business management certifications could help in this regard because certification means that businesses aim to demonstrate a salient strategy to avoid ethical failures. Another major objective we pursue in this chapter is to clarify from a theoretical view of social capital [12,13,14] how businesses benefit from being ethically certified. Following this, we review prior literature to explain the rationales that led us to perceive the current relationships among the different concepts we address herein (i.e. ethical business management certification, tourist local destination, relational social capital) especially as they pertain to the enhancement of corporate reputations and inter-organizational cooperation. Doing so enables us to outline a theoretical model that links all these concepts together to delineate how business opportunities for ethical business management–certified firms are favored. Finally, we discuss the research implications and outline the limitations and future research directions.

2 ETHICAL BUSINESS MANAGEMENT CERTIFICATION

To instill an ethical culture in a company, business managers have at their disposal myriad organizational initiatives that help transmit the importance of ethics and positively influence employees' ethical behaviour. However, consistency in the ethics message transmitted for all organizational procedures and mechanisms is necessary for the successful implementation and superior ethical corporate business performance [15,16]. As such, the implementation of an ethical (business) management system (EMS) is a necessary first step toward gaining a true ethical culture. The correct implementation of an EMS would mean that all mechanisms that are perceptible and serve to transmit values, beliefs, and assumptions (e.g. written documents, training programs, hotlines, myths and stories) are methodically and consistently implemented to foster ethical behaviour [17].

Usually, adoption of an EMS accompanies some 'ethical' or 'corporate social responsibility' standards (Global Reporting Initiative's Sustainability Reporting Guidelines, Social Accountability International's SA 8000, FORETICA's SGE21, Institute of Social and Ethical Accountability's AA1000) created by coalitions of organizations, governments, non-governmental organizations, and/or civil society organizations that help and guide business managers in implementation. These standards are created not only to provide advice to organizations but also to enhance the level of performance for such management systems [18], with the objective of being viewed as legitimate by other organizations and stakeholders. Therefore, when an EMS is implemented according to recognized standards, the firm is able to better guarantee a good reputation to stakeholders. In effect, it is by obtaining certification from certifying authorities, which shows that standards have been correctly applied, that the firm can send a clear sign that it is committed to engaging in ethically and socially sound behaviors and decisions. All others interested in the firm's performance (e.g. shareholders, consumers, competitors, environmental context, suppliers, distributors, investors, government) will also know that the certification process entailed several audits, which proves that the firm truly implemented the system and is committed to developing business activities according to ethical standards in meeting their interests.

When ethical and socially responsible reputation is acquired, the firm is provided with some valuable resources connected to attain competitive advantage. Thus, the firm may attract value in many ways such as by facilitating recruitment of the best human resources and capital [19]; obtaining greater financial funding than other companies, due largely to its ethical and socially responsible reputation, which makes their inclusion in ethical funds of investment easier [20]; receiving favorable treatment by media and other social authorities; and gaining a greater number of sales and production contracts [19]. In short, the high levels of trust attained from stakeholders when a company gains a moral capital reputation [21] can help ethically certified firms acquire valuable resources. In any case, the benefits that these firms might receive in terms of inter-organizational cooperation create excellent business opportunities as well.

3 TOURISM LOCAL DESTINATIONS: CLOSE INTER-ORGANIZATIONAL RELATIONSHIPS

According to the literature, as a consequence of belonging to a territorial cluster, firms can obtain myriad advantages [22, 23]. Within a territorial cluster, there are many interrelationships between different agents. This issue is largely due to the idea that firm success in such a cluster is dependent on the success of the whole cluster. A high level of cooperation among firms in the same cluster is usually considered one of the many resources conferred by simply belonging to the cluster [24].

Although much of the literature on the advantages that firms gain from belonging to certain territorial clusters has focused on the industrial sector, recent research indicates that advantages can also be applicable to the tourist sector [25, 26] and, more specifically, to the tourist local destination context. In effect, tourist firms are usually clustered in tourist local destinations, entailing structural configurations very similar to those appearing in other industrial clusters. In effect, in tourist local destination clusters, tourists firms run their business activities around the same tourist product to make it different and unique to other tourist destinations. As such, firms' feelings of belonging to the cluster might be certainly strong [26, 27] which would foster the need for close interrelationships to offer a competitive product in the destination they are settled. It is not a surprise then that some research defines this type of cluster as an organizational form governed by cooperation patterns [28].

In summary, tourist local destinations, defined as regional concentrations of small and medium-sized firms located around a unique tourist product, make inter-organizational cooperative relationships within the cluster an essential aspect for an efficiently managed business. Such an aspect is even crucial to be carried out for the tourist cluster's sake as tourist firms here compete to make their destination more attractive than other tourist local destinations, which irretrievably needs close inter firm relationships and cooperation to be attained.

4 SOCIAL CAPITAL AND TRUSTFUL RELATIONSHIPS: A QUEST FOR BUSINESS OPPORTUNITIES

The phenomenon of social capital is necessarily implied in regional and territorial clustering issues [23, 29] and refers to '*the sum of the actual and potential resources embedded within, available through and derived from the network of relationships possessed by an individual or social unit*' and includes '*both the network and the assets that may be mobilized through that network*' [13: 243]. Social capital is multidimensional, entailing three key dimensions [13]: structural social capital, cognitive social capital, and, more important for the interests of this chapter, relational social capital.

Although all three dimensions are closely interrelated [30, 31], there are some distinctions among them worth highlighting. The structural social capital dimension indicates how strong and powerful the firm is within the network and how many structural holes the firm covers [32]. The cognitive social capital dimension pertains to the common context and language used in the structure (e.g. shared narratives, language, acronyms, codes, underlying assumptions) that help to support everyday communication among the different agents involved in the network [31, 33]. Finally, the relational social capital dimension refers to the extent to which the different agents within the network are motivated to combine and exchange resources and intellectual capital [13].

This relational dimension is particularly important to the territorial agglomeration phenomenon because it is through the geographical proximity of the different organizations that high levels of this social capital dimension confer to firms. As a result, it is common for these territorial clusters to be perceived as a source of business opportunities for the firms included within them. In effect, the high-quality relationships usually generated in such contexts brings that firms benefit through different aspects. For example, mutual understanding among different agents is increased, time-consuming exchange processes are reduced, and both resource exchanges and knowledge acquisition are fostered [34]. Moreover, because of the relatively high relational social capital in these types of geographically concentrated territories of firms [35], companies gain more opportunities to improve and innovate their offer of (tourist) products [28,31,36]. In addition, cooperation can lead firms to broaden their product offering to consumers and design packaged products that include other specific, specialized products from the other related tourist agents. Finally, the different agents benefit from the multiple advertising actions they themselves would carry out for their own welfare, as well as that of the entire tourist local destination cluster.

However, to achieve highly cooperative relationships among the different agents within a cluster, a trustful climate is an essential element. In effect, the relational dimension of social capital captures the personal relationships that actors have with their contacts, based on a long history of interactions [13]. As such, trust is implicitly necessary to maintain relational social capital [13]. If trust is lacking, the motivation of agents to cooperate and maintain long-standing relationships would be undermined, no matter that the geographical connections in tourist local destination agglomerations provide higher possibilities of interaction between agents [37]. Rather, these relationships would cease if the agents involved perceived that they could not trust one another.

5 HOW BUSINESS OPPORTUNITIES APPEAR THROUGH ETHICAL BUSINESS MANAGEMENT CERTIFICATIONS: PROPOSAL OF AN EXPLANATORY MODEL

The idea that ethics plays an important role in enhancing business opportunities for tourist firms located in tourist local destinations finds salient support. In effect, ethics is a necessary element to any relationship governed by trust [21, 38, 39, 40], and thus to engender trusting relationships among agents, interactions should be absent of ethical failures and opportunistic behaviors, in accordance with their commitment to one another. An important way to preserve trust in relationships and, thus, to facilitate inter-firm cooperation is by obtaining ethical business management certifications.

Although a rigorous process of preparation and evaluation is required for such certifications, and despite the difficulty of evaluating some ethical problems by external audit entities [41], the certified emblem acquired permits the firm to offer others warrantees that ethical commitment is the norm for the daily business activities and behaviors of both the firm and its individual members. In doing so, the firm reflects a moral capital reputation more easily. In addition, acquisition of this certification triggers a process leading to the creation of business opportunities for the tourist firm.

In effect, acquiring an EMS certification entails the implementation of numerous ethics practices, procedures, and systems encrypting a coherent ethics message. Doing so leads to close interactions with consulting entities not only to facilitate EMS implementation but also, more importantly, to adhere to frequent audits and reviews of the EMS that certifying authorities carry out on a periodical basis. Notwithstanding these efforts, once the certification mark is attained, the firm gains the best unbeatable, legitimate "presentation card" to stakeholders, helping to make contacts with potential tourist partners with whom to open new beneficial business opportunities. In effect, an ethical business management certification brings with it a high level of relational social capital, which in parallel, confers a high number of trusting relationships with others. This is a salient aspect for the ethically certified firm because possibilities for cooperation with other agents increase, compared with those of non-ethically certified firms. In the end, a variety of business opportunities (e.g. new tourist products, packaged tourist products, multiple advertising) are more easily gained by the ethically certified tourist firm located in tourist local destination clusters. The theoretical model depicted in Figure 1 helps illustrate this process, in which EMS certifications benefit the tourist firm by open and creating new business opportunities with other agents.

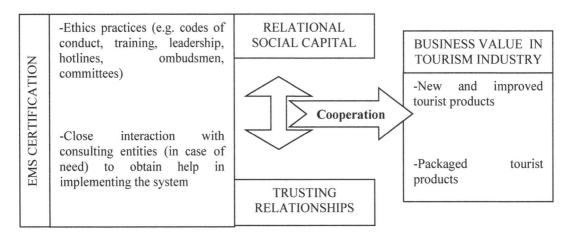

Figure 1. A model for understanding how an ems certification

6 CONCLUSIONS, LIMITATIONS, AND FUTURE RESEARCH DIRECTIONS

Although businesspeople are increasingly considering business ethics in their operational planning, there still seems to be a generalized feeling that efforts to enhance the ethical climate consist of more financial constraints than benefits for the firm. However, although in the short run managers may perceive these efforts as financial impositions to the company, there are sound rationales to believe that these efforts will become invaluable to operate optimally in the market. This is especially true in the tourist sector and, more specifically, in tourist local destination clusters because cooperation seems to play an important role both for the cluster and for the individual firms residing in it to operate optimally [42].

As mentioned, one of the long-term positive aspects for ethically committed firms is trust generated in their immediate environment. Therefore, tourist firms located in specific tourist local destination clusters will benefit from acquiring reputations as ethical firms, specifically in their relationships with other businesses, potential partners, and, ultimately, stakeholders (e.g. suppliers, clients, distributors). Although in this type of agglomeration the high number of necessary interactions among companies usually makes their ethos perceptible in the long run, by obtaining EMS certifications, this process for ethical companies should increase and speed up. In addition, the trust generated from the presence of such certification give opportunities to cooperate with other tourist agents in the short run, providing the company a better competitive position relative to others. In effect, for a tourist company in tourist local destination clusters, the possession of a mark certifying that an EMS has been implemented facilitates the generation of trust and garners enduring and stable relationships with other partners from the outset. These enduring relationships likely confer a series of benefits to the firms involved, and especially for the ethically certified firm. Some of these benefits entail aspects such as new and improved products, the opportunity to offer packaged services, and multiple advertising by other partners located in the same tourist local destination cluster.

This theoretical chapter contributes to the understanding of how ethical business management certifications can help firms generate business opportunities and activities in tourist local destinations, but several limitations need to be addressed. One limitation is the theoretical approach addressed here for examining how an ethical business management certification can benefit firms located in tourism local destinations. However, this work fills a gap in theoretical literature by providing additional insights into how firms can enhance business operations in tourist districts such as those addressed herein. In addition, this chapter represents a first step toward facilitating further research focused on developing theoretical propositions to be empirically tested in a sample of tourist firms operating both in and out of specific tourist local destination clusters.

Another limitation refers to the partial overview taken in the assessment of how tourist firms located in tourist local destinations can create business opportunities. Here, we exclusively analysed one exclusive potential antecedent, the obtaining of EMS certifications, and some invaluable consequences derived from such certifications in gaining an ethical business management reputation in tourist local destination clusters: trusting relationships and relational social capital. However, other factors, such as the structure and configuration of resources and capabilities to acquire new knowledge, could also help to explain how business opportunities are generated [29, 43] even after a tourist firm attains an ethical business management certification. Thus, further research is required to better understand this complex issue, which should include the analysis of the role of other intervening variables in giving more significant meaning and usefulness to the theoretical model proposed herein.

REFERENCES LIST

[1] Treviño, L.K. & Nelson, K.A. (2004). *Managing Business Ethics: Straight Talk about How to Do it Right*. New York: John Wiley & Sons.
[2] Weaver, G.R., Treviño, L.K. & Cochran, P.L. (1999). Corporate ethics practices in the mid-1990's: An empirical study of the Fortune 1000. *Journal of Business Ethics*. **18**, 283-294.
[3] I.B.E. (Institute of Business Ethics) (2008). *The 2008 National Survey: Employee Views of Ethics at Work*. London, UK. Available at http://www.ibe.org.uk/publications/listofpublications.htm [Accessed on November 20th, 2011].
[4] Guillén, M., Melé, D. & Murphy, P. (2002). European vs American approaches to institutionalization of business ethics: the Spanish case. *Business Ethics: A European Review*. **11**, 167-178.
[5] Kaptein, M. & Schwartz, M.S. (2008). The effectiveness of business codes: A critical examination of existing studies and the development of an integrated research model. *Journal of Business Ethics*. **77**, 11-127.

[6] E.R.C. (Ethics Resource Center) (2005). *National Business Ethics Survey, How Employees View Ethics in Their Organizations, 1994-2005*, Washington, DC. Available at http://www.ethics.org/topic/national-surveys [Accessed on July 20th, 2012].

[7] E.R.C. (Ethics Resource Center) (2011). *National Business Ethics Survey, Workplace Ethics in Transition*, Washington, DC. Available at http://www.ethics.org/topic/national-surveys [Accessed on July 21st, 2012].

[8] O'Fallon, M.J. & Butterfield, K.D. (2005). A review of the empirical ethical decision-making literature: 1996-2003. *Journal of Business Ethics*. **59**, 375-413.

[9] Sims R.R. & Brinkman, J. (2003). Enron ethics (or: culture matters more than codes). *Journal of Business Ethics*. **45**, 243-256.

[10] Carroll, A.B. & Bucholtz, A.K. (2008). *Business and Society: Ethics and Stakeholder Management*. Ohio: South Western Cengage Learning.

[11] Michael, E.J. (2007). *Micro-clusters and Networks: The Growth of Tourism*. Oxford: Elsevier.

[12] Tsai, W. & Ghoshal, S. (1998). Social capital and value creation: the role of intrafirm networks. *Academy of Management Journal*. **41**, 464-76.

[13] Nahapiet, J. & Ghoshal, S. (1998). Social capital, intellectual capital, and the organizational advantage. *Academy of Management Review*. **23**, 242-266.

[14] Adler, P.S. & Kwon, S.W. (2002). Social capital: prospects for a new concept. *Academy of Management Review*. **27**, 17-40.

[15] Weaver, G.R., Treviño, L.K. & Cochran, P.L. (1999). Integrated and decoupled corporate social performance: Management commitments, external pressures and corporate ethics. *Academy of Management Journal*. **42**, 539-552.

[16] Selvarajan, R. & Cloninger P. A. (2009). The influence of job performance outcomes on ethical assessments. *Personnel Review*.**38**, 398-412.

[17] Ruiz-Palomino, P., Bañon-Gomis, A. & Ruiz-Amaya, C. (2011). Morals in business organizations: an approach based on strategic value and strength for business management. *Cuadernos de Gestión*. **11**, 15-31.

[18] Peirce, M. (2003). AA1000 series: The challenge of accountability management. In Wieland, J. (Ed.), *Standards and Audits for Ethics Management Systems, The European Perspectives*. Heidelberg: Springer.

[19] Fombrum, C.J. (2001). Corporate Reputation as Economic Assets. In Hitt, M.A., Freeman, R.E. & Harrison, J.S. (Eds.), *The Blackwell Handbook of Strategic Management*. Oxford: Blackwell Publishers.

[20] De la Cuesta, M., Valor, M. & San Martin, S. (2002). *Inversiones Éticas en Empresas Socialmente Responsables*. Madrid: UNED.

[21] Uslaner, E.M. (2002). *The Moral Foundations of Trust*. Cambridge: Cambridge University Press.

[22] Signorini, L.F. (1994). The price of Prato, or measuring the industrial district effect. *Paper in Regional Science*. **73**, 369-392.

[23] Molina-Morales, F.X. (2005). The territorial agglomerations of firms: A social capital perspective from the Spanish tile industry. *Growth and Change*. **36**, 74-99.

[24] Dei Ottati, G. (1994). Cooperation and competition in the industrial district as an organization model. *European Planning Studies*. **2**, 35-53.

[25] Merinero, R. (2008). Micro-cluster turísticos: El papel del capital social en el desarrollo económico local. *Revista de Estudios Empresariales*. **2**, 67-92.

[26] Saxena, G. (2005). Relationships, networks and the learning regions: Case evidence from the Peak District National Park. *Tourism Management*. **26**, 277-289.

[27] Paniccia, I. (1998). One, a hundred, thousands of industrial districts. organizational variety in local networks of small and medium-sized enterprises. *Organization Studies*. **19**, 667– 669.

[28] Novelli, M., Schmitz, B. & Spencer, T. (2006). Networks, clusters and innovation in tourism: A UK experience. *Tourism Management*. **27**, 1141-1152.

[29] Parra-Requena, G., Molina-Morales, F.X. & García-Villaverde, P.M. (2010). The mediating effect of cognitive social capital on knowledge acquisition in clustered firms. *Growth and Change*. **41**, 59-84.

[30] Nahapiet, J. (2009). Capitalizing on connections: social capital and strategic management. In Bartkus, V.O. & Davis, J.H. (Eds.), *Social Capital: Reaching Out, Reaching in*. Cheltenham: Edward Elgar Publishing.

[31] Martinez-Cañas, R., Sáez-Martínez, F.J. & Ruiz-Palomino, P. (2012). Knowledge acquisition's mediation of social capital-firm innovation. *Journal of Knowledge Management*. **16**, 61-76.

[32] Zheng, W. (2010). A social capital perspective of innovation from individuals to nations: where is empirical literature directing us?. *International Journal of Management Reviews*. **12**, 151-83.

[33] Lesser, E. (2000). Leveraging social capital in organizations. In Lesser, E. (Ed.), *Knowledge and Social Capital: Foundations and Applications*. Boston: Butterworth Heinemann.

[34] Yli-Renko, H., Autio, E. & Sapienza, H. (2001). Social capital, knowledge acquisition, and knowledge exploitation in young technology-based firm. *Strategic Management Journal*. **22**, 587–613.

[35] Molina-Morales, F.X. & Martinez-Fernandez, M.T. (2009). Does homogeneity exist within industrial districts?. A social capital based approach. *Papers in Regional Sciences*. **88**, 209-230.

[36] Delgado-Verde, M., Martín de Castro, G., Navas-López, J.E. & Cruz-González, J. (2011). Social capital, relational capital and technological innovation. empirical evidence in spanish high and medium-high technology manufacturing firms. *Cuadernos de Economía y Dirección de la Empresa*. **14**, 207-221.

[37] Gulati, R. (1995). Does familiarity breed trust? The implications of repeated ties for contractual choice in alliances. *Academy of Management Journal*. **38**, 85–112.

[38] Kouzes, J. M. & Posner, B. (2001). Bringing leadership lessons from the past into the future. In Bennis, W., Spreitzer, G.M. & Cummings, T.G. (Eds.), *The future of leadership. Today's top leaders thinkers speak to tomorrow's leaders*. San Francisco: Jossey-Bass.

[39] Ruiz, P., Ruiz, C. & Martinez, R. (2011). Improving the 'Leader–Follower' Relationship: Top Manager or Supervisor? The Ethical Leadership Trickle-Down Effect on Follower Job Response. *Journal of Business Ethics*. **99**, 587-608.

[40] Bull, M., Ridley-Duff, R., Foster, D. & Seanor, P. (2008). Seeing social enterprise through the conceptualisation of ethical capital [On line]. Paper presented at ISBE, *Institute for Small and Entrepreneurship Conference*, 5-7 of November, Belfast, North Ireland, Sheffield Hallan University. Available at http://shura.shu.ac.uk/758/ [Accessed on February 25th, 2013].

[41] Francés, P., Granda, G. & Urtiaga, A. (2003). The ethical management system of FORETICA. In Wieland, J. (Ed.), *Standards and Audits for Ethics Management Systems, The European Perspectives*. Heidelberg: Springer.

[42] Pechlaner, H., Fischer, E. & Hammann, E-V. (2006). Leadership and Innovation Processes-Development of Products and Services Based on Core Competencies. *Journal of Assurance Quality in Hospitality and Tourism.* **6**, 31-57.

[43] Gruber, M., Heinemann, F., Brettel, M. & Hungeling, S. (2010). Configurations of resources and capabilities and their performance implications: an exploratory study on technology ventures. *Strategic Management Journal.* **31**, 1337-1356.

A proposal for of the USALI by inclusion of environmental behaviour indicators and information

A. CIUDAD-GÓMEZ
University of Extremadura, Accounting and Financial Economy Department, Spain

ABSTRACT

At the moment, companies need instruments which allow the effect of their activities on the environment in which they operate and its progress to be measured, and to be able to report their environmental behaviour both internally and externally.
So our aim is to open a debate about the need to develop guidelines related with the presentation of information about environmental matters which allow standardization within the lodgings sector; and to put forward a series of indicators and environmental statements to be taken into account in upcoming updates of the "Uniform System of Accounts for the Lodging Industry"

1   INTRODUCTION

Interest in the environment has increased in recent years and companies responding to stakeholders' new demands have begun to make information about their environmental performance public, leading to the need to define instruments and establish standards for the presentation of reports which allow this performance to be informed of both within and outside the organization. But the diversity of reports and indicators and non-existence of standardized regulations are hampering comparability of environmental reporting as well as its credibility to users.

Concentrating on the lodgings sector with which this study is concerned, we have the *"Uniform System of Accounts for the Lodging Industry"* (USALI) [1] reporting and management system, internationally used by the lodging industry in general, which allows useful information to be obtained for the decision making process, although one of its failings is that it does not includes guidelines related with the presentation of information about environmental matters.

In this respect, we think it is necessary that green or environmental accounting should begin to be included in this uniform accounting system, including rules related with the presentation of information about environmental aspects that might have an effect on business decision-making, because nowadays *"companies are beginning to consider environmental protection as an added value of their business image"* [2], even more in the lodging industry where activity is dependent on the surrounding environment and its conservation. So the purpose of this study is to open a debate about the need to develop guidelines for the presentation of information about environmental matters which allow standardization in the lodging sector, and present a proposal for improvement of the USALI which can be taken into account in upcoming updates, including as minimum amount of information a series of environmental declarations and a set of indicators to measure the environmental performance of companies in the lodging sector.

2 MATERIALS & METHODS

This study has been carried out based on the suggestions and contributions of international organizations, the characteristics of the lodging sector and the USALI itself. The main existing recommendations include those made by the *International Organization for Standardization* (ISO), which divides environmental indicators into two categories [3]: *Environmental performance indicators (EPIs) and Environmental condition indicators (ECIs)*.

One stands out because it has become very well known in recent years, the carbon footprint, about which two standards are being developed: ISO 14067 *"Carbon footprint of products - Requirements and guidelines for quantification and communication"* and ISO 14069 *"GHG - Quantification and reporting of GHG emissions for organizations (Carbon footprint of organization)"*. As a public alternative to the ISO, the European Union has published *The European Eco-Management and Audit Scheme* (EMAS III), the third edition of the European Eco-Management and Audit Scheme, which includes the use of environmental behaviour indicators, focused on these areas: energy efficiency, material efficiency, water, waste, biodiversity, and emissions; and the indicators shall [4].

In addition to these standards, another guideline taken into consideration is the *Global Reporting Initiative* (GRI), extensively used internationally and identified by the European Union as a model to follow [5], establishing the essential aspects that should be covered by environmental indicators [6].

Finally, the *World Business Council for Sustainable Development* (WBCSD) identifies the key elements to be measured in eco-efficiency [7] and in *The Greenhouse Gas Protocol (GHG Protocol)*, published in collaboration with the World *Resources Institute* (WRI), it sets out standards and protocols for the quantification and monitoring of GHG emissions, grouped into three levels, called fields [8]. On the other hand, the *USALI,* a set of regulations published by the *American Hotel & Motel Association* (AHMA), is an accounting system applicable to the lodgings industry which over the years has become a reporting and management system used internationally by the hotel industry in general, though as Harris & Brown [9] point out, it has become the industry standard especially for large hotel companies and international chains.

Its operation is based on the division of hotel activity into departments, to which their direct costs are attributed, and supplying information aimed at internal and external users, establishing simple, clear, precise rules of presentation.

But the USALI, which has facilitated homogenization of information presentation in the lodging sector throughout the world, does not have rules about the presentation of environmental information, only mentioning dispersedly certain costs related with the consumption of resources and the outputs produced, maintenance costs, laundry services, supplies and transport.

3 RESULTS & DISCUSSION

Because of all this, we suggest that future editions of the USALI should include a part dedicated to environmental information, with two sections.

3.1 Section 1. Environmental statements

In this section, we have concentrated on the design of a normalized format for *environmental statements* related with consumptions of resources and emissions generated by hotel activity. All of them should include information at minimum for two consecutive years and the base year.

3.1.1 *3.1.1 Energy consumption*

Companies will be more competitive to the extent that energy consumptions are progressively lower, and this is what we propose for their management (Table 1):

Table 1. Energy Consumed Balance

Energy type	Unit	Current year			Prior year		Base year	
		Amount	Gigajoules (GJ)	%	Gj	%	Gj	%
Non-renewable								
Electricity	kwh		$GJ_{1\text{-}NR}$					
Petrol	Litres		$GJ_{2\text{-}NR}$					
Diesel	Litres		$GJ_{3\text{-}NR}$					
Oil (light)	litres		$GJ_{4\text{-}NR}$					
Oil (heavy)	litres		$GJ_{5\text{-}NR}$					
Propane	litres		$GJ_{6\text{-}NR}$					
Natural gas	m^3		$GJ_{7\text{-}NR}$					
Kerosene	Litres		$GJ_{8\text{-}NR}$					
Coal	Tonnes		$GJ_{9\text{-}NR}$					
Firewood	Tonnes		$GJ_{10\text{-}NR}$					
Other			$GJ_{n\text{-}NR}$					
Total non-renewable energy consumption			$GJ_{TNR} = \sum GJ_{NR}$					
Renewable								
Bioethanol	Litres		$GJ_{1\text{-}R}$					
Biodiesel	Litres		$GJ_{2\text{-}R}$					
Other			$GJ_{n\text{-}R}$					
Total renewable energy consumption			$GJ_{TR} = \sum GJ_R$					
Total sum of energy consumed			$GJ_{TNR} + GJ_{TR}$	100%		100%		100%

3.1.2 Water consumption

Water saving is important because of its scarcity as a resource, so we propose the following report (Table 2).

Table 2. Summary of total water consumption

Water consumption	Current year		Prior year		Base year	
	m_3	%	m_3	%	m_3	%
Purchased water (PW)	M_{3PW}					
Abstracted water (AW) • Groundwater • River or reservoir water • Recovered water	M_{3AW}					
Total water consumption	$M_{TWC} = M_{3PW} + M_{3AW}$	100%		100%		100%

3.1.2

3.1.3   3.1.3 Material consumed

The main impact generated by the products and substances used by lodging establishments is the waste remaining, so this must be managed. In drafting the report, the unit we have chosen initially is tons; other mass units can also be used, but the company would have to parameterize its system to do this (Table 3).

Table 3. Summary of material consumed

Material consumed	Current year		Prior year		Base year	
	Tonnes	**%**	**Tonnes**	**%**	**Tonnes**	**%**
Paper products	Tons$_{PP}$					
Paper						
Toilet Paper						
Napkins						
Tablecloths						
Others						
Cartridges and toners	Tons$_{C\&T}$					
Cartridges						
Toners						
Others						
Plastics	Tons$_{PL}$					
Garbage Bags						
sanitary bags						
Laundry Bags						
Plastic cups						
Plastic plates						
Plastic Cutlery						
Straws						
transparent film						
Others						
Chemicals and cleaning	Tons$_{C\&C}$					
Bleach						
Detergents						
Dishwasher						
Softeners						
Disinfectants						
Shampoo						
Gel						
Others						
Total material consumed	**TMC= Tons$_{PP}$ +Tons$_{C\&T}$ +Tons$_{PL}$ +Tons$_{C\&C}$**	**100%**		**100%**		**100%**

3.1.4   3.1.4 Greenhouse gas emissions (GHG)

The proposed report is an initial step towards calculation of the carbon footprint and will allow companies to manage GHG reduction and increase their operating efficiency.

In preparing it, we have taken two essential matters into account, the gases to be included and their scope: whether to take all gases into consideration or just CO_2, the former providing a more complete view whereas the latter, as Wiedmann & Minx [10] point out, makes calculation easier; and with regard to scope, whether to include scope 1 and 2 or even scope 3 emissions.

In our proposal, we have chosen to take CO_2, NH_4, N_2O, HFC and PFCs into account, and with regard to scope, to include scope 1 and 2 emissions, in order to establish simple, clear, precise rules of presentation, in accordance with the principles of the USALI (Table 4).

Table 4. Summary of CO_2e emissions by category

Source	Current year		Prior year		Base year	
	Emissions (MT CO_2e)	**%**	**Emissions (MT CO_2e)**	**%**	**Emissions (MT CO_2e)**	**%**
Stationary combustion	$A_{1.1.}$					
Mobile Combustion	$A_{1.2.}$					
Refrigerant/ AC Fugitive Emissions	$A_{1.3.}$					
Scope 1 GHG emissions	$A_1 = A_{1.1.} + A_{1.2.} + A_{1.3.}$					
Electricity	$A_{2.1.}$					
Scope 2 GHG emissions	$A_2 = A_{2.1.}$					
Total Emissions (Scope 1 + Scope 2)	$TE = A_1 + A_2$	100%		100%		100%

3.1.5 3.1.5 Solid waste production

The proposed environmental report (Table 5) will be useful in waste reduction management and improving selective collection for later reuse, recycling, regeneration or composting.

Table 5. Summary of solid waste produced

Material category	Current year		Prior year		Base year	
	Tonnes	%	Tonnes	%	Tonnes	%
Selective collection of waste for recycling Leftover food Garden waste and soil Paper and paperboard Plastics Metals Glass Clothing and textiles others						
Total non-hazardous waste recycled	$A_{1.1.}$					
Tones & Accessories Cooking oil used Batteries fluorescent tubes Containers of hazardous substances						
Total hazardous waste recycled	$A_{1.2.}$					
Total Weight recycled waste	$A_1 = A_{1.1.} + A_{1.2.}$					
Total Weight of Solid Waste Disposed to Landfill	A_2					
Total solid waste production	TSWP= $A_1 + A_2$	100 %		100 %		100 %

3.1.6 *3.1.6 Waste water discharges (liquid waste)*

It is important that the amount of waste water produced (Table 7) and its composition (Table 6) be reported.

Table 6. Quality of wastewater discharged

Parameters	Unit	Current year	Prior year	Base year	Effluent limit
Biochemical Oxygen Demand BOD$_5$	mg/L				
Chemical Oxygen Demand - COD	mg/L				
Total suspended solids- TSS	mg/L				
Total Nitrogen	mg/L				
Total Phosphates	mg/L				
pH	-				
Total Coliform	MPN/100 ml				
Residual Chlorine	mg/L				
Oil and grease	mg/L				

Table 7. Summary of waste water discharges

Waste water		Current year		Prior year		Base year	
		m$_3$	%	m$_3$	%	m$_3$	%
Total annual volume of water treated in sewage own	M$_{3WT}$						
Total annual volume of water treated and reused Total annual volume of water treated and discharged	M$_{3WT\&R}$ M$_{3WT\&D}$						
Total annual volume of untreated wastewater and discharged.	M$_{3UW\&D}$						
Total waste water discharge	M$_{TD}$ = M$_{3WT\&D}$ + M$_{3UW\&D}$	100 %		100 %		100 %	

It would be a good idea to be able to separate and differentiate between sullage and sewage (or grey water and black water), there being important differences between the two which mean their treatment and management are also different.

3.2 Section 2. Environmental Performance Indicators

The information about consumption of resources and waste generation, emissions and waste water is useful, but performance comparison between hotels is easier to do intensely, calculating by dividing the consumption or environmental impact by a normalization factor.

For the normalization factor, considering as Thomas et al. [11] point out that "*each industry sector has its own peculiarities and that normalisation measures must be sector-sensitive*", we have used the number of *rooms occupied* (11) and *total guests* (23) defined by the USALI [1], and other metrics such as the area in *square feet* (m^2) of the building could also be included.

We will now describe each of the environmental indicators that we suggest be included in the USALI (Table 8).

Table 8. Environmental indicators included in the USALI.

3.2.1 *ENERGY CONSUMPTION (1) (2)*	
INDICATOR 1:	**Energy Consumption intensity**
Description of Indicator	This indicator measures progress in average energy consumption by the organization in relation to the number of rooms occupied (number of guests).
Measure	Total energy consumption (GJ) per annum[7] Rooms Occupied (11) per annum [Total guests (23) per annum]
Unit	Gj per Rooms Occupied (total guests).
Indicator objective	Minimise overall consumption of energy
INDICATOR 2:	**Renewable Energy Consumption**
Description of Indicator	This indicator measures progress in renewable energy consumption by the organization. It is presented as a percentage of total energy consumption, encouraging the replacement of current fossil fuel energy by renewable energy sources.
Measure	Total renewable energy consumed (GJ) per annum Total sum of energy consumed (GJ) per annum
Unit	%
Indicator objective	Encourage greater use of renewable energy
3.2.2 *WATER CONSUMPTION (3)*	
INDICATOR 3:	**Water Consumption intensity**
Description of Indicator	This is defined as the total volume of water consumed per rooms occupied (number of guests).
Measure	Total water consumption per annum Rooms Occupied (11) per annum [Total guests (23) per annum]
Unit	m^3 per room occupied (total guests).
Indicator objective	Minimisation of water consumption

---

[7] *"Total energy consumption (GJ) per annum"* can be classified into the following sub-categories.

3.2.3 *MATERIAL CONSUMED (4)*	
INDICATOR 4:	**Material consumed intensity**
Description of Indicator	This is defined as the total volume of material consumed per rooms occupied (number of guests).
Measure	$$\frac{\text{Total material consumed per annum}}{\text{Rooms Occupied (11) per annum [Total guests (23) per annum]}}$$
Unit	Tonnes per rooms occupied (total guests).
Indicator objective	Minimisation of material consumed
GREENHOUSE GAS (CO_2) EMISSIONS (GHG) (5)	
INDICATOR 5:	**Greenhouse Gas Emissions intensity**
Description of Indicator	This indicator measures the amount of greenhouse gas that is produced per rooms occupied (number of guests).
Measure	$$\frac{\text{Total weight of } CO_2e \text{ produced per annum (tonnes } CO_2e)}{\text{Rooms Occupied (11) per annum [Total guests (23) per annum]}}$$
Unit	Tonnes CO_2 equivalents per rooms occupied (total guests).
Indicator objective	Minimise the net production of greenhouse gas (CO_2)
INDICATOR 5.a:	**Greenhouse Gas Emissions intensity: stationary combustion**
Description of Indicator	This indicator measures the amount of greenhouse gas (stationary combustion) that is produced per rooms occupied (number of guests).
Measure	$$\frac{\text{Total Emissions } CO_2e \text{ from stationary combustion per annum}}{\text{Rooms Occupied (11) per annum [Total guests (23) per annum]}}$$
Unit	Tonnes CO_2 equivalents from stationary combustion per rooms occupied (total guests).
Indicator objective	Minimise the production of GHG from stationary combustion
INDICATOR 5.b:	**Greenhouse Gas Emissions intensity: mobile combustion**
Description of Indicator	This indicator measures the amount of greenhouse gas (mobile combustion) that is produced per rooms occupied (number of guests).
Measure	$$\frac{\text{Total Emissions } CO_2e \text{ from mobile combustion per annum}}{\text{Rooms Occupied (11) per annum [Total guests (23) per annum]}}$$
Unit	Tonnes CO_2 equivalents from mobile combustion per rooms occupied (total guests).
Indicator objective	Minimise the production of GHG from mobile combustion

INDICATOR 5.c:	**Greenhouse Gas Emissions intensity: Refrigeration and air conditioning equipment Fugitive Emissions**
Description of Indicator	This indicator measures the amount of greenhouse gas (Refrigeration/ AC Fugitive Emissions) that is produced per rooms occupied (number of guests).
Measure	Total refrigerant emissions (MT CO_2e) per annum / Rooms Occupied (11) per annum [Total guests (23) per annum]
Unit	Tonnes CO_2 equivalents from Refrigeration/ AC Fugitive Emissions per rooms occupied (total guests).
Indicator objective	Minimise the production of GHG from Refrigeration/ AC Fugitive Emissions
INDICATOR 5.d:	**Greenhouse Gas Emissions intensity: the electricity use**
Description of Indicator	This indicator measures the amount of greenhouse gas (the electricity use) that is produced per rooms occupied (number of guests).
Measure	Total Emissions CO_2e the electricity used per annum / Rooms Occupied (11) per annum [Total guests (23) per annum]
Unit	Tonnes CO_2 equivalents from the electricity used per rooms occupied (total guests).
Indicator objective	Minimise the production of GHG from the electricity used
SOLID WASTE PRODUCTION (6) (7) (8)	
INDICATOR 6:	**Solid waste production intensity**
Description of Indicator	This indicator measures progress in solid waste generation by the organization.
Measure	Total solid waste production (tonnes) per annum / Rooms Occupied (11) per annum [Total guests (23) per annum]
Unit	Tonnes per rooms occupied (total guests).
Indicator objective	Reduce solid waste production
INDICATOR 7:	**Solid waste disposed to landfill**
Description of Indicator	This indicator measures the weight of waste that has not made a selective collection for recycling and become waste for landfill
Measure	Total Weight of Solid Waste Disposed to Landfill per annum / Total solid waste production (tonnes) per annum
Unit	%
Indicator objective	Reduce solid waste disposed to landfill

INDICATOR 8:	Percentage of recycled waste
Description of Indicator	This indicator measures progress in the selective collection of waste for recycling. It is presented as percentage of total waste production.
Measure	Total Weight recycled waste per annum Total solid waste production (tonnes) per annum
Unit	%
Indicator objective	Increase the selective separation of waste for recycling
INDICATOR 8.a:	Percentage of recycled non-hazardous waste
Description of Indicator	This indicator measures progress in the selective collection of non-hazardous waste for recycling. It is presented as percentage of total waste production.
Measure	Total non-hazardous waste recycled Total solid waste production (tonnes) per annum
Unit	%
Indicator objective	Increase selective separation.
INDICATOR 8.b:	Percentage of recycled hazardous waste
Description of Indicator	This indicator measures progress in the selective collection of hazardous waste for recycling. It is presented as percentage of total waste production.
Measure	Total hazardous waste recycled Total solid waste production (tonnes) per annum
Unit	%
Indicator objective	Increase selective separation.
WASTE WATER DISCHARGES (LIQUID WASTE) (9) (10) (11)	
INDICATOR 9:	Waste water discharges intensity
Description of Indicator	This indicator measures progress in generation of liquid waste from the organization.
Measure	Total waste water discharge (m_3) per annum Rooms Occupied (11) per annum [Total guests (23) per annum]
Unit	M_3 per rooms occupied (total guests).
Indicator objective	Reduce liquid waste production

INDICATOR 10:	Waste water processing in sewage own intensity
Description of Indicator	This indicator measures progress in the process of wastewater.
Measure	Total annual volume of water process in sewage own (m3) per annum rooms occupied (11) per annum
Unit	M3 per rooms occupied
Indicator objective	Encourage the waste water process in sewage own
INDICATOR 11:	Waste water processed and reused intensity
Description of Indicator	This indicator measures progress in the reuse of processed wastewater.
Measure	Total annual volume of water processed and reused (m3) per annum rooms occupied (11) per annum
Unit	M3 per rooms occupied
Indicator objective	Encourage greater reuse of water processed

3.2.4 *ECO-EFICIENCIA (12)*

INDICATOR 12:	Eco-efficiency
Description of Indicator	This indicator combines economic performance and environmental impact evaluation.
Measure	Value of product and service Environmental impacts **Value of product and service:** ▪ Rooms occupied (11) ▪ Total guests (23) ▪ Total revenue (See *Summary Operating Statement*) ▪ ANOI (See *Summary Operating Statement*) **Environmental impacts:** ▪ Energy consumption (Gj) ▪ Water consumption (m3) ▪ Material consumed (t) ▪ Greenhouse gas emissions (MT. CO_2e) ▪ Solid Waste (t) ▪ Waste water (m3)
Unit	€ ($, £ ...) per Gj, m3, t or MT CO_2e
Indicator objective	Enhancing the quality and reducing the environmental impact

4   CONCLUSIONS

Homogenization of the preparation and presentation of information world-wide is fundamental to allow comparability to be achieved, so it is essential that guidelines on environmental information should begin to be included in the USALI.

So by way of a suggestion for improvement we have set out a series of standardized environmental indicators and declarations using simple, easily applicable methods, in accordance with the principles of the USALI.

We also consider that it is essential to use the ***carbon footprint*** as an environmental indicator, which is hampered by the non-existence of a general consensus on its definition and calculation. Therefore, an international process of standardization needs to be initiated encompassing and delimiting the existing proposals, defining and delimiting the scope of its calculation, and resolving the ambiguity and discretionality in scope 3. When a general consensus has been reached, the next step will be homogenization of calculation of the carbon footprint by companies in the lodging sector, and development of their own measurement system.

5 REFERENCE LIST

[1] American Hotel & Lodging Educational Institute (AHLEI) (2006). *Uniform System of Accounts for the Lodging Industry.* Hotel Association of New York City New York City. (Tenth Revised Edition). Lasing, Michigan.

[2] Ripoll, J.V. & Crespo, C. (1998). Costes derivados de la gestión medioambiental. *Técnica contable*, 591, 169-180.

[3] ISO 14031 (1999). "Environmental Management -Environmental Performance Evaluation Guidelines" Switzerland: International Standard.

[4] EMAS III, 2009. *Regulation (EC) No 1221/2009 of the European Parliament and of the Council of 25 November 2009 on the voluntary participation by organisations in a Community eco-management and audit scheme, repealing Regulation (EC) No 761/2001 and Commission Decisions 2001/681/EC and 2006/193/EC.* Available in: http://eurlex.europa.eu/LexUriServ/LexUriServ.do?uri=OJ:L:2009:342:0001:0045:en:pdf [accessed 14 February 2010].

[5] Commission of the European Communities (2001). *Green Paper. Promoting a European framework for Corporate Social Responsibility.* COM (2001) 366 final, Brussels. Available in: http://eur-lex.europa.eu/LexUriServ/site/en/com/2001/com2001_0366en01.pdf [accessed 15 May 2011].

[6] Global Reporting Initiative (GRI) (2011). *Sustainability Reporting Guidelines (Version 3.1).* Amsterdam, The Netherlands. Available in: https://www.globalreporting.org/resourcelibrary/G3.1-Guidelines-Incl-Technical-Protocol.pdf [accessed 22 December 2011].

[7] World Business Council for Sustainable Development (WBCSD) (2000). *Measuring Eco-Efficiency: A guide to reporting company performance.* Available in: http://www.wbcsd.org/web/publications/measuring_eco_efficiency.pdf [accessed 10 May 2010].

[8] World Resources Institute (WRI) & World Business Council for Sustainable Development (WBCSD) (2004). *The Greenhouse Gas Protocol: A Corporate Accounting and Reporting Standard (Revised Edition).* GHG Protocol Initiative. Available in: http://www.ghgprotocol.org/files/ghgp/public/ghg-protocol-revised.pdf [accessed 12 May 2010].

[9] Harris, P. & Brown, B. (1998). Research and development in hospitality accounting and financial management. *International Journal of Hospitality Management,* 17, 161-181.

[10] Wiedmann, T. & Minx, J. (2007). *A Definition of 'Carbon Footprint.* In: C. C. Pertsova, Ecological Economics Research Trends: Chapter 1, 1-11, Nova Science Publishers, Hauppauge NY, USA.

[11] Thomas, C., Tennant, T. & Rolls, J. (2000). *The GHG indicator: UNEP guidelines for calculating greenhouse gas emissions for businesses and non-commercial organizations.* United Nations Environment Programme. Available in: http://www.unepfi.org/fileadmin/documents/ghg_indicator_2000.pdf [accessed 12 December 2011].

The Spanish equestrian routes. Opportunities and pitfalls for developing this new tourism product

M. J. VIÑALS
Universitat Politècnica de València, Cartographic Engineering, Geodesy and Photogrammetry Department, Spain
M. MORANT
Universitat Politècnica de València, Cartographic Engineering, Geodesy and Photogrammetry Department, Spain
M. D. TERUEL
Universitat Politècnica de València, Economy and Social Sciences Departament, Spain
P. ALONSO-MONASTERIO
Universitat Politècnica de València, Cartographic Engineering, Geodesy and Photogrammetry Department, Spain

ABSTRACT

Equestrian routes are one of the most exciting tourism products in relation to horse riding activities. They represent sports-, adventure-, and nature-based activities, and in recent years, several European developments and the Royal Spanish Equestrian Federation have devoted efforts to enhance their tourism potential in Spain.

In spite of the private stakeholder and local authority's interest in Equestrian Tourism, several pitfalls have been identified in relation to marketing and commercialisation. This study reveals that the equestrian sector is not currently organised enough to engage in tourism and discloses key elements for the definitive establishment of this new product.

1. INTRODUCTION

Equestrian tourism in Spain is an emergent activity that may impact two economic spheres: the horse industry and the tourism sector. Consequently, this situation demands a consideration of the difficulties in starting this new activity. Nevertheless, many opportunities have been identified in Spain to enhance the tourism segment.

In recent decades, European countries with the largest number of horses have successfully developed equestrian tourism within the framework of the economic development of rural areas. Among these countries are United Kingdom, France, Germany, Italy and Eastern Europe states, such as Hungary and Romania. Therefore, it seems feasible for Spain to successfully develop these sorts of developments because the possibilities in Spain are very similar to these countries.

Equestrian tourism is a broad concept that covers a multitude of horse-related activities. Activities could be divided into participatory experiences, such as riding properly speaking, as well as spectator activities in which the visitor can observe others perform equestrian shows or events. This study focuses on those activities in which participants are actively involved, especially those related to horseback riding and trail riding, that is, horseback riding in nature.

Trail riding is a guided activity that takes into account the conservation of the natural landscape and cultural heritage and the enhancement of community activities, bringing a breath of fresh air to the rural world, enabling it to diversify and to open up to new perspectives. Trail riding is a high-quality outdoor experience that allows riders to develop personal values, such as the enrichment of human relationships (connections with the local people, bonding with friends, family or other riders), the strengthening of the relationship between man and horse, the enjoyment of beautiful landscapes and wilderness, the practice of physical exercise and the sharpening of skills. The increasing awareness of ecological issues, the educational effects of access to the natural environment, and the understanding of specific challenges related to rural areas are also beneficial consequences of leisure riding. Other emotional benefits can also be added, such as self-esteem, escape, fun, and confidence. By taking part in trail riding activities, it is possible to support the local culture of the rural areas, to contribute to the welfare and survival of animals and to have influence on the employment situation in rural areas and on the equestrian industry.

In general terms, there are different categories of trail riding activities recognised and offered around the world, but it must be noted that only a few recreational or leisure horse disciplines feature in commercial horse tourism products, and fewer still in adventure products. These activities are commonly classified depending on the difficulty, the range of the different prior skills and experience required of the riders, and the length of stay. According to Ollenburg [1], guided commercial trail rides and horse treks are the most marketed, but both can be included in the field of adventure tourism because they require considerable riding skills and are therefore only available to clients who are already skilled recreational riders. Nevertheless, we can currently find other less sophisticated products that constitute the high volume of customers. They are short trail rides for independent tourists and/or local residents with no previous riding experience, characterised as low-price, low-skill and short-duration. These products offer the opportunity to briefly ride a placid horse being led at a gentle pace on level ground. In this framework, there are included "learning experiences" organised by practitioners strongly linked to the equestrian centres or riding schools (beginners and novice riders). The activity usually consists of horsemanship lessons and short leisure ridings (1/2 day), especially during the weekend. Riders are local regular clientele from within a 60-minute driving radius from the main cities. Proximity to high-population areas is a key factor for the equestrian centres. The riding schools and equestrian centres, then, are the real main beneficiaries of this activity.

Another similar user profile is the inexperienced occasional tourist, engaged by a new, attractive option to spend their leisure time in a complementary activity during their holidays in a destination area. These customers rent a horse, and they need specialised associated services to carry out the activity. Customer profiles and motivations are different with this group from the previous group, and the expenditure level can be the same or slightly higher.

The category of one-day trail rides includes experienced riders, and two types of riders in this group may be found. The first type consists of riders who are usually horse owners with their own horses in equestrian centres under different sorts of horse board or kept at home if they live in rural areas. This type of rider usually goes on weekly one-day excursions, especially on weekends and on holidays, using local catering services and, occasionally, horse transportation services to move horses to outstanding natural areas to enjoy different landscapes. The benefit from this group of riders mainly goes to the equestrian centres because they offer the boarding facilities and services. These riders book specialised horse riding products when travelling abroad. The second type consists of riders who are occasional tourists who want to enrich their experience in a destination with a complementary activity such as a one-day horse riding trip. From the point of view of the tourism implications, they are the same as the previous half-day trip customers; but in this case, the riders are more experienced and have better equestrian skills. These riding activities are an interesting source of incomes for the equestrian centres because tourists have to rent a horse and all of the services (e.g., horses, saddle, and catering) to carry out the activity, including the equestrian guiding services, especially if riders are not familiar with the area or are concerned with safety.

These activities fall within the field of excursionism, which according to the World Tourism Organization, means that overnighting is not a part of the offered tourism product. Therefore, tourist horse riding experiences may be horse treks or multi-day backcountry horse-packing trips that include some type of accommodation (e.g., ranches, farms, equestrian centres, country houses, "bed and bale" houses, natural or rural shelters, rural hotels and hostels, and rural inns). This type of activity is a low-volume, high-price, high-skill, and longer-duration equestrian product.

Horse treks are products that involve five to seven hours riding every day for one to two weeks or longer, averaging 20 to 40 km per day. They are a challenging activity for both the horse and the rider, and being fit for the ride is essential. According to Ollenburg [1], clients engaging in these types of tours should be experienced in long-distance endurance riding, be able to control an unfamiliar horse in difficult terrain, and be able to adapt to local horse breeds, riding gear and other customs. This high-experience ride tourist must be familiar with different saddle and bridle designs and different techniques for tethering, picketing, hobbling or yarding horses during stops and at night; they also have to control different signals and commands to communicate from rider to horse. Nevertheless, the most commonly offered activity consists of the two-day horse riding overnight, with accommodation, full board and ride included in the rate. All of these adventure horse treks are offered in a wide range of destinations worldwide. Other type of products includes farm stays and ranches devoted to skilled visitors who want to help with farm work, such as cattle driving.

The United States of America (USA), Canada, Australia and many European Union countries have highly developed equestrian tourism, and currently they offer attractive programs for international tourists. These countries are the main flows of equestrian tourists travelling to worldwide equestrian destinations. According to the American Horse Council [2], in the USA there are 9.2 million horses, and 42% of them are used for recreational trail riding purposes. Over 2 million people are horse owners, and nearly 4.6 million people are involved in the industry as, for instance, owners, breeders, trainers, and service providers. In the European Union, there are 4.4 million horses, and most of them are devoted to recreational purposes [3]. In Germany, approximately 1.6 million riders are recognised, and almost 70% of them practise leisure riding. Bouhaouala & Albertini [4] provide data from France and inform us that the number of riders registered in the Equestrian French Federation has multiplied almost five times in the last twenty-five years (from 145,071 in 1984 to 687,334 in 2010). The importance of leisure to them is predominant; thus, in 2010, only 10.5% of the licences concern competition, which means that almost 90% of the riders practise equestrian pursuits for different types of leisure activities. The French equestrian tourism market is based on 2,423 equestrian centres, and it has an estimated annual turnover between € 220 million and € 245 million. Customers of these equestrian centres (local, French and foreign tourists) account for nearly 45% of their business.

In Spain, equestrian tourism is an activity that has not received much attention until recently. Considering the fact that little accurate data are available about the horse industry, only some institutional studies devoted to horses provide us with figures. Nevertheless, research in this field is based upon different approaches that always reflect underestimated figures. According to Tragsega [5], the number of horses in Spain in 2003 was 424,373, a later study of the General Sub-direction of Livestock Production of the Spanish Ministry of Agriculture, Fisheries and Food [6] gives the number 629.048 (+14.6%) for 2006, and recently a study by Deloitte [7] estimates a volume of, at least, 800.000 in 2011. In all the estimates, Andalucía is the region with the highest number of horses. In 2010 the Royal Spanish Equestrian Federation had 42,255 licenses registered, the dominant number being women riders. It is important to highlight that the real number of practitioners is larger (most likely ten times more) because these activities do not require being registered with a federation because the Royal Spanish Equestrian Federation only registers those who intend to compete in official equestrian races.

Estimates of the real number of riders engaged in horseback riding in Spain put the number at approximately 300.000 people who practise leisure riding or equestrian tourism because those activities do not require riding in a club or being registered with a federation. Additionally, 719 sport equestrian clubs were registered. At the regional level, the Madrid region has the largest number of licenses, followed by Andalucía and Cataluña.

In relation to equestrian tourism, there is little Spanish research available because it is still a fairly new tourism product currently being developed. Excursionism practices are common, and the most notable horse treks activities are localised in the Andalucía and Cataluña regions.

This study focuses on the development of recreational trail riding activities in Spain, taking into consideration three basic axes: the horses, trails and on-route facilities and accommodation and food services. In rural areas in Spain, we can find them all but only separately, not as a marketable tourism product. Therefore, we intend to show that having the endogenous material and human resources is crucial for the success of horse-related tourism products. However, it is also necessary to address certain commercial issues and to plan effective strategies. This paper analyses the opportunities existing in Spain to overcome pitfalls and challenges and reach the level of success achieved by other European countries in relation to equestrian tourism.

The methodology followed in this study is based on quantitative and qualitative techniques based on consultations undertaken with a number of horse riding groups as well as other key stakeholders (including owners/operators of horse businesses, protected areas managers, municipality authorities, suppliers, and professional associations). In addition, in-depth interviews, small focus groups, public meetings with users, on-site surveys with riders, institutional data collection, specialised literature review, and Internet database searches have been conducted.

2. OPPORTUNITIES FOR EQUESTRIAN TOURISM IN SPAIN

There are many opportunities for equestrian tourism in Spain, enabling the country to bring authentic experiences to the market. The cornerstones of these opportunities, according to Viñals *et al.* [8], are: nature, scenery, climate, bridle trails and on-route facilities, horses and tourism infrastructure, culture and people, among others.
Spain presents such a great diversity of natural and rural landscapes that can certainly satisfy practically all types of horse rider expectations. Many suitable landscapes and outdoor settings for riding exist. Viñals [9], in a report analysing the features of the different Mediterranean ecosystems and settings for horse riding purposes, found a very low number of natural and rural areas unsuitable for these activities.

Some figures about the value of our natural and rural heritage include the 6.4 million hectares that cover one-fifth of the territory and include 1,720 protected areas [10] under national and international legal jurisdiction (e.g., natural park, national park, UNESCO biosphere reserves, UNESCO world heritage sites, ZEPA areas,[8] and LIC areas[9]), which represent 12.6% of the Spanish national territory. Also, it is important to note the contribution of the strong cultural heritage that the rural areas provide (architectural heritage, traditional lifestyles and ethnographic assets), in addition to the rich and popular Spanish gastronomy. Moreover, strong links between heritage and horses in the rural areas of Spain must be recognised.

In relation to the climate, it must be noted that it is an element that significantly determines the development of outdoor activities such as trail riding. Spain is a country with a typically Mediterranean climate, characterised by hot, dry summers and mild and rainy winters, registering a low level of climate risks. Climatic factors, such as temperature, hours of sunshine and the absence of rain support the duration of the available period for riding. The hours of sunshine in Spain vary from 1,700 on the northern coasts up to more than 3,000 in the South and the Canary Islands, and the country receives an average of 600 mm precipitation per year. According to Amelung & Viner

---

[8] ZEPA is a Special Protection Area or SPA, a designation under the <u>European Union</u> <u>Directive on the Conservation of Wild Birds</u>.
[9] LIC is a Site of Community Importance, defined in the <u>European Commission</u> <u>Habitats Directive</u> (92/43/EEC) and included in the Nature 2000 Network.

[11], in the summer season, the northern Mediterranean region achieves excellent scores on the Tourism Climate Index and acceptable scores in winter.

The bio-climatic comfort of riders and horses is largely guaranteed many days per year, especially during the spring, autumn and summer seasons because thresholds of temperature and humidity do not exceed 20°C-28°C and 20%-60% of relative atmospheric humidity. Horses' temperature thresholds are a bit lower than humans' because their base body temperature is higher (37.2°C-37.8°C).

Regarding facilities, good "footing" trails are necessary to promote horse riding activities. The quality and quantity of trails in Spain are impressive, approximately 500,000 km on public land, basically due to the long history of the country and the intensive settlement process that took place. The existing network of Spanish trails in natural and rural areas includes different types of paths that are suitable for horse riding. As mentioned above, we find historical paths, such as the ancient cattle trails, bridle paths, rural roads, and forestry tracks, and others more recently created particularly for recreational purposes, such as green-ways running along green corridors, long- and short-length tracks (GR and PR, respectively), old rail tracks, and even trails specifically designed for horse riding, such as the Equestrian Itineraries (IE) (fig.1).

Figure 1. Official Signage of the Certified Spanish Equestrian Trails

Also, there are "Spanish Romerías" or pilgrimages that have strong links with horses and that currently have a tourist vocation due to their similarities to horse treks. One of the most popular is the one devoted to the Virgen del Rocío crossing through the Doñana National Park in Huelva. Another internationally known pilgrimage is "El Camino de Santiago" (St. James Way). This route was declared the first European Cultural Route by the Council of Europe in 1987, and it was inscribed on the list of UNESCO World Heritage sites in 1993. The St. James Way was one of the most important Christian pilgrimages during medieval times stretching across Europe. This route runs along northern Spain, ending at the church of Santiago de Compostela. Currently it is a challenge for both Christian pilgrims, normally travelling by foot, and for many other travellers motivated by sport or adventure, making journeys by foot, by bicycle, or on horseback.

Other traditional routes on horseback in Spain are the "Ruta de la Plata" (Silver Route), a Roman path that runs from Seville to the Cantabrian Sea. It is considered an access route to the St. James Way from southern Spain. The "Camino del Cid", is a route very focused on horse riding that extends across four Spanish regions (Castilla-León, Castilla-La Mancha, Aragón y Valencian Autonomous Region), recalling the feats of the medieval figure of the Cid. The "Santo Grial" route (the Holy Grail Route) is a type of pilgrimage that runs through the Aragon and Valencian territories, recalling the sites where the Holy Grail was guarded. It is a route especially considered to be for horse riders.

The Equestrian Itineraries (IE) are a recent proposal of the Royal Spanish Equestrian Federation (RFHE) that consists of the creation of routes designed specifically for horse riding activities. Currently there are 39 certified RFHE itineraries, both in operation or in the process of creation, providing 1,206 km for riding. The Valencian Autonomous Region has the largest trail riding mileage with six itineraries in the Province of Valencia: IE 001 Monestirs-Pas del Pobre (Alzira), IE 002 Ríos Júcar y Cabriel (Cofrentes), IE 003 Ruta Volcánica (Cofrentes), IE 004 Alcola-Sácaras (Cofrentes), IE 005 Llíria-Montes de la Concòrdia (Llíria), and IE-031 Ruta del Turia (Valencia, Quart de Poblet, Paterna, Manises, Riba-roja de Túria, Vilamarxant) (fig. 2), all of them in operation. These routes benefit the large network of existing trails on public land in Spain by building the appropriate itineraries for the tourist and equestrian sectors to provide the necessary goods and services to guarantee a quality experience. At the same time, a local development goal is pursued by promoting the recovery and restoration of rural heritage and infrastructure and by the reactivation of the labour market. Additionally, this project intends to increase awareness of nature and the traditional heritage of the rural areas, especially focusing on all those aspects related to purebred Spanish horses.

Figure 2. Certified Equestrian Trail IE-031 "Ruta del Turia" (Valencia)

The RFHE and its regional offices provide guidance to both public administrative offices and by private institutions in the approval process of an Equestrian Itinerary. These itineraries are marked in accordance with RFHE fashion [12], and they must guarantee the minimum requirements of safety and quality (e.g., good "footing" trails, horse trailers parking area, beverage for horses, "bed and bale" lodges, veterinarians, and farriers) to receive certification. Alonso-Monasterio *et al.* [13] and Viñals *et al.* [14], after working on the development of some equestrian itineraries, also propose including a Code of Ethics to inform users about the expected behaviour concerning nature and heritage as well as to offer recommendations in relation to other users (Code of Etiquette) (fig.3).

Figure 3. IE-031 Equestrian Trail Map, with Code of Ethics and Etiquette

The RFHE wants to go further with this project, and it is currently working on the development of the National Inventory of Equestrian Itineraries and on the Equestrian Tourism Destination labelling process for the villages and towns involved.

Another great strength for equestrian tourism in Spain is its reputation as a country whose roots are deeply ingrained in the horse culture. The country has an enduring appreciation for horses, and there are many manifestations of this. First, the existence of the Spanish breed of horses, the Purebred Spanish Horse (PRE), famed internationally for its great beauty and harmony, must be noted. These horses have a great gift for learning a variety of competitive styles, easily responding to commands and exhibiting a rapid and intense understanding of the rider. Their main function is as a riding horse, not only with great aptitude for high school performance but also for trail riding because of their gentle disposition, and trustworthy attributes. In Spain, two main reputed breeding associations take care of them: National PRE Breeders' Association (ANCCE), created in 1972, and National PRE Breeders' Federation (FENACE). In 2011, the PRE Stud book registered 199,159 horses [15].

In relation to tourism issues, Spain is one of the most visited tourist destinations worldwide. Despite the fact that the contribution to the Spanish Gross Domestic Product (GDP) has been decreasing in the last decade, tourism it is still very important, ranging from 10% to 11% of the total GDP. The number of international tourists arriving in Spain in 2010, according to World Bank, was estimated at 57,316,000.[10] The reasons are that Spain benefits from a series of competitive advantages. As the most significant advantages, the Ministry of Economics and Competitiveness [16] highlights the "endowment of cultural resources" and "tourist infrastructure", in which Spain ranks first out of 130 countries.

The figures above represent professionalism, and the existing culture Spain has in the tourism sector represents an important strength. However, rural tourism has not been the most developed sector because urban cultural tourism and the sun and beach have mostly taken the spotlight so far, and the majority of the infrastructure and services have been assigned to support these segments of the tourism market. In spite of that, Spain has a large number and wide variety of rural accommodation facilities, according to National Statistics Institute [17]. Thus, in 2011, the number was estimated at 15,037, with a total of 137,727 beds [17]. It is difficult to classify the different types of accommodations, but basically there are rural houses for rent, rural hotels, and rural hostels. These accommodations offer bed and breakfast, half board or full board, and increasingly are offering recreational activities, as well.

To position this new segment devoted to trail riding activities in the tourism market, it is useful to consider the best design for a horse riding tourism product based on the existing rural housing, horse trails and equestrian sector. A good idea would be to adapt any of these rural accommodation facilities to the concept of "Bed and Bale", which means having a place to rest or stay for both rider and horse. In this way, the expectations of horse trekking riders can be met. In France, the Fédération Française des Relais d'Étape de Tourisme Equestre (a brand recognised by the Equestrian Federation of France) regulates these types of establishments and can serve as an example to follow.

---

[10]http://data.worldbank.org/indicator/(Accessed 05/12/2012)

For all these reasons, we can regard the promotion of this new tourism product based on trail riding as more than feasible because the tourism infrastructure and recreational facilities, trained human resources, and institutions for planning and tourism management are already in place. Furthermore, local communities are interested in developing new activities that contribute to their economies with employment and benefits. For this reasons, municipalities are generally supportive of equestrian tourism activities. Nevertheless, they are aware of their heritage and they want to guarantee that activities are agreeable with the environment, ethnographic resources and local traditions. In this sense, trail riding fits perfectly with the expectations of residents and local stakeholders. Currently, towns and villages interested in equestrian tourism are more concerned with the horse activities than with the tourism sector. The interest originates with the equestrian local stakeholders, who attempt to stabilise and diversify their business. Sometimes, this interest represents the best hope to expand and support entrepreneurial activity as a means to revitalise local communities. There are many equestrian tourism stakeholders: breeding farms, coaches and training facilities, riding schools, boarding stables, equestrian centres, and suppliers (e.g., farriers, veterinarians, insurance companies, and the animal feed industry), as well as equestrian associations and sport federations that have a wide range of activities. Without question, Spain has a large number of experienced equestrian professionals. ANCCE has estimated that there were more than 7,500 PRE breeders in 2010, and Villaluenga [18] has counted 600 horse veterinarians in Spain.

Institutional support for equestrian tourism activities is evident at the local, regional, national and international levels. Therefore, many local and regional subsidies have been requested to assist the equestrian sector to reach the levels required to develop high-quality tourism activities. At the national level, an important project was developed in relation to the equestrian inns ("*Posadas Ecuestres*"). It was focused on the creation of appropriate lodges for riders and horses, similar to the concept of "Bed and Bale". This project, developed in 2010, was supported by the Spanish Ministry of the Environment, Rural and Marine Affairs and the Royal Spanish Equestrian Federation. It was developed in the provinces of Andalucía, Navarra, and País Vasco. It was framed within a larger project called the "European Network of Equestrian Inns" in which other European partners, such as Hungary, France and Portugal, took part. We must also emphasise Spain's participation in various EU projects, such as the European INTERREG Program, in relation to horses. Similarly, we should note the Interreg III B "Pegaso" (2005-2008) carried out by Spain, Portugal, United Kingdom and Ireland. Also, the Interreg IV-Sudoe Project "Equustur" (2009-2011) was developed by Spain, France, and Portugal with the objective of creating an equestrian tourism network based on given quality standards.

3. CHALLENGES TO THE DEVELOPMENT OF EQUESTRIAN TOURISM PRODUCTS

As mentioned at the beginning of this paper, equestrian tourism is an issue that involves both the tourism and equestrianism sectors, and it is a new issue in Spain. These two sectors have not worked together until now, and for this reason the results have been inadequate. There is a need for coordination of activity to create the synergies that will transform a recreational equestrian activity into an equestrian tourism product with a clear content and retail and promotional feasibility.

Spanish equestrian enterprises are small and medium-size companies that require the generation of equestrian clustering systems that will allow them to develop better business opportunities through cooperative efforts. Laudable attempts have arisen in recent years in this sense; the creation of "Agetrea", an association located in Andalucía that seeks to guarantee the quality of equestrian tourism products. In Cataluña, there is another equestrian tourism association named "Catalunya a Cavall"; and more recently, "Equitur-Top Cavalls", an equestrian enterprises' cluster devoted to the promotion and dissemination of equestrian tourism products at the national and international levels, was created. It should also be recognised that Equitur, founded in 1978, was the first Spanish equestrian company dedicated to the creation, development, organisation, promotion and sale of services related to equestrian tourism.

Despite all these efforts, Spanish equestrian products are not well positioned in international tourism markets. There are important equestrian tour operators in many European countries (especially in United Kingdom, France, and Germany) that have traditionally managed the international market; Spain has come late to this market and currently needs to be more creative to become competitive. There are several different underlying causes of this situation.

Equestrian authorities and involved stakeholders are not currently organised to engage in tourism, but they are very interested in diversifying their horse businesses to make them more profitable. Based on the in-depth interviews, it is noted that a significant number of equestrian stakeholders do not see a link between their business and the tourism sector, and logically they do not have sufficient technical expertise in tourism management. Many horse enterprises present difficulties to become active tourism companies because they have not reached the required standards and/or they do not possess legal licenses to operate; some of these enterprises do not even satisfy the livestock rules in force in many cases due to reasons related to the scattered, incomplete and confusing existing equestrian legislation.

Moreover, no strategic plan for the horse sector exists in Spain. Consequently, a holistic vision for the medium-term and long-term future of the sector is lacking. Only the Valencian Autonomous Region has recently presented (April, 2013) the Valencian Strategic Plan for the Horse Sector.[11] This plan devotes considerable attention to equestrian tourism in the region, identifying the most important issues to be addressed in the coming years.

From the point of view of the tourism institutions, equestrianism has been underestimated, and the endogenous potential of this segment in Spain has usually been neglected. *Turespaña* is the Spanish national tourism development authority; it provides strategic and practical support to develop and sustain Spain as a high-quality and competitive tourist destination. On its website, this organisation fails to present equestrian tourism among the Spanish marketed tourism products.[12] The only equestrian products promoted

---

[11] This plan has been carried out by the Municipality of Valencia (Fundación Deportiva Municipal) and the Purebred Spanish Horse Valencian Association (PRECVAL).
[12] http://www.tourspain.es/es-es/marketing/Productos/Paginas/default.aspx (Accessed 03/21/2013)

by official organisations in Spain have been international horse events; trail riding, such as many recreational activities, is not allocated a place in the tourism market.

Additionally, legislation related to the operation of equestrian tourism is currently insufficient. Not all Spanish regions have a statute on active tourism, and in the case of those that do, the terms of reference devoted to equestrian tourism are very poor. However, the certification of horse riding guides in Spain is a complex issue that has only been addressed until now by formal training school offerings and by informal training courses. In relation to trail riding, the guide plays a huge role in the success of the trip. For this reason, it is important that this professional has the sufficient social and technical (e.g., horsemanship, first aid, and leadership) skills to drive the development of the activity. Horse guides must either possess a diploma in the field or at least have extensive experience. The Spanish Ministry of Education, conscious of these educational needs, has recently approved professional certification in Horse Guiding, but unfortunately it has not yet been fully implemented.

Safety issues play an extremely important part in equestrian tourism. It should be noted that liability and insurance coverage is compulsory for horses and equestrian activities in Spain. Nevertheless, in the near future, it will be necessary to review the current insurance rates to guarantee that they are comparable to those of adventure tourism activities. Another important, necessary intervention is the preparation of safety guidelines for equestrian tourism providers to inform them how to proceed in commercial trail ridings to guarantee the safety of clients and horses, to prevent accidents and to act in emergency situations.

Another important challenge is to provide leadership in the marketing of the equestrian tourism sector in Spain, which requires major efforts to substantially improve the current situation. First of all, it must be noted that the existence of a corporate brand has been proposed by the Royal Spanish Equestrian Federation, that is, the labelling of certified trails and the companies that operate them, as well as their accommodation and food suppliers. However, this brand is not a trademark for the activity "Trail Riding in Spain". In addition, there is a general lack of official institutional marketing, and there is no marketing strategy to promote equestrian tourism at the national and international levels.

Finally, it should be noted that infrastructure and facilities currently are still scarce. Equestrian tourists seek the highest standards of facilities and services coupled with a unique trail riding experience. The development of more certified riding itineraries (IE), with an appropriate signage system and with good connections to the tourism sector, is necessary to develop real, marketable equestrian tourism products, providing a consistent and well-articulated offer. Furthermore, suitable accommodations for both horse and rider need to be developed and promoted so that riders know where they can stay and can plan their routes accordingly.

4. DISCUSSION AND CONCLUSIONS

The discussion of the opportunities and pitfalls for Spanish equestrian routes raises a number of ideas that can be considered recommendations for further developments and concluding remarks. First, the many elements that favour the development of the equestrian tourism segment in Spain (e.g., nature, scenery, climate, Purebred Spanish

Horses, horse reputation and tradition, and equestrian professionals) must be highlighted. They are truly the strengths and pillars of the tourism system in addition to the certified facilities and the large number of good "footing" trails for riding already in existence. In any case, to achieve success in the creation of marketable equestrian tourism products, some pitfalls and weaknesses must be overcome.

Intense marketing research should be carried out to ascertain which target markets are the best. Therefore, there is an urgent need for reliable data from both the horse and tourism sectors. The lack of statistics and good information prevents serious market research, as well as the economic and social impact knowledge of the horse riding activities at the local, regional and national levels. Similarly, an in-depth study on potential demand traits and on the riders' expectations is necessary to find and efficiently access suitable markets.

A marketing strategy for Spanish equestrian tourism must be developed to promote Spanish equestrian products at the national and international levels. The marketing strategy for international markets should focus on a branding campaign based on iconic, well-known elements, such as: Spanish natural and rural landscapes, Purebred Spanish Horses, equestrian traditions and the Mediterranean climate, in addition to resources, such as gastronomy and ethnography.

Another type of marketing strategy should be better for domestic marketing. The best strategies for national marketing campaigns that promote the popularisation of horseback riding should offer memorable experiences (new sensations and emotions or horse baptism) to novice riders and amazing experiences discovering the many landscapes of the various Spanish territories for skilled riders.

Nevertheless, to be competitive it is important to improve the quality and diversity of the products offered as well as to have professional and educated staff. Quality could be improved by developing a categorisation system for equestrian centres that helps tourists to clearly identify which destinations correspond to their needs and also by creating an equestrian tourism quality control system. Diversity of products is necessary to make the difference. The growing reputation of Spain as a horse country that brings an authentic local experience to riders is a fact. It is also true that strong and growing competition from other European countries (Germany, France, United Kingdom) more consolidated in this market exists. Nevertheless, opportunities have been foreseen due to the non-saturation of the equestrian tourism market, and Spain still has a place.

An important finding of this study suggests that the key operators in Spanish equestrian tourism are those associated with the culture of horsemanship (people involved with the breeding, training and riding of horses) rather than tourism culture. For this reason, improving education and increasing the amount of training opportunities for entrepreneurs is a key point in the development of the equestrian tourism sector.
From the point of view of the commercialisation, it must be noted that product development should be built on the basis of business partnerships and networking because equestrian tourism is in the hands of small or family enterprises, sometimes clustered under the umbrella of entrepreneurial associations. Therefore, new technologies, such as central reservation systems, or local platforms for product distribution seem to be a suitable for commercialisation and distribution. Equestrian tourism products fit perfectly with the e-commerce concept, and marketing on-line seems the best option. Furthermore,

independent service providers or associations can be included in fare aggregates to improve their business opportunities. This should be carried out because now products are sold in a very piecemeal way directly to each provider, and riders must book the majority of the elements separately. Similarly, rural tourism enterprises are linked to websites and other distribution channels, as well as to social networks to achieve better product positioning. The use of new technologies is essential to improve the availability of information on trail riding because it is a crucial issue for horse riders.

It is also necessary to create websites that include lists of equestrian tourism providers and facilitate providing different equestrian services all over the country. Clear product and company descriptions allow clients to find even the smaller service providers who may not have their own websites. This website should obviously be available in English and other foreign languages, depending on the target audience.

Strategies for the development and promotion of equestrian tourism are currently handled by the Royal Spanish Equestrian Federation, which has initiated the process of enhancing these products, especially trail riding with its certified itineraries. In the current situation, however, equestrian tourism needs to be supported by other tourism institutional bodies, particularly organisations such as Turespaña that are fully competent in these issues at the international level. This promotion must be constant and must have clear aims and targets.

REFERENCES

[1] Ollenburg, C. (2005). Worldwide structure of the equestrian tourism sector. *Journal of Ecotourism*. 4 (1), 47-55.

[2] American Horse Council (2005). http://www.manesandtailsorganization.org/American_Horse_Council_2005_Report.pdf (Accessed 05/05/2012).

[3] Muller, H. (2010). *The social impact of the Horse Sector in Europe*. Report presented at the European Horse Network Conference. Brussels.

[4] Bouhaouala, M. & Albertini, F. (2005). Horse-based Tourism: Community, Quality and Disinterest. *Espaces, Tourisme & Loisirs*. 229, 16-18.

[5] Tragsega (2003). *Estudio y caracterización del sector equino en España*. Informe del Ministerio de Agricultura, Pesca y Alimentación. 297 pp.

[6] General Sub-direction of Livestock Production of the Spanish Ministry of Agriculture, Fisheries and Food (2010). http://www.acalanthis.es/doc/EL%20SECTOR%20EQUINO%20EN%20CIFRAS_C%C3%B3rdoba%20y%20Sevilla_Septiembre_2010.pdf (Accessed 09/03/2012).

[7] Deloitte (2013). *Estudio del impacto del sector ecuestre en España*. Ed. Daemon Quest. 321 pp.

[8] Viñals, M.J., Morant, M., Alonso-Monasterio, P. & Ruiz Sancho, S. (2012a): Endogenous potential of Spanish Rural Areas for Equestrian Tourism. *Proceedings 1st EJTHR International Conference on Destination Branding, Heritage and Authenticity*. Organized by Universidad de Santiago de Compostela (España).

[9] Viñals, M.J. (2006). *Manual para el diseño e implementación de rutas ecuestres en áreas mediterráneas*. Informe inédito. Universitat Politècnica València. 68 pp.

[10] MARM (2011). http://www.inmodiario.com/152/11479/millones-personas-visitan-cada-espacios-naturales-protegidos.html (Accessed 05/10/2012).

[11] Amelung, B. & Viner, D. (2006). Mediterranean Tourism: Exploring the Future with the Tourism Climatic Index. *Journal of Sustainable Tourism.* 14 (4), 349-366.

[12] Solis, A. & Solis, J. (2010). *Manual de señalización y homologación de itinerarios ecuestres.* Ed. Real Federación Hípica Española/ QFTurisme. 58 pp.

[13] Alonso-Monasterio, P., Viñals, M.J. & Halasa, Z. (2012). *Mapa del Itinerario Ecuestre IE-005 Llíria-Montes de la Concòrdia.* Universitat Politècnica de València / Ayuntamiento de Llíria.

[14] Viñals, M.J., Alonso-Monasterio, P., Morant, M. & Teruel, L. (2012b). *Mapa del Itinerario Ecuestre IE-031 Ruta del Turia.* Diputación Provincial de Valencia / Universitat Politècnica de València.

[15] Eurodressage (2011). http://www.eurodressage.com/equestrian/2012/05/05/pre-studbook-registered-14000-pre-horses-2011 (Accessed 05/14/2012).

[16] Ministerio de Economía y Competitividad (2008). http://www.investinspain.org/icex/cda/controller/interes/0,5464,5322992_6261977_6279071_4099539_47_0_0,00.html?registrosPorPagina=5&numReg=239 (Accessed 05/12/2012).

[17] INE (2012) http://www.ine.es/daco/daco42/ocuptr/eotr0011.xls (Accessed 05/08/2012).

[18] Villaluenga, J.L. (2010). Encuesta sobre la situación profesional del veterinario de equinos en España. *Equinus.* 26, 64-71.

88

Sustainable performance and tourism: a collection of tools and best practices

Trade shows as marketing tools

A. RODRÍGUEZ
Universidad Nacional de Educación a Distancia (UNED), Economics and Accounting Department, Spain
M.D. REINA
Universidad Nacional de Educación a Distancia (UNED), Economics and Accounting Department, Spain
C. SEVILLA
Universidad Nacional de Educación a Distancia (UNED), Economics and Accounting Department, Spain

ABSTRACT

Trade shows should be viewed as a component of a firm's overall marketing strategy. When a firm decides to participate in an event, the event becomes part of the marketing mix for one, several or all of its product ranges [1]. Some studies (such as those conducted by Exhibit Surveys or the CEIR) underscore the importance of planning for trade shows, just as with any other business activity. To this end, trade show strategies must be designed to meet certain requirements that are developed throughout the chapter.

1. DEFINITION AND FUNCTIONS OF TRADE SHOW MARKETING

Trade show marketing is the most effective medium for reaching new customers and markets; it shortens the buying cycle and offers firms access to customers who are otherwise impossible to reach [2].

Trade shows are simply another tool for firms to meet their marketing goals [3]. Firm's trade show policy is an amalgam of its communication, sales, distribution, and market research policies.

Trade shows bring into play the full range of marketing-mix tools [4], each of which will be more or less important depending on the type of product being sold and the objectives to be met. According to [1], trade show marketing is an essential part of a firm's sales strategy. This is true to such an extent that firms that regularly use trade shows to sell their products must treat them as simply another variable of their marketing mix, along with product, price, distribution and promotion.

1.1. Advantages and disadvantages of trade shows

Trade shows offer certain benefits to exhibitors, visitors – whether professionals or members of the general public – and the economy [5]:

- For exhibitors, trade shows help to encourage and increase sales, while also providing a chance to gather opinions, get ideas and promote projects. Moreover, a large number of personal contacts can be made, some of which will result in new customers for the firm.
- By attending trade shows, visitors can discover the latest developments in the sector, allowing them to stay abreast of any changes and supplement their technological information.
- At the economic level, trade shows generate industrial and business activity that stimulates the transfer and sale of goods and services and boosts technological progress, while at the same time enhancing the national and international image of the host city.

Exhibitors obtain a number of benefits from participating in trade shows [4, 6]: customer acquisition, availability, accessibility, three-dimensional presentation, high return and efficiency.

In addition to the above, participating in trade shows offers more benefits than other marketing instruments (AFE, n.d.): it offers insights into current and future market trends; it makes it possible to determine existing and potential customers' degree of satisfaction with the products offered by the firm and the competition; exhibitors can strengthen their relations with colleagues in the industry in order to discuss problems and new trends; it enables the identification of potential suppliers, representatives, importers and dealers; it constitutes an important step in a firm's internationalization strategy, as it can generate export opportunities; it helps to strengthen the firm's image.

On the other hand, trade shows also have certain disadvantages or drawbacks: according to [7] it is impossible to calculate the return on investment and, thus, to know how effective they are; likewise, it is difficult to compare the performance of trade shows with that of other marketing tools, such as advertising or direct selling; both management and customers often approach these events as obligations instead of an established communication medium ; the costs of participating are high and rising [7]; the excessive proliferation of events, not only in terms of the number and size of the booths, but also with regard to their specialization and regionalization, can dilute the effect of their advantages and benefits [8-9]; large shows often have chaotic and confusing environments that can hinder effective communication between buyers and sellers [8-10].

Trade shows have certain characteristics that set them apart from other communication tools, such as personal selling, advertising and sales promotions. In this sense, they offer the following advantages over other communication tools:

- They enable a direct relationship between the buyer and the seller [11,12]; in fact, it is the only communication medium in which it is the buyer who approaches the seller [13].
- They offer the exhibitor the possibility of making contact with a high number of potential customers in a short period of time. Moreover, they are the ideal environment for gaining access to customers who would otherwise be difficult to reach [14].
- Customers are able to meet members of the management team they would never meet at the firm's regular retail outlets [5, 11].

- Personal two-way contact is made between the buyer and seller [5]. Moreover, the visitor can see, try and touch the product [4].
- Both the buyer and the seller are in neutral territory [11, 15], giving them greater freedom to speak and negotiate freely.
- Other communication media can be used at the same time [4-5, 16].
- At trade shows, the other components of the marketing mix also come into play: the product, which is what the firm is presenting at the show; price, as the sale can be negotiated at the show itself; and distribution, since, given that the product can be sold, the booth itself becomes a point of sale [4-5].

However, trade shows also have drawbacks compared to other communication tools:

- The presence of the competition is inevitable, which can be especially damaging when the firm is presenting innovations or new products [17].
- Participation generally requires a large investment of both human and financial resources, a factor that is more detrimental for SMEs [3] than large corporations [18].
- The proliferation and excessive frequency of trade shows in a single industry considerably increases the costs [8].
- It is difficult for the firm to measure the medium- and long-term return on investment [7].

2. TRADE SHOWS AS PART OF THE MARKETING MIX

Trade shows have not always been regarded as a marketing tool by firms. Consequently, the vast majority of firms only exhibited at them so as not to give up ground to the competition and out of inertia. They neither set objectives for their participation, nor defined a strategy [2, 4, 19-20]. However, in recent decades, the trade show sector has undergone rapid change, and today firms are beginning to realize that exhibiting at a trade show means more than simply setting up a booth and waiting for something to happen [21].

Trade shows are considered to be a marketing tool that firms can use to meet their business objectives [3]. Their functions can be grouped into two categories [3, 7, 11, 22-26]:

- **Selling function**: The exhibitor often conducts business transactions with visitors.
- **Communication function or Nonselling function**: Many firms use trade shows to convey information, whether by describing or demonstrating their products, by answering key questions, or by promoting their image.

Despite the importance of both functions, many SMEs fail to set nonselling objectives [27], and rather focus only on generating new leads and sales. However, due to the increase in competition, some of these firms have begun to rebuild their business model, placing increasing importance on promoting their image.

Although trade shows are unanimously regarded as a communication medium, discrepancies exist with regard to the exact role they play within that variable. Most authors consider them to be a tool for promoting sales [5, 28-31], although some [32, 33], consider them to fall within public relations. Communication is thus the best variable for framing them [34]. Another option has been proposed by [23], whereby trade shows are a mix of direct selling and promotion, depending on the expectations of the different firms in attendance.

According to [3], a firm's trade show policy is an amalgam of its sales, distribution and communication policies and its market research activities. Trade shows have great potential in terms of allowing participants to effectively engage in nearly all aspects of the marketing mix [35]; thus, participation in a trade show must be understood in conjunction with the other aspects of marketing.

The majority of marketing activities that any firm might include in its strategic marketing plan [2] also take place at trade shows, with the only difference being one of scale: the marketing plan for the show is smaller and takes place over a more limited period of time, specifically, the duration of the show. However, the strategic planning for a trade show must focus not only on the period of the trade show itself, but also include the actions to be carried out before and after the event [23-24, 36-38]. The effect of resource allocation [26] on trade show performance, defined as the achievement of both selling and nonselling objectives, is partially mediated by the trade show marketing process (i.e., pre-show promotional activities, at-show selling, and post-show follow-up). According to [35], a firm's communication policy includes the following tools: advertising, sales promotion, personal sales discussions, and public relations. Market research, sponsorship and patronage, and trade shows can also be included.

Trade shows as part of the communication mix: Figure 1 depicts the position of trade shows as a communication medium on two different levels. The first level shows how participation in a trade show can lead to intense contact between exhibitors and visitors, enabling firms to establish good relationships with customers. Dialogue between exhibitors and visitors is invaluable, as it is the only way to develop lasting new business relationships and to improve existing ones. Moreover, firms can provide much more vivid and active information about a product or service in the context of a trade show than with any other medium in the marketing mix.

The second level shows the considerable value of trade shows as promotional events, but also highlights their comparatively low availability to exhibitors (i.e., the comparatively low possibility to exploit the opportunities they offer), due, among other things, to the relative infrequency with which they are held. Trade shows are given great importance compared to other communication media due to their multifunctional nature. No other medium can be used in such a personal and targeted way, and no other situation offers the same chance for such direct communication with customers, whether with a view to creating a new need for information or to meeting existing ones. Participation in a trade show helps firms reach more potential customers and enhance their image among existing ones. It also allows them to detect changes in customer profiles and buying behavior more quickly and directly. Moreover, trade shows allow firms to showcase specific benefits of a product and/or the firm itself, such as reliability, after-sale service or product quality, more clearly.

Direct
advertising

Agent

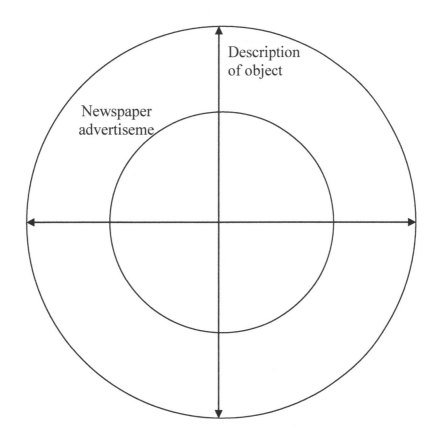

Source: AUMA [35].

The following communication tools are used when participating in a trade show: stand design, preliminary advertising campaign for the event, direct marketing, public relations, marketing events, personal selling, cooperation on communication and IT marketing.

Trade shows as part of the price-and-conditions mix: Participation in a trade show can help to change the conception of the existing price-and-conditions mix, as well as, where desired, to test the waters with regard to new market segments.

The price-and-conditions mix should be designed with the goal of enabling the firm to meet its stated goals and assure its profits.

Separately, with a view to incentivizing customers to visit the trade show and purchase products and services there, special prices can be offered for sales made at the show itself [39].

Trade shows as part of the distribution mix: Through its participation at the show, a firm can determine whether it is necessary to reorganize or make other changes to its sale policy. It is worth noting that in some industries (such as jewelry and watches), trade shows are one of the primary distribution channels and play a very important role in the sale of firms' products.

Trade shows as part of the product mix: Over the last decade, trade shows have positioned themselves in the business market as: one of the most profitable forms of promotion; an important component of the distribution process [3]; one of the marketing media best suited to the small and medium size of, for example, Spanish firms [3, 34]; and the best way for firms to present their latest innovations, as well as a means of detecting new market trends [3, 5].

In short, trade shows are an important part of the sales process [12]. However, despite the importance of this communication tool and the significance of the statistics, trade shows have not received much attention from researchers in Spain [34, 40-42], or internationally [25, 43-46], and there is thus a lack of empirical studies analyzing the trade show industry and the challenges it poses and offering guidance to firms in terms of which strategies and tactics to use and the relative effectiveness thereof. The dearth of research on these issues may be due to the difficulty of isolating their effect from the other factors involved in a successful promotional campaign, which could also be the reason for the great variety of strategies and tactics used, although that could also be due to the intertwined attitudes of the parties involved [47].

3. TRADE SHOW PLANNING

Trade show planning must not focus only on the firm's participation in the show itself, but also on the activities to be carried out before and after the event [6, 24, 36-37, 48]. Table 1 shows the different activities that should be included in the trade show participation plan:

Table 1. Activities to be carried out before, during and after the trade show

PRE-SHOW ACTIVITIES	ACTIVITIES DURING THE SHOW	POST-SHOW ACTIVITIES
Defining the show objectives. Choosing the right show. Identifying the target market. Setting the Budget. Conducting a preliminary advertising campaign. Contracting, design and decoration of the stand. Selecting and training the team for the show.	Carrying out promotional activities during the trade show. Incentivizing the sales force. Identifying, qualifying and closing leads	Following up on leads. Measuring and evaluating the outcome

Source: Own production based on data from [4, 37, 39].

3.1. Pre-show activities
Defining the show objectives. According to [19], objectives are "those concrete, realistic and quantifiable goals that the exhibitor aims to achieve through its participation in a trade

show." The objectives for a given show must be defined in direct relation to the firm's marketing objectives [4]; establishing these objectives is critical to the firm's success at the show [14, 49].

After reviewing several contributions from the specialized literature [3] considered the following trade show objectives to be the most important: generating orders or sales; increasing market opportunities with potential customers; promoting the firm's image and enhancing its reputation; obtaining both general information and information about the competition; presenting new lines or products and gauging the market's reaction; providing information about the firm and its products on the market; maintaining and enhancing the image and provision of services to existing customers; researching new applications and/or ideas for the firm's products; having the firm's specialists demonstrate how to use industrial equipment that is difficult to transport by explaining the technical specifications; hiring new staff and recruiting new sales representatives and dealers; training the new sales staff; attending the event because the competition will be there; funding or sponsoring the industry business association that is working to increase participation in the show; reaching technicians; specialists and professional specifiers who are otherwise difficult to reach, achieving free publicity or coverage in the media; making personal contact with buyers, boosting morale at the firm in general and among the regional managers from the show's catchment area in particular by ensuring the parent firm or central offices provide personal and financial support and drawing up lists of prospective customers.

Opinions differ with regard to the objectives of a trade show; in fact, the number of objectives varies dramatically, from the one hundred defined by [50], to the thirty-three proposed by [35], to the eight posited by [4]. The explanation for this broad discrepancy quite likely lies in the fact that the objectives can vary depending on the industry and type of show under study.

Selecting the type of show. Not all trade shows will be able to meet all desired objectives. It is thus essential to choose the right event in which to participate [38, 51]. Such a choice will require reliable and abundant information on the following factors: the type of show, the visitors, the competitors to be in attendance, and the relationship between the show's organizers and the industry's professional and business associations.

Identifying the target market. When a firm decides to participate in a trade show, it must first identify its target audience and its expectations for it. This can sometimes be complicated, above all when dealing with general events in which it is virtually impossible to divide the visitors into different segments [38].

Setting the budget. The creation of a budget is a necessary part of trade show planning. The amount of money allocated to participating will largely depend on the firm's previously established objectives and the trade show's potential for meeting them [21]; it will also depend on the firm's corporate objectives and overall budget.

A study conducted by [36] analyzed whether the most successful firms had larger trade show marketing budgets than less successful ones. The most successful firms allocated 28% of their marketing budget to participation in trade shows, while less successful firms allocated 20% or less. According to several authors [4, 21, 52-54], the following costs must be taken into account when planning for a trade show: space rental; products for display; design (conception, furniture, decoration), assembly and disassembly of the booth; booth maintenance (cleaning, upkeep); transportation and insurance; shipping and storage; promotional activities (brochures, gifts, advertising, invitations, direct mail, e-mail marketing, announcements, stickers, banners, posters, press conferences, PR agency fees, etc.); staff expenses (wages, bonuses, accommodations, travel, meals, transportation); utilities (gas, electricity, water, telephone); services for customers (food and beverages, accommodations, travel, entertainment); other expenses (employee training, security, photography, consumables for the booth, gardening, etc.).

Preliminary advertising campaign. It is a mistake to think that a firm can generate all its desired contacts simply by being present at the show [20]. Promotional activities must be carried out beforehand to ensure that the target audience knows the event is taking place and that the firm will be participating in it [21]. This is even more important for small firms [55], as it helps to offset the lack of knowledge that many visitors have of them. A variety of media can be used to this end, including: telemarketing; direct mail and e-mail marketing; faxes; personal invitations; trade journals; local or national media; the internet; advertisements in the official exhibitor catalog; sending press kits or press notes to trade journals and local media, as well as invitations to attend the event; newsletters; special events; the firm's own sales network.

Contracting, design and decoration of the stand. The stand is the firm's calling card. Consequently, its size, design and appearance must all be in keeping with the image and products the firm aims to offer at the show [35]. However, exhibitors must not stop there. In addition to ensuring that their stand is attractive to visitors, they must also ensure that it has a focus and a specific message that conveys the firm's offer; it must make an impression on visitors. In this sense, the stand can be regarded as a very effective marketing tool [20, 56].

Selecting and training the team. The selection of the most suitable employees to work at the trade show must be made based on their specialist knowledge and capacity to forge and maintain relationships and present the products [35]. The chosen staff will be the face of the firm at the trade show and, often, the only point of reference for potential customers. It is thus essential to choose the right people [56].

The trade show team must understand the relationship selling process, i.e., the need to maintain communications with customers over time. Depending on the buyer, the show may take place in the initiation, development or conversion stage of the relationship process. Often, existing and potential customers who are not looking to buy from the outset are ignored. This leads to a failure to start a relationship with new prospects or maintain the relationship with dormant ones, a situation that will often be capitalized on by the competition.

One of the most important goals of the training is to teach the team members to convey to visitors that they are always available.

3.2. Activities during the show

The success of this stage will depend on how much effort went into the pre-show activities. At the event, three main factors must be taken into account:

Promotional activities. The common purpose of the promotional activities carried out before and during the show is to increase the number of visitors to the booth. At professional trade shows, the pre-show activities are more important, because professional buyers usually plan their time at a show using the information obtained in the lead-up to it [48]. However, at consumer shows, it is the activities carried out during the show that are critical, as even visitors who come with the idea of visiting certain booths will stop at others, too, if a given promotional activity at the event catches their eye.

The sales force. The team chosen to attend the trade show represents the entire firm. Every member must thus strive to be in top form throughout the entire trade show process. Attending a trade show must not be regarded as a reward; it is very hard work requiring prior preparation [35]. In short, participating in a trade show requires a lot of time, work and effort from employees. Therefore, if the firm believes that it is important to participate in a show, it must make sure that its booth is staffed with qualified professionals who can suitably represent it and know how to take advantage of any opportunities that might arise [20].

Leads. As already noted, choosing the right team and ensuring it receives the necessary training is essential to creating an environment adapted to visitors' needs [10, 57]. It is especially important to determine whether or not visitors belong to the firm's target audience, as well their level of professional authority [58]. It must be borne in mind that the selling conditions at a stand are quite different from the usual conditions; the communication process is much faster. If possible, at the end of the conversation, attempts should be made to improve the situation with those leads with whom no agreement has been reached, for example, by arranging for a visit or sending a quote or technical specifications. All information gathered about a visitor must be recorded immediately so as not to forget anything important [35] and to be able to follow up on the lead once the show is over [36].

3.3. Post-show activities
The final stage of trade show planning consists of the activities that must be carried out once the event is over. Well-planned post-show activities are of great help in achieving the established objectives for the show [35]. Moreover, carrying out such activities effectively is the only way to capitalize on both the financial and human investment made during the event [59].

The main aims of this stage are twofold (logistical activities must also be carried out, such as disassembling the stand or transporting the products for display; these aspects must be taken into account beforehand during the planning stage):

- **Following up on leads:** Once the show is over, the exhibitor must use the information gathered during the show to follow up with potential customers. Customers who spent some of their time at the show visiting the firm's stand must be contacted personally and made to feel like their needs are being seen to quickly and efficiently [60].

- **Measuring and evaluating the outcome:** Evaluating the outcome (the following authors have conducted empirical research to measure and assess the outcome: [9, 18,

22-24, 26, 36, 47, 55, 61-71] is generally considered to be the most complicated part of trade show marketing for three main reasons [60]: Many of the firms attending a trade show do not set objectives for their participation in it; When such objectives are defined, they are often quite heterogeneous, making them quite difficult to measure; When a firm participates in a trade show, it generally uses other marketing media, too (direct mail, advertising, or personal selling), making it vastly more difficult to calculate the real return on investment.

Ideally, quantifiable objectives should be defined in the pre-show period so that performance on them can be evaluated once the show is over [61]. However, the return on investment must not be measured only in monetary terms, as solely taking the sales made into account will considerably limit the evaluation of the firm's performance at the show. Other factors, though hard to evaluate, must be taken into consideration, too, including, among others, building customer loyalty, the strength of the firm's commitment to its customers, the exchange of experiences and perspectives, and boosting team spirit. According to [19], the return can be measured in both the short and long term. The most common technique for evaluating the return on the trade show investment (ROI) tends to use a short-term approach:

$$Return\ on\ investment\ (ROI),\ short\text{-}term = \frac{Turnover\ at\ the\ show}{Cost\ of\ participating\ in\ the\ show}$$

In contrast, the following formula can be used to measure the show's long-term ROI:

$$ROI,\ long\text{-}term = \frac{Turnover\ resulting\ from\ the\ show}{Cost\ of\ show\ +\ Cost\ of\ follow\text{-}up\ and\ sales\ calls}$$

Finally, the performance of a country's trade show industry should be taken into consideration. This can be measured taking into account different economic indicators, the event's impact on the economies of the city or region in which it is held, and the sum total of the turnover registered by the fairgrounds and the stand design and assembly firms. Even so, it is very hard to determine the exact investment in this industry, and even harder to calculate its performance and efficiency.

4. CONCLUSIONS

The data in this study and the different analyses performed give rise to several interesting considerations. At times like the present, when trade shows in certain industries are undergoing major structural changes, suffering cut-backs due to the economic crisis and declining numbers of exhibitors, it is especially important to be able to maximize the benefits for firms that a show can offer.

Trade shows have two main functions as a marketing tool: to promote the firm's image and to foster the sale of goods and services. To this end, the trade show marketing plan must be drawn up within the context of the firm's overall marketing plan, the right show must be chosen, and the firm's target audience must be identified. Trade shows can be used to achieve multiple objectives, which can be grouped into two main categories that correspond to the basic purposes of any show, namely: promotional objectives, aimed at maintaining and enhancing the image of both the firm and its products, and selling objectives, aimed at attracting new customers and increasing sales.

To optimize the outcome of a trade show, firms must plan for the show accordingly, carrying out the necessary activities before, during and after the event to take full advantage of the show's capacity as a highly effective tool. It is much harder to justify the cost of simply attending the show without planning. In the pre-show period, firms must above all establish the objectives they hope to achieve by participating in the event, as these objectives will determine the outcome. Only with a clear understanding of what it hopes to accomplish will a firm be able to determine what actions to take during and after the show. At consumer shows, promoting the firm's image is quite important; firms hoping to raise consumer awareness of their brand should thus consider attending that type of show. At the show, a record should be kept of all the visitors to the stand in order to facilitate the subsequent follow-up on leads. Given the large number of SMEs that exhibit at shows, it is crucial to use promotional activities to catch visitors' attention. This might include promotional giveaways that help to keep the firm's image alive in visitors' memories. Exhibitors view trade shows as an effective tool both for attracting new customers and for retaining existing ones. Greater importance should thus be given to the post-show analysis, as it is essential to enabling appropriate follow-up of the leads generated at the show and, thus, to subsequently designing an increasingly tailored strategy for promoting the firm's image and selling products at the fairgrounds.

Finally, quantifiable objectives should be established in the pre-show period to enable assessment of the firm's performance once the show is over. The return on investment must not be measured solely in monetary terms, but rather taking into account other factors, too, which can be quite difficult to evaluate, including, among others, building customer loyalty, the strength of the firm's commitment to its customers, the exchange of experiences, and boosting team spirit.

REFERENCES

[1] Ferre, J. M. (2000). El entronque de la feria dentro del plan de marketing, *IPMARK*, 537, 48-49.

[2] Pitta, D. A., Weisgal, M. and Lynagh, P. (2006). Integrating exhibit marketing into integrated marketing communications. *The Journal of Consumer Marketing,* 23(3), 156-166.

[3] Munuera, J. L., Ruiz, S., Hernández, M. and Mas, F. (1993). Las ferias comerciales como variable de marketing: análisis de los objetivos del expositor. *Información Comercial Española,* 718, 119-138.

[4] Puthod, L. (1983). Análisis y objetivos de marketing en la participación en ferias. *ESIC Market,* 42, 31-64.

[5]Jiménez, J. F., Cazorla, I. M. and Linares, E. (2002). Ferias comerciales en España. Un análisis sectorial. *Distribución y Consumo,* 61, 61-71.

[6] Le Monnier, F. (1998). Marketing ferial: la comunicación integral. *Marketing y Ventas,* 121, 6-12.

[7] Bonoma, T. V. (1983). Get More out of Your Trade Shows. *Harvard Deusto Business Review,* 15, 109-118.

[8] Herbig, P., Palumbo, F. and O'hara, B. (1996). Differences in Trade Show Behaviour between Manufacturers and Service-oriented Firms. *Journal of Professional Services Marketing,* 14(2), 55-79.

[9] Herbig, P., O'hara, B. and Palumbo, F. (1998). Trade Show: Who, What, Why. *Marketing Intelligence & Planning,* 16(7), 425-435.

[10] Bello, D. C. and Barksdale Jr., J. C. (1986). Exporting at Industrial Trade Shows. *Industrial Marketing Management*, 15(3), 197-206.

[11] Shoham, A. (1992). Selecting and evaluating trade shows. *Industrial Marketing Management,* 21(4), 335-341.

[12] Center for Exhibition Industry Research (CEIR). (2003). *Role and Value of Face-to-Face Marketing*. Retrieved from: http://www.ceir.org/store_products.view.php?id=567.

[13] Munuera, J. L. and Ruiz, S. (1999). Trade fairs as service: a look at visitors' objectives in Spain. *Journal of Business Research,* 44(1), 17-24.

[14] Bellizzi, J. A. and Lipps, D. J. (1984). Managerial Guidelines for Trade Show Effectiveness. *Industrial Marketing Management,* 13(1), 49-52.

[15] Rufín Moreno, R. (2008). *Introducción al marketing*. Madrid: Editorial Sanz y Torres.

[16] Blythe, J. (2002). Using Trade Fairs in Key Account Management. *Industrial Marketing Management,* 31(7), 627-635.

[17] Bello, D. C. and Barczak, G. J. (1990). Using Industrial Trade Shows to Improve New Product Development. *The Journal of Business & Industrial Marketing,* 5(2), 43-56.

[18] Herbig, P., O'hara, B. and Palumbo, F. (1994). Measuring Trade Show Effectiveness: An Effective Exercise? *Industrial Marketing Management*, 23(2), 165-170.

[19] Navarro, F. (2001). *Estrategias de marketing ferial*. Madrid: ESIC Editorial.

[20] Mottard, E. (2003a). ¿Cuánto es de rentable participar en una feria? *Marketing y Ventas ,*182, 44-47.

[21] Miller, S. (2003). *Saque el máximo provecho de las ferias*. Barcelona: Ediciones Urano.

[22] Kerin, R. A. and Cron, W. L. (1987). Assessing Trade Show Functions and Performance: An Exploratory Study. *Journal of Marketing,* 51(3), 87-94.

[23] Gopalakrishna, S. and Lilien, G. L. (1995). A Three-stage Model of Industrial Trade Show Performance. *Marketing Science,* 14(1), 22-42.

[24] Gopalakrishna, S., Lilien, G. L., Williams, J. D. and Sequeira, I. K. (1995). Do Trade Shows Pay Off? *Journal of Marketing,* 59(3), 75-83.

[25] Tanner Jr., J. F. and Chonkon, L. B. (1995). Trade show objectives, management, and staffing practices. *Industrial Marketing Management,* 24(4), 257-264.

[26] Ling-Yee, L. (2008). The effects of firm resources on trade show performance: how do trade show marketing processes matter? *Journal of Business & Industrial Marketing*, 23(1), 35-47.

[27] Fu, H., Yang, G. and Qi, Y. (2007). Factors Affecting Trade Show Effectiveness for Chinese Small and Medium-sized Exporters. *International Management Review*, 3(3), 84-96.

[28] Santesmases, M. (1996). *Marketing: Conceptos y Estrategias*. Madrid: Pirámide.

[29] Tellis, G. J. and Redondo, I. (2002). *Estrategias de Publicidad y Promoción*. Madrid: Pearson Educación, S.A. (Addison-Wesley).

[30] Randall, G. (2003). *Principios de Marketing*. Madrid: Thomson.

[31] Kotler, P., Kevin, L., Camara, D. and Mollá, A. (2006). *Dirección de marketing* (12th

ed.). Madrid: Prentice-Hall.

[32] Esteban, A., García De Madariaga, J., Narros, M. J., Olarte, C., Reinares, E. M. and Saco, M. (1997). *Principios de marketing.* Madrid: ESIC.

[33] Rodríguez, I. A., De La Ballina, J. and Santos, L. (1997). *Comunicación comercial: conceptos y aplicaciones.* Madrid: Cívitas.

[34] Gázquez, J. C. and Jiménez, J. F. (2002). Las Ferias Comerciales en la estrategia de marketing. Motivaciones para la empresa expositora. *Distribución y Consumo,* 66, 76-83.

[35] Association of the German Trade Fair Industry (AUMA). (2011). *Successful Participation in Trade Fairs.* Retrieved from: http://www.auma.de/_pages/e/12_Download/download/TradeFairPreparation/Successfu lParticipation.pdf

[36] Tanner, Jr., J. F. (2002). Levelling the playing field: factors influencing trade show success for small companies. *Industrial Marketing Management,* 31(3), 229-239.

[37] Mesonero De Miguel, M. (2004). Identificación de las variables explicativas del éxito obtenido en una feria industrial. In: *Actas del Encuentro de Profesores Universitarios de Marketing,* Alicante, 621-637.

[38] Moreno, M. F., Reinares, E. M. and Saco, M. (2006). *Planificación estratégica de las ferias comerciales.* Madrid: Dykinson, S.L.

[39] Dallmeyer, B. (2013). *Successful Exhibit Marketing.* Retrieved from: http://www.ufi.org/Medias/pdf/thetradefairsector/howtoexhibit.pdf.

[40] Berné, C. and García-Uceda, M.E. (2008). Criteria Involved in Evaluation of Trade Shows to Visit. *Industrial Marketing Management,* 37(5), 565-579.

[41] Puchalt, J. (2008). La actividad ferial en el contexto europeo. *Información Comercial Española,* 840, 29-50.

[42] García, D., Madrid, A. and Munuera, J. L. (2008). Crecimiento, endeudamiento y rentabilidad de las instituciones feriales en España. *Revista de Economía,* 840, 105-122.

[43] Hansen, K. (1996). The Dual Motives of Participants at International Trade Shows: An Empirical Investigation of Exhibitors and Visitors with Selling Motives. *International Marketing Review,* 13(2), 39-54.

[44] Seringhaus, F. H. R. and Rosson, P. J. (2001). Firm experience and international trade fairs. *Journal of Marketing Management,* 17, 877-901.

[45] Gopalakrishna, S., Roster, C. A. and Sridhar, S. (2010). An Exploratory Study of Attendee Activities at a Business Trade Show. *Journal of Business & Industrial Marketing,* 25(4), 241-248.

[46] Rinallo, D., Borghini, S. and Golfetto, F. (2010). Exploring Visitor Experiences at Trade Shows. *Journal of Business & Industrial Marketing,* 25(4), 249-258.

[47] Blythe, J. (1999). Exhibitor Commitment and the Evaluation of Exhibition Activities. *International Journal of Advertising,* 18(1), 73-88.

[48] Lee, C. H. and Kim, S. Y. (2008). Differential effects of determinants on multi-dimensions of trade-show performance: by three stages of pre-show, at-show, and post-show activities. *Industrial Marketing Management,* 37(7), 784-796.

[49] Cavanaugh, S. (1976). Setting Objectives and Evaluating the Effectiveness of Trade Show Exhibit. *Journal of Marketin,* 40(4), 100-103.

[50] Siskind, B. (1997). *The Power of Exhibit Marketing* (4th ed.). North Vancouver, B.C.: Self-Counsel Press.

[51] Kane, W. (1989). So You Want to Exhibit at a Trade Show. *The International Executive,* 31(3), 21-23.

[52] Latorre, J. L. (1990). *Ferias y exposiciones en el exterior. Manual práctico.* Madrid: ICEX.

[53] Shipley, D., Egan, C. and Wong, K. S. (1993). Dimensions of trade show exhibiting management. *Journal of Marketing Management, 9*, 55-63.

[54] Vanderleest, H. W. (1994). Planning for international trade show participation: a practitioner's perspective. *S.A.M. Advanced Management Journal, 59*(4), 39-44.

[55] Williams, D. J., Gopalakrishna, S. and Cox, J. M. (1993). Trade show guidelines for smaller firms. *Industrial Marketing Management, 22*(4), 265-275.

[56] Friedmann, S. A. (2002). Ten Steps to a Successful Trade Show. *Marketing Health Services, 22*(1), 31-32.

[57] Bello, D. C. (1992). Industrial buyer behaviour at trade shows: implication for selling effectiveness. *Journal of Business Research*, 25(1), 59-80.

[58] Bendow, B. (1992). Evaluating Trade Promotions. *International Trade Forum, 28*(3), 12- 17, 32-33.

[59] Urruela, J. V. (1992). La post-feria. *Marketing y Ventas, 60*, 22-24.

[60] Mesonero De Miguel, M. and Garmendia, F. (2004). Comunicaciones integradas feriales o cómo planificar con éxito una feria industrial *Revista de Dirección y Administración de Empresas, 11*, 109-129.

[61] Smith, T. M. and Smith, P. M. (1999). Distributor and End-User Trade Show Attendance Objectives: An Opportunity for Adaptive Selling. *Forest Products Journal*, 49(1), 23-29.

[62] Carman, J. M. (1968). Evaluation of Trade Show Exhibitions. *California Management Review* 11(winter), 35-44.

[63] Gopalakrishna S. and Williams, J. D. (1992). Planning and Performance Assessment of Industrial Trade Shows: An Exploratory Study. *International Journal of Research in Marketing, 9*(3), 207-224.

[64] O'hara, B. S. (1993). Evaluating the effectiveness of trade shows: a personal selling perspective. *The Journal of Personal Selling & Sales Management, 13*(3), 67-77.

[65] Bello, D. C. and Lohtia, R. (1993). Improving Trade Show Effectiveness by Analyzing Attendees. *Industrial Marketing Management*, 22(4), 311-318.

[66] Poornani, A. A. (1996). Trade-show management: budgeting and planning for a successful event. *Cornell Hotel and Restaurant Administration Quarterly, 37*(4), 77-84.

[67] Dekimpe, M. G., François, P., Gopalakrishna, S., Lilien, G. L. and Van Den Bulte, C. (1997). Generalizing about Trade Show Effectiveness: A Cross-national Comparison. *Journal of Marketing, 61*(4), 55-64.

[68] Hansen, K. (2004). Measuring Performance at Trade Shows. Scale Development and Validation. *Journal of Business Research, 57*, 1-13.

[69] Berné, C. and García, M. (2005). *Origen y consecuencias de los resultados de la exposición en ferias profesionales*. Congreso Internacional "La Tendencia del Marketing", ESCP-EAP, Paris.

[70] Ling-Yee, L. (2006). Relationship learning at trade shows: its antecedents and consequences. *Industrial Marketing Management, 35*(2), 166-177.

[71] Tafesse, W. and Korneliussen, T. (2011). The dimensionality of trade show performance in an emerging market. *International Journal of Emerging Markets, 6*(1), 38-49.

A review of eco-innovation from a research-line perspective

LL. MIRET-PASTOR
Universitat Politècnica de València, Social Sciences Department, Spain
J. MONDÉJAR-JIMÉNEZ
Universidad de Castilla-La Mancha, Statistics Department, Spain
A. PEIRÓ-SIGNES
Universitat Politècnica de València, Management Department, Spain
M. SEGARRA-OÑA
Universitat Politècnica de València, Management Department, Spain

ABSTRACT

This paper reviews the main analyses carried out by its authors relating to eco-innovation. Most of these works have focused on an analysis of eco-innovation facilitators, and of environmental certificates and their impact on business results. The authors indicate that studies into energy efficiency help in continuing to improve indicators of eco-innovation, as well as to deepen knowledge of the facilitators and the environmental and economic effects of eco-innovation.

1. INTRODUCTION

Eco-innovation is the introduction of any new or significantly improved product (good or service), process, organisational change or marketing solution that reduces the use of natural resources (including materials, energy, water and land) and decreases the release of harmful substances across the whole life-cycle [1].

Eco-innovation plays a key role in the move towards a more sustainable economy and society, since it connects both pillars of sustainability: environmental quality and economic well-being. Eco-innovation enables an increase in the value of producers and consumers, while simultaneously reducing environmental impacts [2].

Incentives for environmental innovation go beyond regulatory pressure [3] and environmental benefits [4]. Moreover, it is becoming increasingly necessary for firms to include sustainability as a strategic factor in their management style [5].

A great deal of studies into eco-innovation focus on searching for indicators that effectively and feasibly measure it. Kemp and Pearson [6] have centred their methods on the analysis of surveys, patents and variable documentation; Arundel and Kemp [7] have tried to adapt the theory of innovation systems and their indicators in accordance with eco-innovation; meanwhile, Huppes et al. [8] try to establish a model framework for the analysis and indicators of eco-innovation.

Much of our research has focused on the study of eco-innovation. The objective of this paper is twofold. On the one hand, we wish to present some of the main conclusions of our work, especially in two fields in which we have focused our research: the identification and analysis of innovation facilitators; and the effect of environmental certifications on business results. On the other hand, our second objective is to connect the study of eco-innovation with what is known as the economics of energy efficiency. Both areas of study are two sides of the same coin. One way of more fully examining eco-innovation is to focus on savings, efficiency and the search for clean energy. A study of the indicators and facilitators, environmental effects, financial costs and final results for the companies, as well as the design and the possible effects of new clean energy or energy efficiency certificates, are some of the outcomes of a deeper understanding of eco-innovation and environmental and competitive policies' more effective and efficient design. In order to achieve the objectives proposed in this first introductory section, we will now present two theoretical sections in which we describe our work on eco-innovation and propose the main conclusions that we have reached. In the second section we will focus on eco-innovation facilitators, while in the third section we will review the effect of environmental certification on enterprises. Finally, the last section is dedicated to how we tried to establish connections between the study of eco-innovation and energy efficient economy, possible consequences of our investigation and new lines of research.

2. ECO-INNOVATION FACILITATORS

One of the key issues in the study of eco-innovation is the discovery of factors which facilitate or hinder its implementation in enterprises. This issue has been (and still is) the subject of a wide-ranging debate in the field of innovation in general [9,10,11]. In fact, our studies are based on much of the extensive existing literature on the subject.

The objective of our work has been to shed some light on this key aspect to aid the implementation of effective policies of eco-innovation promotion. An example of this is the database "Panel de Innovación Tecnológica" (PITEC, edition 2007), which consists of a statistical tool to monitor the technological innovation activities of Spanish companies. The database was built by the INE (Spanish National Statistics Institute) with advice from academics and experts. The first data came from 2004, and it has since been updated yearly to include a comprehensive list of Spanish companies characterised by the type of innovation that they undertake (classified by the Oslo Manual, [12]), as well as by industry (in line with the Spanish National Activities Classification, CNAE) or geographical location. A total of 255 variables were analysed. Affiliate level information was not available, as data was taken from an anonymous macroeconomic survey.

In a paper first published in the *International Journal of Environmental Research* [13] focused on determining which aspects were decisive for corporations that had a proactive environmental attitude and the identification of the factors that affect the eco-innovation.

This research adopted a two-step quantitative methodology applied to a large sample of 11,686 industrial Spanish firms, so that the results could be eventually extrapolated to a larger population [14]. In line with Dubé and Pare [15], well-known standardised statistical analysis methods, such as analysis of variance and regression analysis, have helped researchers confirm or reject hypotheses in quantitative research. Thus, a factorial analysis method was applied to reduce data variables. This technique allowed us to obtain homogeneous correlated variable groups. Moreover, a linear regression model with previous factor analysis identification fitted with the data.

The analysis allowed us to identify four major facilitators of eco-innovation: market size; the size of the company; formal innovative activity; and technology spending.

Studies focused on innovation have historically identified firm size or market orientation as the main drivers of innovation. The main conclusion of our work is that formal innovation appears to be the main moderating factor of eco-innovation. These results are in line with numerous studies that suggest that the same factors that influence innovation also influence eco-innovation.

Subsequently, it was considered that the facilitators identified in this first analysis were related to the size of the company and the market or the formal activity [16-20]. We therefore decided to focus on technological intensity. In a paper published in *Environmental Engineering and Management*, [21], using the same database, confirmed the positive correlation between the technological level and environmental orientation that was detected in an earlier work. However, the authors wanted to go further and relate the technological level of industries with the rest of variables that we considered as influential in environmental attitude.

This research adopted a two-step quantitative methodology. A factorial analysis method was applied to reduce data variables. This technique allowed us to obtain homogeneous correlated variable groups uncovering the latent structure of a set of variables. Moreover, a multinomial logistic regression (MLR) model was used to predict the probabilities of the different possible outcomes of a categorically distributed dependent variable (OBJET11), i.e. a firm's eco-orientation when innovation is given a set of independent variables previously identified using factor analysis identification. This analysis was subsequently applied to every technological subsector. The MLR model ranked the relative importance of the independents [22-24] by comparing each level of the dependent with the reference category for each independent variable.

As shown in the paper, the empirical results demonstrate that eco-innovation levels are not only influenced by the industry's technological intensity, but this technological intensity also influences the type and importance of the eco-innovation drivers.

The size of the company is a key marker for eco-innovation in all industries analysed; therefore, for most technologically advanced companies, the most significant (and sometimes sole) eco-innovation driver is related to firm size. However, other variables, such as formal activity, R&D type and market size, also affect it in different ways.

Formal innovation levels have an influence in sectors with intermediate technology levels, especially in medium-high technology companies where innovation plays a major role. In contrast, the key role in low-technology companies seems to be the "type of investment in RD" (although this factor is also important in medium-technology industries). A third piece of work in this field, which also had a similar methodology and was based on the same database (PITEC), was published in *Boletín de la Sociedad*

Española de Cerámica y Vidrio [25]. This study delved into a specific manufacturing sector as it is the one of the producers of ceramic tiles. The objective was to identify the moderating factors influencing behaviour in eco-innovative enterprises. The results were very similar to the previous work.

The factors that the literature identified as drivers of innovation, such as the firm size and its openness to the market, can also be considered drivers of eco-innovation. In fact, innovation can be formally measured both through the number of patents and by the launch of new investment products, and can thus be deemed the main factor influencing eco-innovation moderators.

In a later work in the same sector, we examined [26] key aspects of the environmental strategy of ceramic enterprises more deeply. Their study approach was different to the above-mentioned work in that it used a qualitative methodology and in-depth interviews with different managers.

Three internal company facilitators were observed through an analysis of the realized surveys: the size of the company (small, medium or large); the characteristic of the company regarding its internationalization (i.e. international or national); and the degree of implication for executives and shareholders.

On the other hand, the main obstacles faced by companies when attempting to adopt a more proactive environmental strategy are: a lack of institutional support (65.71 %); insufficient financial support (54.29 %); lack of tools information (51.43 %); lack of technical solutions (37.14 %); and lack of qualified human resources (33 %).

Finally, the companies identified significant benefits arising from the implementation of proactive environmental management actions. The most important of these is to avoid sanctions, followed by improvements to the corporate image, the saving of long-term costs, and obtaining new business opportunities.

3. THE EFFECTS OF ENVIRONMENTAL CERTIFICATION ON BUSINESS

Environmental certification can be defined as a voluntary process that checks, audits and validates whether a process, product or service meets a set of specific standards. In regards to environmental management, these standards serve as guide for implementing an environmental management system (EMS).

We can define an EMS as a cycle of planning, action, review and improvement of the environmental performance of a company. An EMS is based on the realization of an environmental diagnosis that identifies, assesses, reduces and prevents environmental impacts on the environment. The two most commonly used environmental certification systems are ISO 14001 and the EcoManagement and Audit Scheme (EMAS). These two systems are cited by several authors as indicators of eco-innovation [6]. This is the reason why we have been analysing the effects of adopting environmental certificates on business results.

Firstly, we analysed a key industrial sector: the food industry [27]. Through the SABI (Iberian Balance-Sheet Analysis System) database, we analysed economic data on 6,118 companies in the sector, of which 150 were ISO 14001 certified. Our findings show that the use of ISO14001 as an environmental management tool had a significant impact on several economic performance variables, which led us to conclude that there is a direct relationship between ISO 14001 and corporate performance. In an analysis of the sample which was segmented by size, it was confirmed that size is a distinguishing factor too.

The data analysed in this research seems to be in agreement with other studies. The results show that firms with proactive practices exhibited a significantly positive economic performance [28,29]. In addition, the findings support the theory [30] that small firms need support systems to help managers in their development needs, while larger firms can afford to have a team of specialists. In a parallel study of PITEC, we can conclude that the more companies focus on innovation, the more eco-innovation is supported, given that both formal innovative activity (patents) and total innovation investment (total expenditure in R&D and number of R&D employees) are good indicators of the level of innovation, as well as by the fact that there are significant differences between the groups considered. Another important conclusion relating to the analysis is that company size determines the sustainable innovative proactivity of the firm. Furthermore, higher export orientation is a characteristic of eco-innovative firms.

So far we have focused our research into industries in the service sector, specifically the hospitality industry. In doing so, we have looked at different ways of measuring eco-innovation in the tourism sector, and analysed three main environmental certificates used in the sector [31].

Subsequently, we attempted to analyse the relationship between the implementation of a proactive environmental management tool – the ISO 14001 standard – and the generation of economic revenues in the Spanish hotel industry [32]. We also considered the possible effects on the business results of moderating factors such as company size and the market sector where the hotel operates. We analyzed data from 2008, regarding 2,116 Spanish. A total of 108 properties had implemented the ISO 14001 certification. Quantitative analysis techniques show significant differences in the economic performance of ISO-certified hotels and those which are not certified, particularly for urban and beach hotels. The results show the influence that company size and organizational factors have on revenue. Only small rural hotels saw no difference in revenues due to the presence or absence of ISO certification.

Another study [33] sought to analyse the impact of environmental certification on hotel guest ratings. Based on a comparison of customer ratings at 6,850 hotels in Spain with and without ISO 14001 certification, guests rated the hotels with ISO 14001 certification higher overall than those without this certification. These results are stronger for hotel comfort and hotel services compared with other hotel attributes. Moreover, the most significant differences were found in the upscale four-star hotels. While the study does not reveal causes for these findings, the implication is that the high-end five-star luxury hotels do not gain distinctive differentiation by having the ISO 14001 certification, while guests' price sensitivity overrides environmental concerns for three-star hotels. At the four-star level, however, hotels seem to be able to gain a distinct market advantage from environmental certification. For all hotels, the management discipline provided by ISO 14001 can provide a competitive advantage.

Finally, a recent study analysing the effects of the ISO 14001 environmental certification on manufacturing industries and services attempted to ascertain the effects of other ecological certificates in primary industries, particularly the effect of the MSC (Marine Stewardship Council) certificate in fisheries and all its auxiliary subsectors.

4. EXAMINATIONS OF ECO-INNOVATION FROM THE ENERGY EFFICIENCY PERSPECTIVE

Both the European Commission and the OECD consider one of the greatest challenges for the effective implementation of policies that promote eco-innovation is how to improve benchmarking and create better indicators [34]. As such, measuring economic and environmental performance is necessary.

Until now, much of our work has focused on measuring the economic impact of eco-innovation, but another challenge is how to measure its environmental impact. For this purpose, a number of different indicators have appeared: MIPS (Material Input per Unit of Service), the ecological footprint and the carbon footprint.

As can be seen, many of these environmental indicators refer to energy issues. In fact, one of the challenges reported by the Observatory of Eco Innovation [35] is the building of energy productivity indicators that express the amount of economic value generated by one unit of energy input of consumption.

This line opens important study directions for eco-innovation and energy efficiency. From a business viewpoint, the reduction of energy costs is one of the main incentives for the implementation of eco-innovative measures. Research by the Carbon Trust showed that large UK businesses undervalue the financial returns from investments in energy efficiency by more than half. This leads them to waste at least £1.6bn every year on energy they could easily save through simple energy-saving measures [36]. From an environmental point of view, a priority is a reduction in the carbon footprint, i.e. the consumption of energy and resources.

Therefore, public institutions should promote innovative eco-policies that allow performances and results to be reviewed from three aspects of sustainability: economic, environmental and social development. Similarly, energy efficiency policies incite greater competitiveness and a better environment for businesses, while reducing the energy dependency of countries and facilitating the achievement of environmental commitments to climate change. The EU is aiming for a 20 % reduction in Europe's annual primary energy consumption by 2020. The Commission has proposed several measures to increase efficiency at all stages of the energy chain, including generation, transformation, distribution and final consumption.

The measures focus on the public transportation and building sectors, as these are where the potentials for savings are greatest. Other measures include the introduction of smart meters (which encourage consumers to manage their energy use better) and clearer product labelling.

Within the framework of the EU's Competitiveness and Innovation Framework Programme (CIP), the CIP Eco-innovation Initiative addresses European companies that have developed new ways of reducing the industry's ecological footprint and their attempts to make better use of natural resources. This initiative supports the market entry into and further uptake of new "green" products, services and technologies.

In fact, the promotion of eco-innovation policies in other countries (e.g. Canada) has focused solely on eco-efficiency. The ecoENERGY Innovation Initiative (ecoEII) was launched in 2011 by the Canadian government. The program's objective is to support energy technology innovation in order to produce and use energy in a cleaner and more efficient way. This initiative is a key component of the Canadian government's attempts to achieve real emissions reductions, while maintaining the country's economic advantage and its ability to create jobs for Canadians. The ecoEII will also help in the search for long-term solutions to reducing and eliminating air pollutants from energy production and use.

Activities funded under ecoEII concern five strategic priority areas:
- energy efficiency;
- clean electricity and renewables;
- bioenergy;
- electrification of transportation;
- unconventional oil and gas.

In short, there are many initiatives for the promotion of eco-innovation, and most of them come from a more efficient and responsible use of energy. An in-depth study of eco-innovation specifically requires the study of many aspects of energy such as: What factors encourage or impede energy savings? How we can promote energy saving actions? How can we measure environmental impacts and economic energy efficiency measures? Does energy certification or labelling have an impact? The challenges facing the study of eco-innovation are numerous, but many of them are shared by the study of the economics of energy efficiency.

AKNOWLEDGEMENTS

The authors would like to thank the Spanish Economy and Competitiveness Ministry for its support through the research projects (ECO2011-27369 & ECO2012-36685).

REFERENCE LIST

[1] EIO (2010) Eco-innovation Observatory Annual Report 2010. Pathways to a resource-efficient Europe, available at: http://www.eco-innovation.eu/index.php?option=com_content&view=article&id=200&Itemid=258

[2] Van Berkel, R. (2007): Eco-innovation opportunities for advancing waste prevention. *International Journal of Environmental Technology and Management*, 7, 527-550.

[3] Brunnermeier, S. B. & Cohen, M. A. (2003) Determinants of environmental innovation in US manufacturing industries. *Journal of Environmental Economics and Management*, 45, 278-293.

[4] Carrion, C. & Innes, R. (2010).Environmental innovation and environmental performance. *Journal of Environmental Economics and Management*, 59, 27-42.

[5] González-Benito, J. & González-Benito, O. (2008) Operations management practices linked to the adoption of ISO 14001: An empirical analysis of Spanish manufacturers. *International Journal of Production Economics*, 113, 60-73.

[6] Kemp, R. & Pearson, P. (2009) Final report of the project 'Measuring Eco-Innovation (MEI).Working paper series. United Nations University, Maastricht

[7] Arundel, A. & Kemp, R. (2009). Measuring Eco-innovation. Working paper series. United Nations University.

[8] Huppes, G., Kleijn, R., Huele, R., Ekins, P., Shaw, B., Schaltegger, S. & Esders, M. (2008) Measuring eco-Innovation: Framework and typology of indicators based on causal chains. Management summary of the final report of the ECODRIVE project. www.eco-innovation.eu/wiki/images/Ecodrive_management_summary.pdf

[9] Rennings, K., Ziegler, A., Ankele, K. & Hoffmann, E. (2006) The Influence of Different Characteristics of the EU Environmental Management and Auditing Scheme on Technical Environmental Innovations and Economic Performance, *Ecological Economics*, 57, 45-59.

[10] Bercovitz, J. & Mitchell, W. (2008) When is more better? The impact of business scale and scope on long-term business survival, while controlling for profitability. *Strategic Management Journal,* 28, 61-79.

[11] Crespi, F. & Pianta, M. (2008) Demand and innovation in productivity growth. *Int. Rev. App. Econ.,* 22, 655-672.

[12] Oslo Manual. (2005) Guidelines for collecting and interpreting innovation data. Third edition. OECD and Eurostat organization for economic co-operation and development statistical office of the European Communities.

[13] Segarra-Oña, M., Peiró-Signes, A., Albors-Garrigós, J. & Miret-Pastor, L. (2011) Impact of innovative practices in environmentally focused firms: moderating factors. *International Journal of Environmental Research*, 5, 425-434.

[14] Gelman, A. & Hill, J. (2007) Data Analysis Using Regression and Multilevel/Hierarchical Models. Cambridge University Press.

[15] Dubé, L. & Paré, G. (2003). Rigor in IS Positivist Case Research. *MIS Quarterly* 27, 597-635.

[16] Biondi, V., Iraldo, F. & Meredith, S. (2002) Achieving sustainability through environmental innovation: the role of SMEs. *International Journal of Technology Management,* 24, 612-626.

[17] Mir, D. F. & Feitelson, E. (2007) Factors affecting environmental behaviour in Micro-enterprises. *International Small Business journal*, 25, 383-415.

[18] Rehfeld, K., Rennings, K. & Ziegler, A. (2007) Integrated Product Policy and Environmental Product Innovations: An Empirical Analysis. *Ecological Economics*, 61, 91-100.

[19] Nidumolu, R., Prahalad, C., & Rangaswami, M. (2009) Why Sustainability Is Now the Key Driver of Innovation. *Harvard Business Review,* 87, 57-64.

[20] Demirel, P. & Kesidou, E. (2011) Stimulating different types of eco-innovation in the UK: Government policies and firm motivations. *Ecological Economics*, 70, 1546-1557.

[21] Peiro-Signes, A., Maria-del-Val Segarra-Ona, Miret-Pastor, L. & Verma, R. (2011) Eco-Innovation Attitude and Industry's Technological Level-An Important Key for Promoting Efficient Vertical Policies. *Environmental Engineering of Management Journal*, 10, 1893-1901.

[22] Long, J. S. (1997) *Regression models for categorical and limited dependent variables*. London: Sage Publications

[23] Hosmer, D. W., Lemeshow, S. (2000), Applied Logistic Regression, 2nd Ed., New York, John Wiley & Sons Inc.

[24] Hox, J. (2002) Multilevel Analyses: Techniques and Applications. Mahwah, NJ: Erlbaum, Jamison RN, Raymond.

[25] Segarra Oña, M., Peiró Signes, Á., Miret Pastor, L. G. & Albors Garrigós, J. (2011) ¿Eco-innovación, una evolución de la innovación? Análisis empírico en la industria cerámica española. *Boletín de la Sociedad Española de Cerámica y Vidrio*, 50, 219-228.

[26] Carrascosa-López, C., Peiró-Signes, Á., Miret-Pastor, L. & Segura-García-del-Río, B. (2013). Is It Possible To Generate Added Value Through A Higher Environmental Proactivity Orientation? A Practical Analysis of the Spanish Ceramic Industry. In *EcoProduction and Logistics*, 57-71, Springer Berlin Heidelberg.

[27] Segarra-Oña, M., Peiró-Signes, A., Miret-Pastor, L., & Albors-Garrigós, J. (2011). Uncovering non-obvious relationship between environmental certification and economic performance at the food industry. In *Information Technologies in Environmental Engineering*, 325-338. Springer Berlin Heidelberg.

[28] Aragón-Correa, J. A., Hurtado-Torres, S. Sharma, N. & García-Morales, V. (2008) Environmental strategy and performance in small firms: A resource-based perspective. *Journal of Environmental Management,* 86, 88-103.

[29] Martín-Tapia, I., Aragón-Correa, J. A. & Rueda-Manzanares, A. (2009) Environmental strategy and exports in medium, small and micro-enterprises. *Journal of World Business,* 45, 266-75.

[30] Kroeger, C. V. (1974) Managerial development in the small firm. *California Management Review,* 17, 41-47.

[31] Miret Pastor, L., Segarra-Oña, M. & Peiró-Signes, Á. (2011) ¿Cómo medimos la Ecoinnovación?: análisis de indicadores en el Sector Turístico. *Tec Empresarial,* 5, 15-25.

[32] Segarra-Oña, M., Peiró-Signes, Á., Verma, R., & Miret-Pastor, L. (2012). Does environmental certification help the economic performance of hotels? Evidence from the Spanish hotel industry. *Cornell Hospitality Quarterly*, 53, 242-256.

[33] Peiró-Signes, A., Verma, R., Mondéjar-Jiménez, J., & Vargas-Vargas, M. (2013). The Impact of Environmental Certification on Hotel Guest Ratings. *Cornell Hospitality Quarterly*, Published online before print October 9, 2013, doi: 10.1177/1938965513503488.

[34] OECD. (2009) The OECD Project on Sustainable Manufacturing and Eco innovation. Framework, Practices and Measurements. Synthesis Report.

[35] EIO and CfSD. (2013) Eco-innovate! A guide to eco-innovation for SMEs and business coaches. Eco-Innovation Observatory. Funded by the European Commission, DG Environment, Brussels.

[36] Carbontrust. (2013) The Business of Energy Efficiency. Available at http://www.carbontrust.com/media/135418/cta001-business-of-energy-efficiency.pdf

Geographic information systems (GIS) and new business opportunities for ecotourism

A. MOYA-FUERO
Universitat Politècnica de València, Urbanism Department, Spain
R. MARTÍNEZ-CAÑAS
University of Castilla-La Mancha, Business Management Department, Spain
P. RUÍZ-PALOMINO
University of Castilla-La Mancha, Business Management Department, Spain

ABSTRACT

Geographic Information Systems (GIS) have become a powerful group of tools for improving location decisions, process improvements and resources management. From a spatial point of view, GIS have enhanced interactive queries such as geographic information processing, the geo-referencing of alphanumeric data, data storage, maps elaboration, and more importantly, GIS tools have developed the presentation and interpretation of the results derived from spatial information. In this paper we develop an analysis of the geographical position of ecotourism businesses in the mountain area of the province of Cuenca (Spain) in order to determine the different opportunities for ecotourism through indexes of sustainability.

1 INTRODUCTION

Actually Geographic Information Systems (GIS) are a widespread mainstream technology with a growing and vital use across all industries, including natural resources, military, environment planning, education, insurance, logistics, land management, tourism, business, utilities and many more [1]. Accordingly, this set of tools are typically focused on coding and storing data which a geographic location, undertaking analysis of that data in order to integrating with other data types and presenting for decision support, usually in the form of a map [2].The origin of GIS backs to the late 1970s when an increasing number researchers were interested in improving their decision take process guided by spatial data [3]. However, in a large number of cases it remains under-utilized and often has not provided the business benefits originally desired [1].This technology has created a huge industry together with software developers and vendors [4]. Therefore GIS tools work with just a simplistic software approach – it requires understanding the business environment of the host organization and how this technology can be used to address real tourist business issues [5].

This paper explores the successful use of GIS for Ecotourism activities. Therefore, is based in the necessity to link economic development of a rural area with the environmental conservation and responsible management of his environmental resources.

Accordingly, the aim of use GIS technologies is related with improving the planning and management of environmental areas with an important economic future development [6]. These special tools are the cornerstone for studying ecotourism opportunities together with other indicators proposed in geographical studies methodologies. All these indicators identify the relationships between tourism, land and environment under the perspective of sustainable development [7]. Therefore, this paper uses these indicators for ecotourism activities in some municipalities located in a range of mountains of Cuenca province (Spain). Also, the paper set-up a reference framework for future studies related to aspects of sustainability indicators, models of pressure-state-response environmental and other ancillary and more complex sustainability indicators. Then we analyse the advantages and disadvantages of measuring factors in the establishment of a system of indicators. In the fourth section of the paper is presented the methods and GIS maps made with key indicators considered. Finally, the paper raises a number of basic conclusions regarding entrepreneurial opportunities for rural tourism activities, sustainable activities and rural development that can be utilized for future entrepreneurs, institutions and mediators in general.

2   THEORETICAL FRAMEWORK OF REFERENCE

Sustainable development is about *"meeting the needs of the present without compromising the ability of future generations to meet their own needs"* [8]. In the Conference on Environment and Development of Rio de Janeiro [9] started the change of mentality about responsibility of governments around the world for implementing these principles of sustainable development. This open debate has allowed a major impact on some principles of sustainability as opposed to the negative effects of uncontrolled growth and development [10]. In recent years this concept is not new in the field of planning and resources use and also has been applied for the preparation of General Management Plans that actually are including a novelty for study: the use Geographic Information Systems (GIS). This methodology, and particularly for this paper, is based in the use of "sustainable indicators" for eco-tourism.

The World Conference on Sustainable Tourism arranged in Lanzarote (Spain) in 1995 resume the main ideas of use GIS for eco-tourism activities [11]:

- It must create a long term perspective in order to be ecologically, economically viable and equitable social to local communities.
- It requires an overall management to ensure the conservation of the natural and cultural resources.
- It should ensure, for tourism activities, an acceptable evolution regarding the impact on natural resources, biodiversity and assimilation of impacts and waste of resources.
- All options for tourism development must effectively affect the positive quality of life of the population.
- Promote a more equitable distribution of the benefits and burdens from tourism, which involves changes in consumption patterns.
- It has to pay special attention to the effects of transport and means for reducing the use of non-renewable energy, promote recycling and waste minimization.

- It has to use economic instruments, legal and tax to ensure sustainable use.

Truly, these definitions are just statements of interest that have been signed in various documents of various international organizations [10]. However, it can be appreciated the interdependence of economic growth and environmental conservation and the need for equitable distribution of development benefits [12]. These three points are the key balance of sustainable tourism or ecotourism. Also, these statements must be materialized through general indicators (for instance: biodiversity or social marginalization) or just more specific items for taking into account local and spatial information. For this reason, has been developed an "unofficial" model of Pressure-State-Response of environmental indicators (See Figure 1).

The OECD and the European Environment Agency recommend this model as a start point to generate indicators. The model is based on the principle of causality where human activities exert pressures on the environment and change its quality and quantity of natural resources. Therefore, it is assumed that there is a constant interaction between the pressure on the environment and social responses.

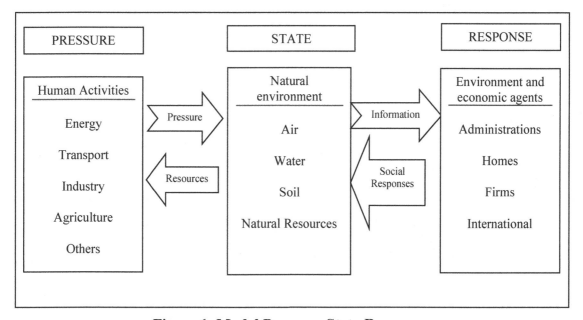

Figure 1. Model Pressure-State-Response

Usually, pressure indicators reflect the direct and indirect pressure over administration. State describes the environmental conditions at a given time, and the quality and quantity of natural resources managed. And finally, response mechanisms correspond to the degree to which society responds to environmental changes.

Accordingly, to know the status of these indicators at a given time must establish reference values describing the sustainability threshold for the different variables. This fact has a great complexity because it depends on the objective situation of the environment and perception of environmental problems, so it is needed to consider these guidelines to establish the framework of value:

- Set parameters that can be easily objectified from a scientific and technical point (air quality, water, etc. ...).
- Evolution of these parameters in time and trend. To analyse the approximation to the desired state (e.g. tourist expenditure/day or demand response to tourist investments).
- Comparison of the values in a territorial context that allows its homogenization from a territorial, economic, political, cultural and social point of view.
- Consensus values from a process of social participation.

For ecotourism in this paper are calculated the following indicators (Table 1):

Table 1 Indicators for ecotourism

Simple Indicator	Measure
1.- Place protection	Place protection according to an International Law for nature resources protection
2.- Pressure on the place	Number of tourists per year
3.- Intensity of use	Intensity of use in peak season
4.- Social impact	Ratio between tourists and local residents.
5.- Monitoring and control of development	Process for monitoring environment or formal control mechanism of place development and density of use.
6.- Residue management	% of wastewater treatment in the receptor site
7.- Planning process	Existence of a regional plan for the place
8.- Critic Ecosystems	Number of rare/in danger species
9.- Tourism satisfaction	Level of satisfaction among visitors
10.- Satisfaction of local natives	Level of satisfaction among local natives
11.- Contribution of the Tourism to the local economy	% of economic local activity generated only for tourism activities

For a good measure of ecotourism indicators it is needed to consider some factors:
- It requires a lot of reliable and continuous information throughout the whole study. It can be obtained by surveys or secondary data elaborated by an administration.
- Information must be separated into administrative units, usually in municipalities, as organisms normally collect data in this unit. When information is in cluster levels (for example, a natural park that belongs to several municipalities) must be separated.
- It is desirable to have the information series. The calculation of indicators with time series can help to define real and achievable targets and discover deviations.
- Data indicators must interrelate with normalizations in order to be comparable and create new composite indicators from these. In this paper we use two techniques, one for the generation of values using the Shannon formula (used in biodiversity studies) and the other normalization based on average values grouped into three ranges of 1 to 3.

3   METHODS, INDICATORS AND RESULTS

The statistical information was obtained from 34 villages included in a tourism improvement plan for the mountain area of Cuenca province (Spain)[13]. An ad-hoc database was built with the raw information available in the website. These small villages have a total population of 18.000 people with a population density of only 3 habitants for Km^2. Villages are part of the "Serrania de Cuenca" National Park and also near "Alto Tajo" National Park. Data and information required "The number of Backpackers, Apartments, Rural Cabins, Campings, Country Houses, Hostels, Hotels, Lodgings and Restaurants" (See Table 2 and Figure 2). Also were included some Points of Interest (POIs) related to sustainable tourism (See Table 3). All data were processed using the software ARCGIS (Version 10.1). This software was used to geo-reference all tourism infrastructures we from their address and have been linked to the coverage of municipalities available in the Spanish IGN (National Geographic Institute).

Table 2. Tourism infrastructure

Infrastructure	Number	Accommodation capacity
Backpackers	2	75
Apartments	15	398
Rural Cabins	4	83
Campings	3	520
Country Houses	75	844
Hostels	15	401
Hotels	9	320
Lodgings	1	13
Restaurants	27	1177

Table 3. Points of Interest

Infrastructure	Number
Monuments	41
Museums	9
Active and Sport Tourism Business	4
Leisure Zone	28

3.1 Site protection

This indicator is calculated according to the index proposed by the International Union for the Conservation of Nature and created through categories of protection. In the case of the Serrania de Cuenca, as seen in Figure 3, there is no space qualified as special protection. Site Protection Index is based on whether the municipality's tourist establishment Nature Park, Nature Reserve or Natural Monument, SPAs (Special Protection Area for birds) and RAMSAR Wetlands LICS (Community Attractions). All information was obtained from the Ministry of Agriculture of Castilla-La Mancha [13].

---

[13]http://www.serraniaaltadecuenca.es (Retrieved on January 15th)

For each element in the town is awarded with a point. Once posted, all values are normalized by ranks 1 to 3 using the following formula:

- Rank 1: 0 in the mean value.
- Rank 2: average value over the 25% in the same point.
- Rank 3: from the limit of the above point to the best value.

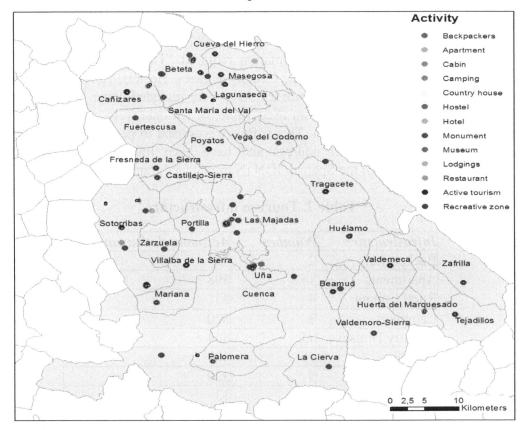

Figure 2. Tourism Activity

3.2 Site pressure

This second indicator is calculated using the number of year visits to every tourist infrastructure. The data were taken from the INE (Spanish National Statistical Institute) [14; 15] and the Chamber of Commerce of Cuenca Province. Unfortunately the secondary data of the survey is elaborated by municipality and not by the whole province. Figure 4 shows the time series (from 2000 to 2011) of the total number of visitors, number of nights and average stay. Data show that there is a clear growing trend until 2008 on then decrease to 2001 levels.

3.3 Intensity of use

This third indicator shows the quantity of use measured in persons per hectare. We use the cartographic base MTN200 of the IGN to get the contour of the urban centres of the municipalities' accommodation infrastructure [15]. In this geometry measure were obtained the acres of land. Also were calculated the number of night stays in the peak months of the statistical basis of INE. As statistics is provincial, is distributed proportionally with the number of night stays divided by the number of places. The indicator is the ratio between overnight stays and hectares. Results were calculated with the same weighting method that has been used for the first indicator. Map with results is showed in Figure 4.

3.4 Social Impact

This indicator measures the ratio between residents and tourists. For this calculation we will consider not only the hotel rooms but also the restoration business of the area. Data were downloaded from the database of the INE, more specifically, the population census of 2011 [14]. The ratio is the tourists between local population (Figure 5).

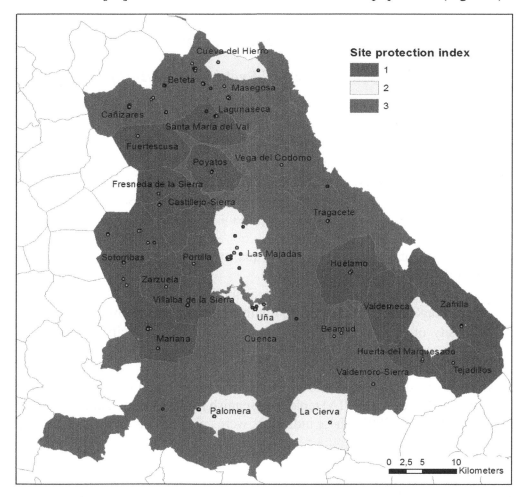

Figure 3. Site Protection Index

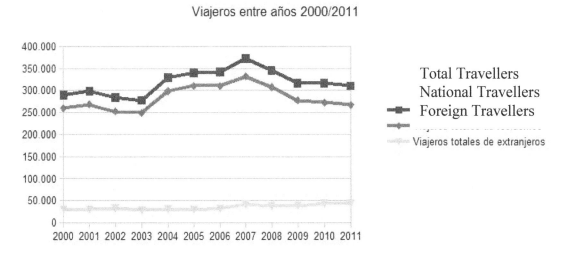

Figure 4. Travellers´ Evolution (2000/2011)

3.5 Control of development

This indicator assesses the existence of any environmental review and legal procedures or formal controls for site development and for densities of use. These indicators are used to provide public information on important environmental issues. Indicators have a manageable number of parameters that encompass the vast amount of scientific information available. Among the most important parameters to estimate are:

- Environmental indicators (water quality, waste management, transport and mobility, energy, air pollution, etc.).
- Local development indicators (contribution to the local tourism economy, percentage of total employment, number of facilities, endowments, etc.).
- Density of use indicators (number of tourists per municipality with respect to supply, seasonal usage statistics, ratio of tourists by local people, etc.).

Data were obtained from the Ministry of Agriculture of Spain through the Public Bank Environmental Indicators (BPIA) replacing Spanish for Environmental Indicators System (SEIA) from the year 2003. These indicators were calculated at the municipal level.

3.6 Waste management

This indicator measures the percentage of water wasted in 2000 through European Directive of Water Waste Management where regions had to adapt their water recycling process in order to renew water management. This directive promotes prevention, tries to reduce pollution, promote sustainable use of water, promotes environmental protection, improves aquatic ecosystems and mitigates the effects of droughts and floods. Therefore, municipalities have to monitor these parameters: water consumption, reservoir water reserves, water resources, desalination of brackish and sea water, nitrate pollution in groundwater, etc.

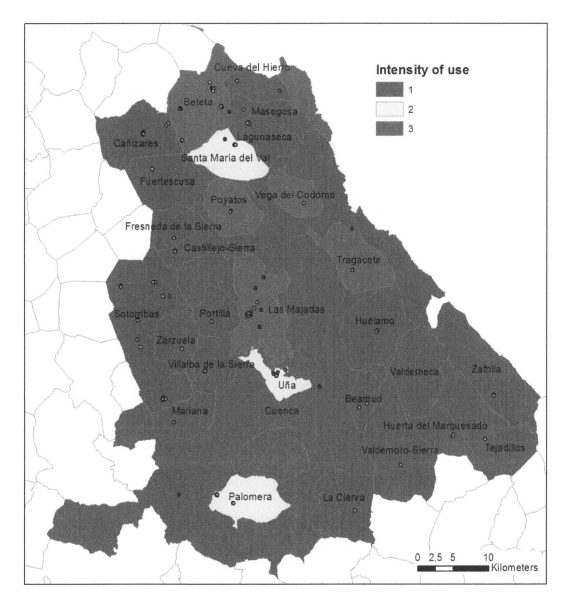

Figure 5. Intensity of Use

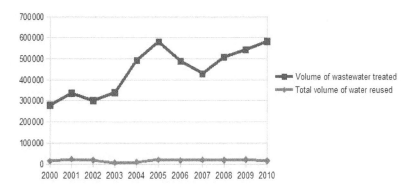

Figure 6. Evolution of wastewater

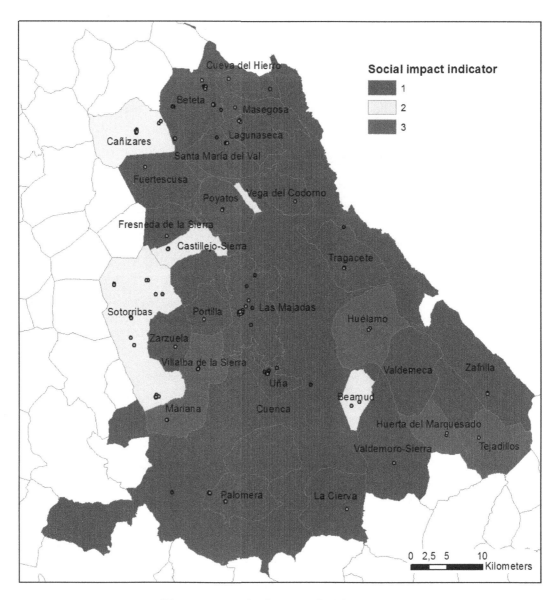

Figure 7. Social Impact Indicator

3.7 Planning process

This indicator deals with the ability to ensure the sustainability of tourism in the Mountain area of Cuenca. Accordingly, it is necessary to create and arrange an organized regional plan for the region as a tourist destination. In 2006 started a "Promotion Plan" for municipalities in order to implement a tourist reservation centre, improving tourist infrastructure, creating internet value and promotion of the area. In 2008 was approved a "Plan for Sustainable Rural Development of Castilla-La Mancha" that was a continuation of the previous and intended to increase the number of tourist accommodations and restaurants, as well as setting the local population, tourism being a key of local economies. This plan was supported by the European Funds for Regional Development (FEDER).

In 2012 there was an extensive and high elaborate plan for the sustainable development of the "Area of the Serranía de Cuenca". This document characterize rural areas in areas of action according to three aspects: population densities, distance to the town of over

30,000 inhabitants, average people of the municipality and the number of people employed in agricultural activities. These three groups identified priority areas for intervention makes a start point or "diagnosis of sustainability". This diagnosis of sustainability is taken as a basis for the characterization of the current situation of the territory and its future trends. It is done through an analysis of the weaknesses and strengths of the area in order to determine which circumstances can be taken into account in order to shape the sustainable rural development strategy of the area. Therefore the main points of the plan are divided into the following four sections: Economic aspects, social aspects, Environmental aspects and infrastructures.

The general conclusions related with ecotourism of this plan are:

- Poor infrastructures and isolation of the territory have contributed to the actual natural environment that is an important heritage relatively well preserved.
- Main sustainable resources of the territory and the landscape can be exploited for tourism activities, can be used for renewable energy, etc.
- Craftsmanship and quality food products can help to create a great potential for the area.

Also the plan includes some corrective measures related to four areas:

- Diversification and strengthening of productive activity for creating new employment opportunities.
- Improvement of telecommunications and transport infrastructures in order to support productive activity.
- Ensure basic services for avoiding work discrimination. Also, improve the quality of life and social cohesion of the population in the area.
- Correct most serious environmental problems for sustainability of the territory taking into account the value of natural resources.

3.8 Critical Ecosystems

This indicator measures the number of rareness or endangered species in the area. Within this Natural Park exists a high biodiversity, it have been listed more than 220 species of vertebrates (4 are in serious danger of extinction). There are populations and colonies of golden eagles and vultures. Also there are a vast quantity of pines, oaks, mosses, fungi and lichens. The park belongs to the Nature 2000 network of National Parks in order to preserve his biodiversity and minimize the impact of human activities. This directive lists two types of soil to protect Special Areas of Conservation (SACs) and Special Protection Areas for Birds (SPAs). Figure 8 shows the evolution of the amount of protected land in Spain.

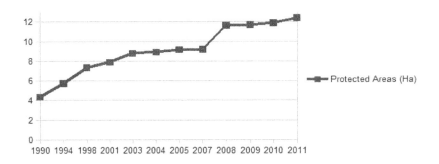

Figure 8. Evolution of Protected Areas

3.9 Tourist satisfaction

This indicator measures the level of tourist satisfaction. It is a complex indicator and usually is obtained through surveys. For the elaboration is needed to divide tourists (nationals and foreigners). The periodicity of this measure must be seasonally adjusted and divided in quarterly results. The mechanisms for obtaining data range from telephone surveys, in collaboration with tourist establishments, with tourist information points and with local administrative authorities.

The variables to measure are related with: consultation and information search, reservation, transportation, mobility, accommodation, food offer, cultural environment, social environment and natural environment. All this information refers to specific tourist establishments and geographical areas and it must be introduced as a GIS geo-referenced variables in order to ease the decision process to identify factors to improve short-term (treatment, kindness, service, ..) as well as medium to long term (road safety, safety, communication, information level. ..).

3.10 Level of satisfaction of local population

This indicator measures the level of satisfaction of local population with the current model of tourism. Main items reflect:

- Perception of the local community about the tourist activity
- Increased conflict and crime in peak season
- Changes in traffic accidents in peak season.
- Level of educational for tourism sector workers
- Level of participation in cultural activities.
- Participation rates and management
- Tourism development plan (by terms).
- Level of local tourism associations (number of local business partners in the total).

These indicator shows if development plans are developed correctly and it also shows the perception of population about whether they are being managed effectively.

3.11 Contribution of tourism to the local economy

The last indicator highlights the importance of tourism to local economies.

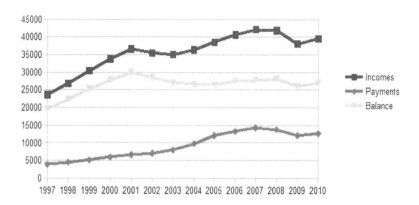

Figure 9. Tourism receipts and payments

Therefore, this is one of the greatest assets to avoid depopulation and survival of many rural municipalities. This tourism indicator should be developed in response to sustainability factors to ensure proper development and ensure economic activity. For assessing the contribution of tourism on overall economic activity in these municipalities it have to measure the "Income and tourism payments per indicator and period". This information is available in the INE database. The evolution of this indicator in the period 1997/2010 is shown in Figure 9:

The real impact on the area should consider:

- Income generated by tourism in terms of time and number of people employed.
- Degree of increased tourism sustainable from the rest.
- Volume of tourists in peak season.
- Occupancy level of accommodation.
- Diversification of the tourism product.
- Total direct employment generated by tourism in contrast to other activities.
- Change in employment generated in peak.
- % tourism revenue/total revenue.
- Number of licenses for tourism establishments.

With available data and with the type of tourist business per municipality it has been created Figure 10 that monitors the diversity of the tourist business according to a 1 to 3 scale. In this indicator it is also used the Shannon Index (Used in biology for determining the biodiversity degree). Index calculated by the formula is as follows:

$$H' = -\sum_{i=1}^{S} p_i \log_2 p_i$$

- S. - Number of Species
- P_i. - % of de specie's individuals in the total population

Accordingly it is been taken into account the total number of species together with the relative quantity of every kind of individual in the area. Results in Figure 11 show, with the normalized index, that areas considered as 1 have the worst index and with 3 with the best index.

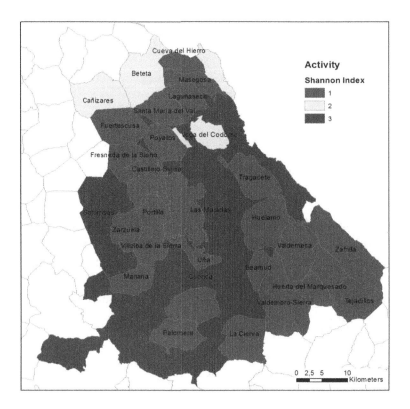

Figure 6. Shannon Index

4 CONCLUSIONS

In recent years the word "sustainable" has been applied to all work planning, regional planning and management of economic activities such as tourism, both in its planning and management. Despite its acceptance, it suffers from ambiguity and difficulty mainly because it is difficult to find some objectively quantified indicators that ease comparison of values for different activities. Regarding the management of eco-tourism activities it has to considerer environmental, cultural and social factors and productive for these indicators. Therefore, GIS have become in a widely accepted tool for data collection, processing, representation in order to develop further research. As this paper show, the analysis of eco-tourism activities using an indicator system is a powerful tool to evaluate the progress of economic development and environmental conservation, as well as for identify the quality of their services, the impact on the local economy and the detection of strengths and weaknesses. However, there is no perfect indicator system and its efficiency depends on the factors used. Fortunately, in recent years much has been achieved in this field, in particular, this work is based on the indicators proposed that has been applied to the Serrania de Cuenca area in this paper. Indicators used can show tourism entrepreneurs some the strengths and weaknesses of each municipality. Without any doubt entrepreneurs should use the indicators together with the support of the sustainable development plan of the area in order to increase their chances of success.

REFERENCES

[1] Douglas, B. (2008). *Achieving success with GIS*. Chichester: Wiley.

[2] Dangermond, J. (2002). Web services and GIS. *Geospatial Solutions*. **12**, 56-9.

[3] Bahaire, M. & Elliot-White, M.P. (1999). The application of Geographical Information Systems (GIS) in sustainable tourism planning: A review. *Journal of Sustainable Tourism*. **7**, 159-174.

[4] Chen, R.J.C (2007). Geographic Information Systems (GIS) applications in retail tourism and teaching curriculum. *Journal of Retailing and Consumer Services*. **14**, 289–295.

[5] Farsari, Y. & Prastacos, P. (2004). GIS applications in the planning and management of tourism. In Lew, A. A., Hall, C. M. & Williams, A. M. (Eds.), *A Companion to Tourism*. Oxford: Blackwell.

[6] Elliott-White, M.P. & Finn, M. (1997). Growing in sophistication: the application of geographic information systems in post-modern tourism marketing. *Journal of Travel and Tourism Marketing*. **7**, 65–84.

[7] Gil, P. (1992). Conceptos para interpretar el turismo rural en España. *Documentación social*. 87. Available online at http://www.caritas.es, (Last retrieved 15th May 2012).

[8] United Nations (1987). *Brundtland Report. World Commission on Environment and Development*. Oxford: Oxford University Press.

[9] United Nations Conference on Environment and Development (UNCED) (1992), Rio de Janeiro, 3-14 June.

[10] Page, S.J. & Dowling, R.K. (2002). *Ecotourism*. New York: Pearson Education.

[11] World Conference on Sustainable Tourism (1995). Lanzarote, Canary Islands, Spain, 27-28 April.

[12] Fung, T. & Wong, F.K.K. (2007). Ecotourism planning using multiple criteria evaluation with GIS. *Geocarto International*. **22**, 87-105.

[13] Junta de Comunidades de Castilla-La Mancha (2012). Plan de Zona de la Serranía de Cuenca. Available at http://www.jccm.es, (Last retrieved 10th April 2013).

[14] Instituto Nacional de Estadística. (2013). Banco de datos estadísticos. Available at http://www.ine.es, (Last retrieved 15th January 2013).

[15] Ministerio de Alimentación, Agricultura y Medio Ambiente (2011). Información ambiental - indicadores ambientales. Banco Público de indicadores ambientales (BPIA). Available at http://www.magrama.gob.es, (Last retrieved 10th March 2013).

The service vision: a case study in how to reposition a terrace.

J. RUBIO
Universitat Politècnica de València, Product and Service Management Master, Spain
C. MIÑANA
Universitat Politècnica de València, Product and Service Management Master, Spain
J. MEYER
Universitat Politècnica de València, Product and Service Management Master, Spain
C. GRANDI
Universitat Politècnica de València, Product and Service Management Master, Spain
J. GARCÍA
Universitat Politècnica de València, Product and Service Management Master, Spain
S.DIETZ
Universitat Politècnica de València, Product and Service Management Master, Spain

ABSTRACT

The current economic crisis has affected the financial situation of many companies. We explain a real case where the manager of a hotel's terrace needs to find solutions for repositioning it on the market. We worked in close cooperation with the hotel to discover the internal difficulties the hotel has to deal with. Theoretical research and benchmarking analysis with local and international competitors gave the project group ideas about how to improve the hotel's overall situation. Based on this, the group formulated different proposals in the areas of strategy, marketing, service, atmosphere and entertainment.

1.-INTRODUCTION

The economic crisis that has struck Europe and other parts of the world, especially Spain, is affecting companies that have to deal with circumstances such as unemployment, and insolvency. The number of tourists going on holiday to Spain has decreased which has had a negative influence on businesses depending on tourism. Considering this background the attention of the project group was caught by the situation of a hotel located in Valencia, which has been affected by the economic crisis. One of the group's members used to work for this hotel and knew its current situation and the management's aim to rebuild a terrace belonging to the hotel.

A decision was made to try to help this hotel by finding solutions for repositioning the hotel, and particularly the terrace, on the market and therefore improving their revenues. The following paper will show the steps that were taken by the project group, as the affluence of customers was not enough for it to be profitable (see Figure 1).

The consequences of this problem were a decrease in revenues, a reduction in opening hours (in comparison with previous years) and a diminution in staff. There was a chain effect, in which each problem worsened the others. In order to overcome these problems, we needed to find innovative ideas and alternatives that could attract potential clients, reposition the hotel and improve the service they offer.

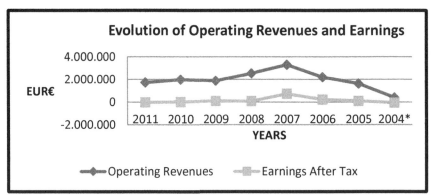

Figure 1: Economic performance of the hotel (2004-2011)
Source: Own elaboration from the data provided by SABI

The hotel in which the terrace is located is a private family hotel in the city of Valencia, at "Las Arenas" beach. The hotel is surrounded by the port, the venue for the America's Cup Park (the largest sailing competition in the world) and F1 Urban Circuit. Because of its location, the hotel enjoys a privileged position having a dual capacity as a beach hotel and a city hotel. It is located just minutes from the historic city centre and the "Ciudad de las Artes y las Ciencias". It is therefore located in the area of main cultural activity and business in Valencia.

2.- COMPETITIVENESS ANALYSIS

The hotel is a five floor building with a terrace. Its structure is new, modern and sophisticated, because the owners wanted to create an atmosphere with contemporary architecture and an art internal design.

Remarkably, the interior design of the hotel was created by a renowned interior designer, resulting in a luxury hotel which is geared to attract customers with high economic status, and guests are offered the opportunity to enjoy a cosmopolitan ambiance, staying in an environment of comfort and luxury.

The core of our project is the *Beta Bar-Terrace* (see Figures 2a and 2b).

Figures 2a-2b. Beta Terrace

2. THEORETICAL FRAMEWORK TO SUPPORT THE IMPROVEMENTS.

This is a place created with the idea of offering guests, and other customers unrelated to the hotel, a place where they can relax with a snack or drink or eat a quick meal. Every type of customer is welcome in this space.

The terrace is "self-service"; customers need to go to the bar to make their order, the staff will not go to each table taking the orders. This is one of the processes that will be assessed by this project in order to potentially find other possibilities, or consolidate the process being used. We will consider whether self-service is an appropriate process by which to take the orders for the products offered on the terrace: meals, drinks and snacks.

Beyond differentiating its physical form, a company can also differentiate its services and make them better and unique compared to their competitors. A company can differentiate its offers from those of competitors along the lines of product, services, channels, people or image. Differentiation can also be carried out through trained people and the use of specific expertise. The image of a company also plays an important role as, following Kotler et al. [1], "A company or brand image should convey the product's distinctive benefits and positioning". A brand image can be created by using symbols, characters and other image elements that reflect the company's personality and that are communicated through advertising.

When it comes to choosing the right competitive advantage a company needs to avoid three major positioning errors. Under-positioning, or failing to ever really position the company should be avoided. In contrast over-positioning is also dangerous for a company since it gives buyers too narrow a picture of the company and its value for the customer. The third error to be avoided is confused positioning, which leaves buyers with a confused image of the company.

Once those errors are understood and avoided there is the question of which differences should be promoted. The difficulty here is to find differences that are meaningful and make a good differentiation from other companies. To avoid choosing differences which are not worthwhile, a company must carefully select the differences that will distinguish itself from competitors (see Table 1).

Table 1: Differences to promote to be competitive

Important	The difference delivers a highly valued benefit to target buyers
Distinctive	Competitors do not offer the difference, or the company can offer it in a more distinctive way
Superior	The difference is superior to other ways that customers might obtain the same benefit
Communicable	The difference is communicable and visible to buyers
Pre-emptive	Competitors cannot easily copy the difference
Affordable	Buyers can afford to pay for the difference
Profitable	The company can introduce the difference profitably

Source: Kotler et al. [1]

The choice of the right differences may be crucial to the success of a company. It has to be noted that despite following a strategy for choosing competitive advantage, change can be difficult and customers might not like the idea of how the company tries to position itself on the market. To be able to compete, companies try to obtain a good position in the market [2]. To achieve this goal and to be able to plan effective marketing strategies, a company needs to discover as much information about the competitors as it can: competitor analysis is a helpful tool through which to analyse a company's competitors. In this way the company is able to find out about areas of potential competitive advantage or disadvantage. In this analysis competitors are first identified, and then the competitors' objectives, strategies, strengths and weaknesses, and reaction patterns assessed. Finally a selection of competitors to attack or distract is made, as seen in Figure 3.

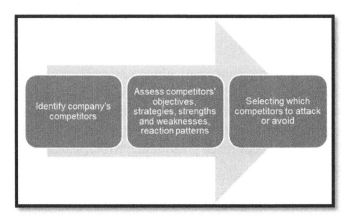

Figure 3. Steps in Analysing Competitors
Source: Kotler et al. [1]

The first step of the competitor analysis is to identify competitors. Not only local competitors should be considered, but also competitors from further afield, to obtain a better impression of the market situation. Companies should also analyse their competitors from a market point of view. That means they should look for companies that are trying to satisfy the same customer need or try to attract the same target group [3].

Once the competitors have been identified they should be assessed in terms of objectives, strategies, strengths and weaknesses, and how they might react to the company's actions. The last step of the competitor analysis includes selecting which competitors the company should compete against most vigorously. Depending on the selected competitor/s, different marketing steps have to be taken to be able to compete [1].

3.- SERVICE INDUSTRIES SPECIFIC CHARACTERISTICS

Evaluating a service before purchase can often be very difficult. In the case of buying a tangible product, the customer usually has the ability to return the product, if they is not satisfied with the good. Tangible characteristics that consumers can evaluate before purchase are called search attributes. Most services emphasize experience attributes such as reliability and customer support, which inexperienced purchasers can discern only during delivery and consumption. Attributes which customers find very hard to evaluate - even after consumption – are credence attributes.

These attributes can help customers to evaluate a service even before purchasing it. Prospective consumers can test the product for texture, taste and sound prior to buying it. Buyers are able to try their product in advance to reduce the sense of uncertainty or risk associated with the purchase occasion. Search attributes can also be found in the physical environment, such as type of food, location and so on. Some attributes can't be evaluated before purchasing the goods, a customer has to experience the service as it is being given. Especially in restaurants, these attributes depend on the particular day or evening. In most cases many circumstances differ from day to day, such as the service provided, the waiter or the atmosphere.

These attributes are nearly impossible to evaluate confidently even after purchase and consumption. Customers have to rely on conditions they aren't able to assess, such as hygiene in the kitchen and the healthiness of the cooking ingredients.

The Marketing Communications Mix (MCM) is an umbrella term for numerous forms of communication service to which marketers have access. Relative to the types of messages they can convey and the market segments most likely to be exposed to them, different communication elements have distinctive capabilities. Elements that are included in the MCM (see Figure 4) will be relevant to our proposals for the terrace.

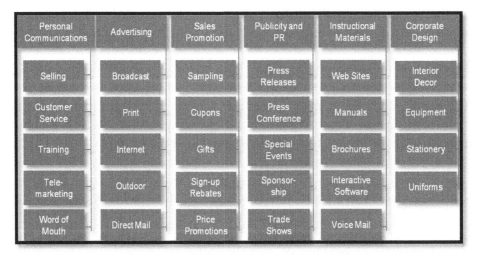

Figure 4: Marketing Communications Mix.
Source: Lovelock and Wirtz [4]

Advertising is often the first point of contact between the marketer and the customer, as it is a dominant form of communication. It is very important, as it informs the client about product features and capabilities.

Direct Marketing includes tools such as mailings, faxes and emails. These strategies are most likely to be successful when marketers possess a detailed database of information about customers and prospects.

A very important marketing channel for Beta Terrace is communication with the customer through **sales promotion**. Typically, the aim is to motivate the customers to buy a product or use a specific service sooner, in greater volume, or more frequently. Sales promotion for service firms such as Beta Terrace could include samples, coupons and other discounts and competitions with prizes.

Public Relations involve all the instruments that stimulate positive interest in a company and its products by sending out new press releases, holding press conferences and staging special events. The most basic element is to prepare and distribute press releases that feature stories about the company, its products, and its employees [4].

Marketing through the internet should create consumer awareness and interest, provide information and offer the ability to measure the effectiveness of specific promotional or advertising campaigns. It's not only about running a website but also placing advertisements and banners all over the internet.

4.- THEORY APPLIED TO THE HOTEL STUDIED AND THE BETA BAR-TERRACE CASE

Marketing is essential for the success of a service company nowadays. The hotel understands the need for marketing and has already taken some action. It is presented online with a homepage which gives information about the hotel and also shows pictures. The homepage is essential for the success of a hotel because many customers will only see the information presented there before going to the hotel personally. The presentation on a homepage can make customers make decisions for or against the hotel. Therefore the design and the customer friendliness of the homepage are very important. Even though the homepage of this hotel gives some information it is not clearly laid out and it is not easy for customers to find the required information.

In addition to the homepage, the hotel is presented on Facebook where it has its own profile. The hotel seems to be quite active here, since upcoming events are often promoted and pictures are uploaded, albeit not very regularly. The hotel also organises some events within the hotel and also in the terrace itself. For example there was a Mercedes event to which many people were invited. These events are very helpful for the hotel to promote itself, and to inform people about the hotel and the terrace. Smaller events such as the public viewing of football matches are also offered in the terrace. The problem here is that those kinds of events are not strongly publicised; in the case of the football matches there is only a flyer at the door of the terrace that informs potential customers about the event. The promotion of these events is very important and should be improved so as to attract more customers.

It must be mentioned that in comparison to many other companies the hotel does not have its own marketing department but only has one employee who takes care of marketing processes for the whole hotel. The director of the hotel also wants to become involved, and has tried to put his own ideas for marketing into action. This means that not only does the hotel not have a marketing department but responsibility for marketing actions is not clearly distributed. Even though the hotel knows about the importance of marketing and takes some action, it is not clear whether they follow a market-oriented-mission and know about all the needs of their customers. As there is only a single person working in this area, marketing does not seem to be treated as of great importance, and the marketing actions being taken could be improved drastically [5].

5.-METHODOLOGY

During the course of the project, the team collected theoretical and practical data, through meetings with hotel managers and readings of interesting articles and books related to the problems and issues perceived. The team had several meetings with the manager, who explained the current situation of the terrace, how it worked and the expectations of the project. Each member of the group then began collecting theoretical data on which to base the study and differentiate the problems. An in-site practical view, for this exercise some members of the team went to the terrace to try at first hand the services offered at the terrace, as well as observing the working strategies from the outside.

Following this, the team shared their findings and experiences, and the next step was a comparison between the terrace and its competitors, a benchmarking analysis [6]. We analysed the information available: the type of menu and how it was displayed, opening hours, offers and promotions, distribution of tables, cleanliness, location, and quality of the product offered. The same comparison procedure was made with the bests terraces in the world, however for them, the team had to search for the information on the internet. Once the above mentioned was complete, we analysed the results, drawing conclusions about what the terrace does and does not do, and suggesting proposals to improve their service on the terrace, so as to achieve their expectations.

6.- FINDINGS

Our results show that in general the terrace had the best scores but despite this some characteristics did not receive high individual sores, and others were only acceptable. For location and atmosphere, the *Beta Bar-Terrace* has the best position in comparison with its competitors, because it is the first local in the beach and it has a view of two aspects over the beach. Opening hours received a high score, but the opening hours of competitors are better, so this is something that can be improved. The interior can also be improved, because although cleanliness is excellent, the distribution of the furniture is not consistent - there are two different types of tables and only one sofa. The concept of 'a terrace' seems unclear, because some tables appear to be for eating inside, as in a restaurant, whilst others are only arranged for snacks. Competitors at *Atuaire* and *Destino56* have more comfortable tables and sofas, and their concept is well defined, so the hotel should change this.

The *Beta Bar-Terrace* has the worst score for menus, in comparison with its competitors: the menu is plastic, and is not attractive to customers, and there are menus pasted on the wall, which takes away from the glamour and quality of the terrace. Some competitors, such as *Gabanna, Vivir sin dormir* or *Destino56*, have very attractive menus for the clients of higher quality, and also promote the menu better at the front of their terraces.

For price value and the type of food and drinks the hotel received similar scores to its competitors, because on the beach walk of Las Arenas Beach almost all the restaurant terraces have similar prices for the location. The menu specific to the Beta Bar-Terrace offers only a few rice dishes; if customers wish for an expanded selection they will be brought a menu from the hotel's Tridente restaurant. This is problematic for the terrace.

The quality of food and drink at the *Beta Bar-Terrace* is the highest, without competition it has very good quality preparation, and the best flavours on the beach walk of Las Arenas Beach. As a result, and because prices are slightly higher the majority of clients are people with high or medium incomes, which differs from competitors such as Vivir sin dormir, who include more offers for young people. In general, however, the terraces all have the same type of clients, which include many tourists of different nationalities, which change depending of the season.

Finally, the extra services offered are similar to those of the hotel's competitors. This needs to be improved, however, because, for example, they have outdated football match promotions on the walls of the terrace, whereas some competitors are two steps ahead by promoting things such as weekend concerts in the *Atuaire*, or with the flyers and posters in *Gabanna* or *Vivir sin dormir*.

In conclusion, obtaining the best overall score does not mean achieving more competitiveness. When applying a benchmarking analysis those aspects that can be improved also appear what offers wide possibilities to enhancement.

7.- CONCLUSIONS

The project group tried to find solutions for how to reposition the terrace, following poor performance and a lack of customers. After meetings with the hotel management, observations, and theoretical research, the group had some ideas which were then clarified and supported by the results of the benchmarking analysis. Based on the research findings, and especially the benchmarking analysis, which compared the hotel with its local and international competitors, the project group then formulated proposals in the different areas of strategy, marketing, service, atmosphere and entertainment, which clearly show the hotel management which processes can be improved.

In summary, *Beta Bar Terrace* is quite well located, and could gain many customers and augment profit by changing and introducing new strategies and ideas recommended by the project team. By implementing some of the proposals in the right way the situation of the *Beta Bar Terrace* will most likely improve and their competitiveness on the market will increase. This will lead to better positioning in the market and the number of customers will increase. The staff and opening hours will not have to be reduced any further due to financial reasons. All in all the implementation of the above proposals will lead to better revenues and help the *Beta Bar Terrace* to find the way out of their financial crisis.

Table 4.- Benchmarking analysis results

Characteristics	Terrace Omega	Score	Gabbana	Score	Atuaire	Score	Vivir sin dormir	Score	Pura Vida	Score	Destino 56	Score
					LOCAL COMPETITORS, "LAS ARENAS" BEACH							
Location	First location on the beach walk, two windows, two sides	8	Middle position on the beach walk, close to a street (good for parking)	7	Middle position on the beach walk, next to a street (good connection), two open sides	7	Middle position on the beach walk, direct walkway to the beach	8	Final position on the part of restaurants on the beach walk	5	Final position on the part of restaurants on the beach walk	5
Opening Hours	Winter: 10:30am-12:00 (Sunday to Thursday) and 10:30am-1:00am (Friday, Saturday) Summer: 10:30am 2:00am (Sunday to Thursday) and 10:30am-3:00am (Friday, Saturday)	8	9:00am-2:00am (Winter: close one day a week)	9	10:00am-1:00am	7	11:00am-3:00am (In the week) 11:00am-4:00am (On the weekend)	8	10:00-19:00 (winter) 10:00am-1:30am (summer)	6	9:00am-3:00am (all year, every day)	10
Atmosphere	Good atmosphere	9	Ok but not 100% inviting	8	Great atmosphere, very inviting	9	Atmosphere is ok, place is very busy	6	Good atmosphere, inviting	8	Good atmosphere, inviting	8
Interior	Furniture not consistent (chairs silver and white), new couches (not like in internet), nice bar, bar table in the middle, nice decoration, lighting and music, screens in the night	7	Different furniture, plastic chairs, sofa (looks old), bar chairs look cheap, lighting and music	5	Very nice, trendy and stylish decoration, looks inviting and comfortable (many pillows), private area with curtains and wooden tables, lighting and music	9	Basic, only chairs and tables, no decoration, loud music, TVs		Basic furniture, wicker chairs, palm tree decoration, lighting and music, TVs	6	Modern interior, all in white, colorful menu, many plants, simple decoration (fits the style), catchy, lighting and music	8
Cleanliness	Very clean	10	Not so clean	6	Clean	8	Not so clean	6	Clean	8	Very clean	10
Kind of menu	It is pasted on the wall of the terrace in a paper (don't look so good), Menu of the day, Omega's rice menu, Hamburguer's Menu, in English and Spanish, plastic menu on the tables, no self-service	5	Put the menu outside the terrace, nice menu, blackboard with cocktails at the entrance, different kinds of food, no self-service	8	Separate plates, sushi menu. Blackboard with the drinks outside. Nice menu, but not well maintained, no self-service	5	Menu outside on a board nice. Good offer with a lot of options. Hamburguer menu. No self-service	7	We don't see a menu for cocktails, they offer a menu of paella, no self-services	6	The menu outside and on the tables. Menu of food drinks and breakfasts. Different kind of food and drinks. No self-services	9
Value price	Omega's rice menu 19.50 euros. Menu of the day 10 euros, Cocktail of the day 8 euros. minimum 2 people.	8	Long drinks 8 euros. Aperitif 6 euros. Tapa + drink 14 euros.	9	Crepes 4 euros. Pinchos 2 euros each. Sushi menú: 10 units 20 euros.	8	Tapa 5 euros. Bocadillo 5.50 euros. Hamburger and Sandwich 8 euros (the most expensive)	8	Menú paella 12 euros.		Cocktail 8 euros. Pizza 9 euros.	7
Types of food and drinks	Just one kind of rice and food, don't have a lot of options. Tapas and sandwichs. Different types of cocktails with or without alcohol. Drinks to take away, have cocktail of the day.	7	Tapas, complete menus, fish, meat, paella. Different kinds of cocktails with and without alcohol.	9	Complete menu with a lot of options and cocktails. Offers cocktails, juices, tapas, pinchos, hamburgers, crepes, salads, desserts.	9	Bakery, salads, desserts, cocktails, tapas hot & cold, bocadillos, hamburgers, sandwiches.		The menu paella includes salad + brave potatoes + paella + drink.	7	Aperitifs, salads, bocadillos, hamburgers, pizza, dessert, tapas, cocktails and breakfasts.	9
Quality of food	Very good, good relation between prices and quality, regular breakfast	10	Poor relation between prices and quality	5	Good	7	Poor quality of the food, and bad relation between prices and quality	4	Regular quality of the food	6	Good	7
Quality of drinks	Very good, good relation between prices and quality	10	Bad relation between prices and quality	5	Good	7	Bad quality of the drinks, and bad relation between prices and quality	4	Regular quality of the drinks	6	Good	7
Types of clients	People with high and medium income level, 60% tourists (Italian, English, German, Duch and French by seasons)	8	Young people, couples, a lot of tourists	7	Young people, couples, a lot of tourists	7	People with high and medium income level, young people in the weekends, a lot of tourists in summer	9	Couples, a lot of tourists in summer	8	Couples, a lot of tourists in summer	8
Extra services	Free WiFi. Football games. (Champions League and BBVA League)	8	Free WiFi	6	Concerts in the weekends	9	Football games. (Champions League and BBVA League)	8	Free WiFi	6	Free WiFi	6
Promotions	No promotions at all	5	They have offers 4 units of tapas + 2 drinks 14 euros.	7	No promotions at all	5	No promotions at all	5	No promotions at all	5	No promotions at all	5
Flyers and posters	Some outdated flyers of football games in the windows.	3	They have blackboards outside with a lot of announcements	10	No flyers, no posters.	2	In the walls have posters offering the food and drinks they have. Announcements of a new product: "come and taste the new beef 100%"	10	The announcement is different from a simple blackboard	10	A lot of blackboards outside, not very good design of the boards.	6
TOTAL	106		99		99		96		90		103	

138

REFERENCE LIST

[1] Kotler, P., Brown, L., Adam, S., Burton, S., & Armstrong, G. (2004). Marketing. Pearsons Education Australia.

[2] Armstrong, G., Kotler, P., & Merino, M. J. (2011). Introducción al marketing, 3ª edición. Ed.

[3]Olson, P. (2006). Comportamiento del consumidor y Estrategia de marketing. Edición Mc Graw Hill.

[4] Lovelock, C., & Wirtz, J. (2007). Services Marketing: People, Technology, Strategy, Pearson Prentice Hall, New Jersey.

[5] Withiam, G. (2011). Social Media and the Hospitality Industry: Holding the Tiger by the Tail. *Cornell Hospitality Reports*, 3, 3, http://www.hotelschool.cornell.edu/research/chr/pubs/roundtableproceedings/roundtable-15500.html

[6] Verma, R., & McGill, K. (2011). 2011 Travel Industry Benchmarking: Marketing ROI, Opportunities, and Challenges in Online and Social Media Channels for Destination and Marketing Firms, *Cornell Hospitality Reports*, 11, 9, http://www.hotelschool.cornell.edu/research/chr/pubs/reports/abstract-15562.html

140

Stock market performance of the tourism enterprises in Spain during the economic crisis.

P. MOYA MARTÍNEZ
University of Castilla-La Mancha. Department of Economic and Financial Analysis, Spain
R. DEL POZO RUBIO
University of Castilla-La Mancha. Department of Economic and Financial Analysis, Spain
R. MARTÍNEZ CAÑAS
University of Castilla-La Mancha. Department of Business Organization, Spain

ABSTRACT

The negative impact of the current economic crisis is indubitable in Spain. Four years later its inception, there is no final sign or turning point of change yet. One sector that is surviving and pulling the Spanish economy is tourism, which despite having been affected, continues to make a significant positive contribution to macroeconomic concepts of income, wealth, GDP and employment. In this chapter we analyze the stock market performance of the tourism sector in the IBEX 35 during the economic crisis, and comparisons with other sectors and behavioural patterns of the overall economy, analyzing potential competitive advantages.

1. INTRODUCTION.

Tourism sector has a fundamental role in the Spanish economy in terms of GDP, unemployment, taxes and social security. Only point out that in 2008 the weight of tourism sector was 10.4% of GDP provides us an insight into its importance in the national economy [1] and world economy [2].

Table 1 shows macroeconomic indicators related to tourism during the period 2008-2011 and provided by Economic and Social Council of Spain [3]. Firstly can be observed negative change indicators between 2008 and 2009 but later, in the subsequent years and except for the ratio travel agencies/tour operators a slowly recovery with positive sign can be seen. Interestingly changes between 2008 and 2011 are in many cases positive. An in-depth analysis elucidate that reduce in number of tourists is much more pronounced than in the hikers and a slower recovery in the first group than in the second. One possible explanation for this fact is that until 2008 foreign tourists on the one hand was afflicted by the global financial crisis and with fear of consumption; on the other hand they could see Spain as an economically insecure destination.

One of the most important measures of tourist sector is the tourism expending. As the same manner of tourist movements in borders, expending suffer go down in 2009 but rebound in 2010 to exceed in 2011 the amounts of 2008. The impressive return to the path of growth with an increase of nearly 8 percent between 2010 and 2011 we should see the great strength and importance of this sector in the Spanish economy and more if we consider that not yet loom startup recovery.

Table 1. Tourism movements in borders and employment in Spain. 2008-2011

Tourist movements in borders	2008	Changes (%)			
		2009-08	2010-09	2011-10	2011-08
Tourist	57.192.014	-8,77	0,96	7,63	-0,87
Hikers	40.477.777	-1,87	3,39	5,13	6,66
Total foreign visitors	97.669.791	-5,91	2,01	6,53	2,25
Tourism expending					
Expending (M€)	51.694	-7,22	2,01	7,91	2,09
Employment					
Affiliates in touristic activities	1.959.557	-2,15	0,77	0,84	-0,57
Accommodation and travel agencies	1.364.045	-3,37	0,97	1,06	-1,39
Accommodation services	279.124	-7,27	0,13	0,75	-6,45
Food and beverage services	1.024.718	-2,26	1,60	1,32	0,62
Travel agencies/tour operators	60.203	-4,15	-6,14	-2,30	-12,10

Source: Economic and Social Council of Spain (2012).

The number of employees is also reduced in 2009, but in 2010 the trend changed again in 2011 surpassing the amounts offered in 2008. Undoubtedly, this sector has significantly content job losses that have suffered other economic sectors.

Respect to the balance of payments shows a similar behavior: reduced tourism receipts in 2009, marking a turning point because from 2010 increase that income held constant payments during the reference period. We can observe this behavior in Figure 1: the income payments show an increasing trend since 2001, obtaining maximum amounts on the years 2011 and 2012, both years when Spain is in recession.

Figure 2 shows two profitability ratios of the hotel sector, which serve as a guide to find some performance statistical in the tourism sector during the crisis period started in 2007. This figure shows the average daily rate and the revenue per room available rate. By obviating accented character seasonal, we find a constant profitability during the reference period of recession.

On the other hand, it is a real fact that Small and Medium Enterprises (SMEs), represent a huge portion of the firms of many developed countries providing large amount of employment. Despite of the great importance of this category of firms, not always receive the joust attention that they really deserve [4].

In this line, it is no wonder that the European Commission manifest that in a globalized world, in which technological advances occurs rapidly, the prosperity, well being and social cohesion in European Union depends on SMEs. This fact is of especial relevance on the southern countries such Spain or Italy due to SMEs represents the 99% of business. Furthermore, when it focuses on the tourism sector this percentage does not change noticeably. Data from The Tourism Satellite Account from 2008 to 2011 in Spain with source in Central and Business Directory published by the Spanish National Statistics Institute found that 3% of the tourism enterprises have more than 100 employees.

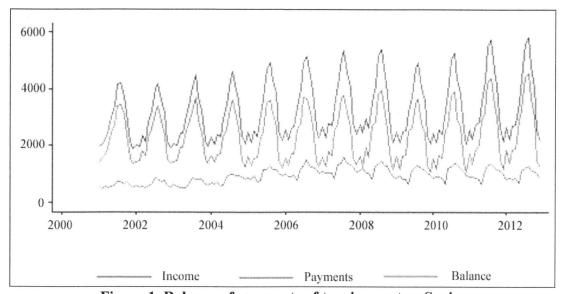

Figure 1. Balance of payments of tourism sector, Spain.
Source: Institute of Tourism Studies of Spain and the National Institute of Statistics.

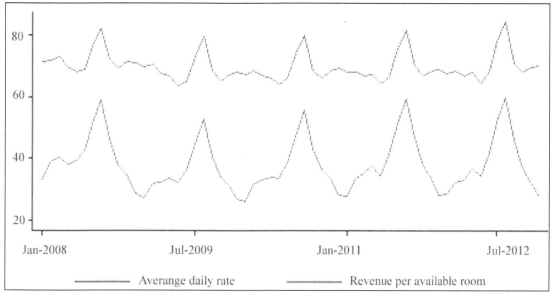

Figure 2. Profitable indicators of Spanish Hospitality Sector from 2008 to 2012.

Source: Institute of Tourism Studies of Spain and the National Institute of Statistics.

Given this fact, be considered that before further analysis on stock market performance of the tourism enterprises during the economic crisis is important to provide an insight into the relationship between SMEs and larger firms which can raise capital in the equity markets more easily [5]. This funding allows greater stability and hence these firms could be representatives of the general evolution of Spanish tourism industry and their behavior in macro-economic events of the current economic and financial crisis.

In this context, the aims of this study are designed: firstly, to analyze the stock market performance of the tourism sector compared to a market portfolio or index in Spain during recession period; secondly, to study the tourism industry behavior in terms of size, examining the possible interrelationships between them.

These two objectives are very important in response to importance of SMEs in the economy of a country like Spain and as larger firms of tourism sector may be an indicator of economic growth or decline of the sector in general. The study of this relationship will make inferences about causality in both groups

2. METHODS

This study examines exposure of Spanish tourism sector to the international financial crisis over the period January 2006 to December 2012, a time interval in which experienced large swings and high volatiles. Thus, also examines the relationship between SMEs and larger firms which can raise capital in the equity markets from tourism sector.

To perform the first task is carried out an analysis of the Spanish tourism industries included on the stock market in relation to portfolio market. The sample consists of five firms listed on the Madrid Stock Exchange and the proxy for portfolio market is the IBEX-35, the broadest Spanish market index. Equity market data are collected from the Madrid Stock Exchange database.

The five firm analyzed were:

CODERE, is a multinational with approximately 20,000 employees over the world. Its main activity, private game, is much related to leisure, tourism and hospitality sector with a great number of posts machines, gaming rooms, racetracks and bets points. It is the only company gaming in the stock market and listed on it since October 2007.

Meliá Hotels International was founded in 1956 in Spain and was one of the biggest hospitality enterprises over the world with more than 350 hotels. Furthermore, is interesting to note that the company is also concerning Sustainability and Social Responsibility being the only company in the sector included in the index of the Spanish stock market responsible FTSE4Good.

NH Hotels is an important enterprise over the world too but not at the level of Meliá Hotels International. Its activity is centering in urban business hotels with high quality of service. The free-float of NH Hoteles represents about 32% of the capital, while the main shareholders include among others Hesperia (25%) and some Spanish banks.

Amadeus is a reference enterprise in technology solutions for the travel and tourism sector. Its distribute travel products and services, offering real-time search, pricing, booking and ticketing to customers between other similar services. Amadeus is listed since April 2010 in the Stock Markets of Madrid, Barcelona, Bilbao and Valencia.

And finally, Sotogrande is the largest resort in Southern Europe offering homes, apartments, plots and luxury home in an environment in which the enterprise have golf courses, beach clubs, a marina, polo fields and spas. Therefore, its business includes high quality hotels in a privilege tourism Spanish location as the Costa del Sol.

To construct the tourism portfolio, the returns of each enterprise were annually weighted based on their market capitalization at December of every year included in the study. Some of the firms included in the tourism portfolio are not quoted for all the years of study, so that the weighted portfolio firms consisted of NH Hotels, Meliá Hotels International and Sotogrande from January 2006 to October 2007. From this date included CODERE and finally from May 2010 also included Amadeus. From 2010 to 2012, Amadeus represented approximately an 80% of tourism portfolio subsequently to test the variability and sensitivity of tourism portfolio to this enterprise another portfolio was created excluding Amadeus. Figure 3 shows the weights of each enterprise in the tourism portfolio 1 (with include all enterprises) and in the tourism portfolio 2 (excluding Amadeus enterprise) in the sample study.

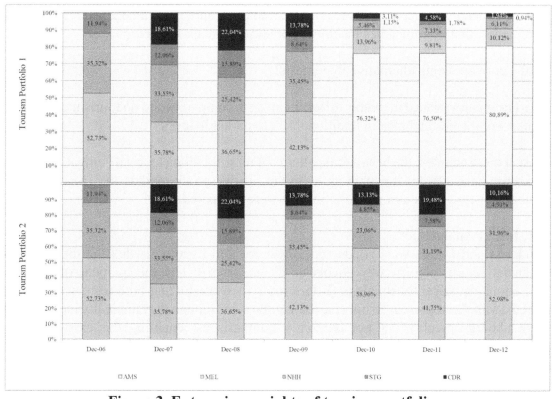

Figure 3. Enterprises weights of tourism portfolios.

Once value-weighted industry stock indexes are calculated, returns are calculated by taking the log difference of the weekly values, a total of 238 observations. The weekly returns are calculated using Wednesday closing stock prices, adjusted for dividends and splits, to eliminate the possible bias induced by the weekend effect. Weekly data are utilized instead of daily or monthly data for several reasons. Further, weekly data significantly reduce the problems of non-synchronous trading bias for less actively traded stocks and too much noise typically associated with higher frequency data. In the second place, weekly data are used rather than monthly data because the former provide a number of observations large enough to yield more reliable results.

The analysis of Spanish tourism portfolio allows to know the sensitivity and response of this source of business activity to the last financial and economic crisis, considering that tourism industry plays a significant role in the economic development of country highly dependent on tourism activity, which may have important implications for portfolio management, asset pricing and risk management.

In turn, we suggest that tourism companies will present more profitable and less sensitive to extant market oscillations than companies do not belong to tourism sector. To test the hypothesis, as mentioned above, IBEX 35 index was used. The capitalization-weighted index consists of the 35 most liquid companies listed on the four Spanish Stock Exchanges (Madrid, Barcelona, Bilbao and Valencia). In the same way that the tourism portfolio, changes were calculated as the log difference between consecutive Wednesdays.

The null hypothesis proposes that financial return and risk differences exist between tourism companies and no tourism companies and thereby formulate:

H_0: The mean/variance in returns is comparable in tourism companies and no tourism companies, that is, companies included in traditional stock market indexes.

And a corresponding alternative hypothesis:

H_1: The mean/variance in returns differs in tourism companies and no tourism companies, that is, companies included in traditional stock market indexes.

To test these contrast, the behavioral patterns of returns belong tourism companies against the same measures for the main index in the Spanish stock market, the IBEX 35 stock exchange value index as a portfolio market were compared.

2.1. Initial Analysis.

Student t and F tests were conducted to test the null hypothesis that the difference of financial returns significantly equals or differs from 0 and the quotient of financial deviations significantly equals or differs from 1. In conducting both tests, we assumed that the samples represent an only paired sample since though they are really independent, they undergo weekly but not randomly comparisons, entailing the existence of a conditioned relationship.

Both intra-sample independence and normality criteria were not a problem in this study. First, the indexes are elaborated according to diametrically different inclusion criteria (liquidity vs. social and environmental standards), thus intra-sample independence criterion was assumed to be met even though if a large percentage of securities were included in both indexes. Second, the distribution of frequencies for weekly returns of a typical security over time does not differ significantly from a normal distribution.

The Student t-test was useful to determine whether there are differences in financial returns/profitability between the indexes, which can reveal which index is more profitable. According to Peña [6], for the bilateral contrast of the t-test:

$$H_0 : \mu_{IBEX35} - \mu_{TOURISMPORTFOLIO} = \mu_y = 0$$
$$H_1 : \mu_{IBEX35} \neq \mu_{TOURISMPORTFOLIO} ; \mu_y \neq 0$$

Where the independent variable is defined as "Y = IBEX35 – TOURISM PORTFOLIO" returns, and we estimate the variance using the quasi-variance of the sample ($\hat{S}_y^2$):

$$\hat{S}_y^2 = \frac{\sum (y_i - \bar{y})^2}{n-1}$$

,for which the acceptance region of H_0 is:

$$|\bar{y}| \leq t_{\alpha/2} \frac{\hat{S}_y}{\sqrt{n}},$$

and the Student t has n – 1 degrees of freedom.

The F-test instead tested whether there are significant differences in the variability of financial returns (risk) between index and portfolio, to reveal which index is more risky. In line with Peña [6], the bilateral contrast in this situation is:

$$H_0 : \sigma^2_{IBEX35} = \sigma^2_{TOURISMPORFOLIO}$$
$$H_1 : \sigma^2_{IBEX35} \neq \sigma^2_{TOURISMPORFOLIO}$$

where the coefficient for variances is:

$$d = \frac{\hat{S}^2_{IBEX35}}{\hat{S}^2_{TOURISMPORTFOLIO}} = F_{(n_1-1;n_2-1)},$$

and the acceptance region of H_0 is:

$$P(F \leq F_C) = 1 - \alpha,$$

such that the Fisher F has $n_1 - 1$ and $n_2 - 1$ degrees of freedom.

Both intra-sample independence and normality criteria were not a problem in this study. We assume that the distribution of indexes and portfolios returns present a normal probability distribution because the t-test, has a sufficient number of observations (and therefore degrees of freedom), make it approximate a normal distribution.

2.2. Subsequent Analysis.

It is noteworthy that most of the Spanish tourism sector consists of SMEs (see DIRCE database in Spanish National Institute of Statistics website for more information). In this subsequent analysis is considered that given the larger and long-term trajectory of the companies discussed above they results can be provide faithful representative of the entire Spanish tourist industry health. This is including SMEs.

To explain the second issue, the relationship between large firms and SMEs, data from the Tourism Satellite Account in Spain, mentioned above, were used and a graphic analysis of the changes in the average business volume stratified by firm size (measured as the number of employees) during the years 2004-2010 we performed.

3. RESULTS AND DISCUSSION.

The line characteristic traced by the tourism portfolio, using the IBEX 35 as a reference stock index, shows a considerable positive correlation between the pairs of returns for both portfolios, which indicates that both the sign and size of the behavioral patterns are similar in most cases (Figure 4).

In table 2 we provide the descriptive statistics for the IBEX35 and tourism portfolio, together with the results of the t-tests and F-tests conducted. Apparently, both means and standard deviations of the two indexes are similar. On the one hand, the t-test cannot offer sufficient evidence to reject the null hypothesis, so the difference of means is significantly equal to 0. Thus, the average performance observed during the sample period is similar for both indexes, according to their behavioral patterns.

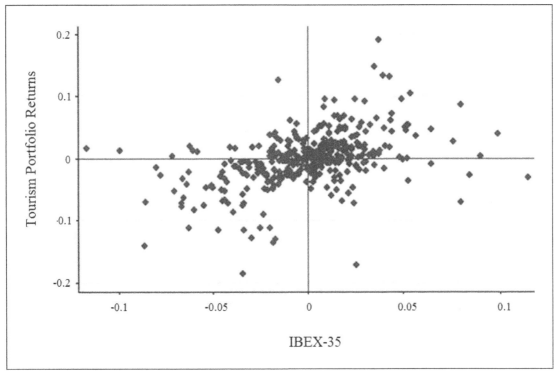

Figure 4. Characteristic line of IBEX 35 and Tourism Portfolio.

However, on the other hand, in terms of return risk and variability, the F-test implies evidence to reject the null hypothesis of equal variances. The volatility in the performance of the indexes is not similar; in particular, the variability and fluctuations experienced by the tourism portfolio appear greater than IBEX 35 stock exchange index. Therefore, though the financial performance of these portfolios tends to be similar, the volatility of financial returns is higher for tourism portfolio.

These data indicate that companies listed in the IBEX 35 stock exchange index are safer and more stable for investors. Nevertheless, because tourism portfolio has a company (AMADEUS) which represent more than 80% of total weight, we find interesting to create another portfolio, to assign the possible differences in returns and risk terms more clearly between IBEX 35 and tourism portfolio without AMADEUS.

Table 2. Descriptive statistics for IBEX35 and Tourism Portfolio

	IBEX35	Tourism Portfolio
Observations	363	363
Mean	-0,0006101	-0,0020347
Standard Deviation	0,0312545	0,0444569
t-test (paired means)	-0,6554 (0,5126)	
F-test (variance)	2,0233 (0,0000***)	

*, **, *** denote statistical significance at the 10%, 5% and 1% levels, respectively.

The line characteristic traced by the new tourism portfolio, using again IBEX 35 as a reference stock index, once more shows a significant positive correlation between the pairs of returns for both, by repeating the same behavioral patterns than previous portfolio shows (Figure 5).

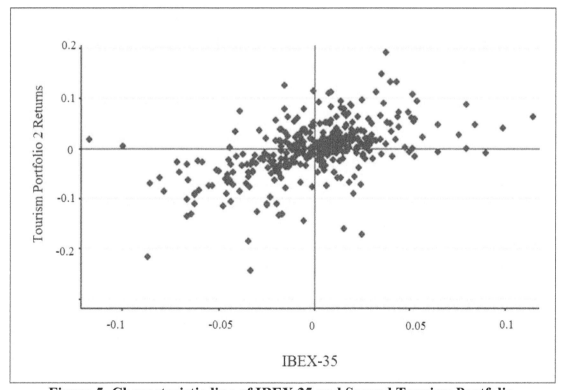

Figure 5. Characteristic line of IBEX 35 and Second Tourism Portfolio.

To analyze significant differences in terms of average financial returns and risk between new tourism portfolio and Ibex 35, we conducted new t- and F-tests. In Table 3, new results are shown.

Table 3. Descriptive statistics for IBEX35 and Tourism Portfolio 2

	IBEX35	Tourism Portfolio[1]
Observations	363	363
Mean	-0,0006101	-0,0038703
Standard Deviation	0,0312545	0,0547415
t-test (paired means)	-1,3285 (0,1849)	
F-test (variance)	3,0677 (0,0000***)	

[1] It is not included AMADEUS.

*, **, *** denote statistical significance at the 10%, 5% and 1% levels, respectively.

We observe that the findings do not differ from those in Table 2. Companies that operate exclusively in the tourism sector would achieve inferior performance compared with companies included in the IBEX 35. Nonetheless, the t-test cannot offer, another time, sufficient evidence to reject the null hypothesis, so the difference of means is significantly equal to 0. Thus, the average performance observed during the sample period is similar for both portfolios (Ibex 35 – second tourism portfolio). However, the null hypothesis of equality of variances should be rejected; the second tourism portfolio induces greater variability and fluctuation in average financial returns, thus it offers a greater investment risk again.

This last result is in line with previous studies that find a lower risk investment for such securities [7] but is in line with expectations about the nature and links of profitable securities. That is, securities generally should react with greater sensitivity to market oscillations if they provide a higher market premium, which is confirmed in previous research that finds a positive association between risks and returns [8, 9].

These results are shown as is highlighted in Figure 6 IBEX-35 trend affect the tourism portfolio volatility, and furthermore is highly correlated. We observe that until May 2008, while IBEX-35 index swift growing moderately there is high volatility in tourism portfolio. When the index begins to decrease until approximately March 2009 and later to grow approximately until November 2009 and relatively quick, the volatility in the tourism portfolio is very high. Later there is a relative stability in the IBEX-35 whose reflection in the portfolio tourist is less volatility. Finally, from November 2011 we can observe the decreases and increases of IBEX-35 generating greater tourist portfolio volatility.

The upper line represents the IBEX-35 index and the lower the changes in the portfolio of tourism.

Respect to second aims established, figure 7 shows that the larger firms (over 99 employees) seem to show the evolution of the tourism sector on a larger scale or long-term scale (with less volatility). In general, is noted that until 2007 decreases the business volume but from 2005 is smoothed. In 2008, and subsequent years, the changes are positives involving grows in business volume although it seems to fall slightly in 2009 year, which shows the strong resistance to the economic crisis of the tourism sector, highly referred throughout the paper.

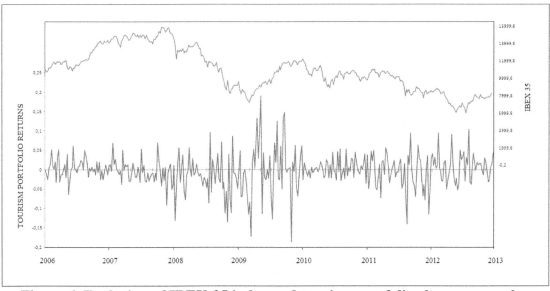

Figure 6. Evolution of IBEX-35 index and tourism portfolio changes over the period 2008-2012.

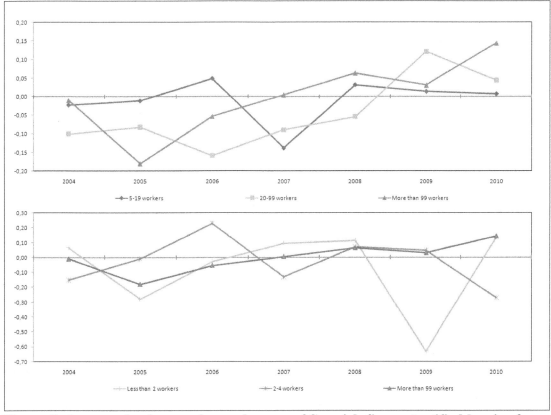

Figure 7. Average business volume changes of Spanish firms stratified by size from 2004 to 2010.
* More than 99 workers firms are in the two graphs with comparison proposal.

On the other hand, in the bottom of the figure, the smaller companies (less than 2 workers and 2-4 workers) are compared against the larger firms (over 99 employees). Higher volatility is observed in the changes if business volume due to the higher risk inherent to smaller companies. It is also noted that in 2009 the business volume of SMEs with less than 2 workers suffer a sharp decline of over 60%.

In any case we can conclude that larger firms can be a faithful representative of the general or mean evolution of Spanish tourism industry and therefore it is important to not only know what the stock market performance of a portfolio of tourism industry in a period as complex, but also evaluate and assess which is the influence of the Spanish market in overall tourism sector. In any case, future research should clarify in greater depth the relationship between the largest tourism companies listed on the stock market and SMEs.

4. CONCLUSIONS.

In the current and deep economic crisis and financial recession, the tourism sector holds an important role of resistance in terms of wealth and job destruction, because both show amounts higher than those previous to the crisis. It`s interesting to analyze in this context the stock exchange evolution of tourism sector respect a reference portfolio. Furthermore, it is important to note that in order to extrapolate our results to the entire Spanish tourist industry, large enterprises and SMEs, we analyze the relationship between the two groups to the conclusion that the economic performance of large companies is that followed by SMEs and therefore, the analysis of large firms can be a faithful representative of the sector movement. But these results should be taken with caution still needed further research.

The first part of our analysis in which a tourism portfolio and the IBEX 35 index were analyzed can conclude that, during the global financial crisis, the behavioral pattern for both portfolios show a similar evolution in terms of returns showing more fluctuating and volatile in the returns of tourism companies than IBEX35 companies.

The second part of the analysis allows us to extrapolate the previous results on the relationship between the IBEX-35 and the tourist portfolios presented to the entire Spanish tourist industry. In this sense, the evolution of the IBEX-35 index allows us to approximate the overall evolution of tourism in Spain, and therefore, as the IBEX-35 consists of the 35 most liquid companies in the Spanish stock markets and also be enterprises with great stability as Grupo Santander, Telefónica, BBVA and Iberdrola, it is worthy to say that, although with more volatility and therefore risk, the Spanish tourist sector (SMEs and large firms) has a strength comparable to that of large IBEX-35 companies.

We also acknowledge several limitations of this study. We included only information relative to stock exchange performance and evolution: additional research might use more clarified or objective data related to performance, such as pay-outs, dividend distribution, or alpha and beta coefficients. Also, tourism portfolio includes a reduced number of enterprises, which may be not representative of general behavior of tourism sector.

In any case, we believe that this paper launches investigation into economic developments in this important tourism sector for the Spanish economy, which should be investigated further to clarify the relationships.

REFERENCE LIST.

[1] Harrison, J. (1995). The Spanish Economy: From the Civil War to the European Community. *Cambridge University Press.* Vol 22.

[2] Brida, J.G., Pereyra, J.S., Such, M.J. & Zapata, S. (2008). La contribución del turismo al crecimiento económico. *Cuadernos de Turismo,* 22: 35-46.

[3] Peña-Pinto, M. (2012). Memoria sobre la situación socioeconómica y laboral. España 2011. *Consejo Económico y Social España.* ISBN: 978-84-8188-333-6. url: http://www.ces.es/documents/10180/205054/MemoriaCES2011.pdf

[4] Sogorb, M.F. (2002). On Capital Structure in the Small and Medium Enterprises: The Spanish Case. *Collection reports from European Economic Observatory of the Institute of European Studies.* url: http://www.ceu.es/idee.htm. ISBN: 84-95219-49-2.

[5] Beck, T., & Demirguc-Kunt, A. (2006). Small and medium-size enterprises: Access to finance as a growth constraint. *Journal of Banking & Finance*, 30(11), 2931-2943.

[6] Peña, D. (2008). Fundamentos de Estadística. *Alianza Editorial*: Madrid.

[7] Orlitzky, M. & Benjamin, J.D. (2001). Corporate social performance and firm risk: a meta analytic review. *Business and Society*, 40: 369–396.

[8] Campbell, J.Y. & Hentschel, L. (1992). No news is good news: an asymmetric model of changing volatility in stocks returns. *Journal of Financial Economics*, 31: 281-318.

[9] French, K.R., Schwert, G.W. & Stambaugh, R.F. (1987). Expected stock returns and volatility. *Journal of Financial Economics*, 19: 3-29.

Co-management and ecoinnovation in traditional fishing. A case study

LL. MIRET-PASTOR
Universidad Politécnica de Valencia. Departamento de Economía y CCSS. Spain.
P. HERRERA-RACIONERO
Universidad Politécnica de Valencia. Instituto de Gestión Integral Costera. IGIC. Spain.
C. MUÑOZ-ZAMORA
Universidad Politécnica de Valencia. Instituto de Gestión Integral Costera. IGIC. Spain.

ABSTRACT

Focusing on a case study as it is the harbor of Gandia, we analyze with a qualitative methodology as fishermen have a real environmental concern that allows eco-innovations through their own institutions: the *Cofradías*. Concluding that the failure of fisheries policy is due in part to the lack of consideration of traditional knowledge and the fishermen own institutions. We propose the adoption of a new fisheries policy based on a genuine co-management.

1 INTRODUCTION

The traditional fishing sector in Spain is going through a critical time, with serious environmental, economic and social problems. To face this situation, the different fishing policies have led to the imposition of ever more restrictive and conservationist legislation, out of a desire to protect the marine environment and ensure the sustainability of the fishing industry. However, many of the measures put in place fail due to the difficulty of implementing and monitoring them, in the face of a sector which is very hostile to legislation.

Given these circumstances, there are ever more voices calling for the replacement of the current centralist, generalist, top-down models with co-management fishing models, which are decentralised, local and able to involve the fishermen themselves in the management of their own resources. This new fisheries management model is based in institutional economics [1], [2] or in the theories of social capital [3], [4].This call to action is even more pressing when one considers the traditional fishing sector, where local features and the specific wishes of the fishermen seem a long way away from the case of large-scale industrial fishing, at which all of European fishing policy seems to be aimed.

In this respect, the Spanish fishermen's associations (*cofradías de pescadores*) are examples of century-old institutions which have played a key role in the management of local fishing resources. This study examines the impressions of fishermen, which reveal not only their concern for the environment, but also the individual and collective initiatives aimed at achieving a more responsible kind of fishing and which might well be considered to be eco-innovations.

Therefore, by focusing on an exhaustive analysis of one of these associations and using a qualitative methodology, our aim is to validate the hypothesis that the real eco-innovators in traditional fishing are the fishermen themselves, who, acting in their own interests, formalise and manage those innovations through a co-management system based on their own institutions, the fishermen's *cofradias*.

In order to validate this hypothesis, this study has this introductory section; then a descriptive section which details the main theoretical concepts that the analysis is based on; the third section justifies and lays out the methodology to be used; the fourth section analyses three of the eco-innovations identified, examining their origin and current management; and the fifth section details the study's main conclusions.

2 ECO-INNOVATION AND CO-MANAGEMENT IN THE FISHING INDUSTRY

In most industries, innovation aims to achieve increases in productivity [5], [6], [7]. This has also been the case for many years in the fishing industry, leading to a technological transformation which the traditional fishing sector has also participated in. Examples of this include the use of radar, sonar, nylon nets, high horsepower engines, etc.

However, both in the literature and in our interviews, fishermen do not link their current problems to productivity. There is a consensus amongst fishermen about what the industry's main problems are:

Reduced catches (which they put down to overfishing)
High costs (which they put down to the high price of diesel)
Low fish prices

These problems require innovation to occur in a completely different way to the traditional one. The industry's current problems do not concern how to increase production, but how to ensure fishing production over the next few years. The industry requires innovations aimed at cutting energy costs, increasing the value of the product and ensuring sustainable fishing models over the long term. All of these goals drive ecological innovation and are part of what has become known as "eco-innovation".
We can define eco-innovation as "a change in economic activities that improves both the economic performance and the environmental performance of society" [8]. Equally, eco-innovation can be defined more simply as any innovation which reduces environmental damage [9].

One thing that we can conclude from the different definitions is that eco-innovation can occur at any time during the life cycle of the product or service in question and that, it is not simply "curative technology" [10], but a wide-ranging process that covers different types of innovations (of process, product or system) and which is not limited to solely environmentally-motivated innovations [11]. The benefits of environmental innovation in companies has been widely studied [12], [13] and goes beyond regulatory pressure [14] or simple environmental benefits [15].

In any case, if eco-innovation has become an issue of strategic importance in many industrial and service sectors [16], [17], in fishing it is a matter of survival.

Given the overexploitation of fishing grounds [18], it seems obvious that the fishing industry must change the way it works and better manage its resources: it must be able to innovate by seeking new technology, new methods of management or new procedures which are more environmentally friendly. The urgent and serious nature of the problem has led to a situation in which much of fishing policy involves the imposition of ever more restrictive and bureaucratic regulation, justified on environmental grounds.

One of the problems for the implementation of environmental innovations is the double externality problem [19], as eco-innovation improves environmental quality and is an improvement from which society in general benefits, but the cost is borne solely by the innovator.

These difficulties in benefiting from innovation can be a major disincentive, reducing the motivation to innovate. Researchers such as Rennings [20] or Kanerva [9] agree on the fact that eco-innovation has an impact on three areas: the technological, the social and the institutional. Social and institutional changes linked with eco-innovation have been widely studied [11], [21-22], underlining the need for eco-innovation to be supported by social and institutional change in order for it to make its impact properly felt [23].

Until now, the imposition of environmental policy has been met with a hostile reaction from fishermen, limiting its effectiveness or even condemning it to failure. Much of this negativity has resulted from the implementation of a centralised, authoritarian, top-down fishing management system. In the case of the traditional fishing sector in the Mediterranean, this negative reception has been exacerbated by the imposition of a system which ignores multiple local differences and rich and wide-ranging traditional knowledge, as well as the importance, tradition and idiosyncrasy of their own management institutions, such as the fishermen's associations.

In fact, all over the world studies have been carried out on different mechanisms used by fishermen themselves for the management of their own resources, something which in the literature is referred to as co-management [24]. These co-management systems represent a significant institutional innovation [25] and they are especially important for traditional fisheries [26-27], as they enable governmental concern for the efficient use of resources to be married with local concern for self-management [28]. In the case of traditional fisheries, there are examples of co-management scattered throughout the world (the Spanish fishermen's associations, the French Prud'homie, the Indian Mazopyat, the Indonesian Sasi, etc.) and, in fact, for many researchers "co-management" is simply a recognition and formalization of what already happens informally at a local level between government agencies and fishermen.

In this same sense, this study aims to analyse the role played by the fishermen's *Cofradías* in the management of environmental innovation within traditional fishing in the Spanish Mediterranean. In contrast with a fishing policy model that imposes eco-innovations via legislation, this study proposes the hypothesis that the real eco-innovators in traditional fishing are the fishermen themselves who, acting in their own interests, formalise and manage those innovations through a co-management system based on their own hundred-year old institutions, the fishermen's associations.

3 METHODOLOGY

The exploratory nature of our study makes it appropriate to use a qualitative methodology which, along the same lines as the "rapid rural appraisal" or "RRA" of small-scale fishing communities, can provide us with a general framework through which to understand the perspective of the social group our research focuses on. Our aim with this is not to seek laws which correspond to social reality, but rather to seek out the meaning behind the action, its socio-cultural significance, and to reach into the meaningful contexts in which the group operates. As well as enabling the interpretation of many results deriving from surveys on particular phenomena, a qualitative approach facilitates a more profound examination of the process of socio-environmental change and a better understanding of the role of nature and social stakeholders within a wider context of social changes and conflicts. Such transformations do not occur in a cultural or ideological vacuum; rather, they are the expression of profound cultural and symbolic mutations which acquire their meaning from the particular significance subjects give to them and from the ways in which the latter modify, accept, reject or avoid permanent features and changes, novelties and traditions, according to the particular contexts and situations they find themselves in.

However, this methodology has constantly attracted strong criticism, principally for its perceived lack objectivity, for the impossibility of reproducing its results, or for its triviality or relativism. Yet, frequently, this kind of criticism is more revealing of prejudice and/or ignorance regarding such methodologies rather than of an interest in entering into a serious debate on the background and theoretical and epistemological origins of qualitative practices. Over the years, qualitative methodological approaches have managed to establish themselves, just as critical theories have also emerged in parallel, and they have demonstrated the greater suitability of all those analytical instruments which are based on interpretation, which seek to comprehend social processes, rather than predict them, and try to understand their nature, rather than explaining it. Official bodies are also giving more and more support to methodologies of this kind, as a way in which to integrate all of the different viewpoints [18].

The main body of empirical material in our study is made up of 15 interviews with fishermen of the involved in small-scale fishing Gandía. One of the greatest advantages of an interview is the opportunity to collate a great deal of detailed, in-depth information from the viewpoint and in the words of people who share the same social setting, as well being able to describe and interpret elements which are not directly observable (feelings, impressions, events from the past, and so forth). Yet it is also its great disadvantage, as it makes fact-checking difficult and, especially in more excessively open-ended interviews, comparisons between different informants may be problematic. For this reason, we opted to undertake semi-structured interviews, using a previously designed script, focusing on those issues which were most relevant to our study. Once the interviews had been carried out and transcribed, a careful examination of them took place and this allowed us to refine the object of analysis and flesh out the pathways the analysis could take.

These interviews are, on the one hand, a valuable source of information regarding the aspects of the true context which might otherwise go unnoticed; on the other, they also constitute a body of representations and motivations which can serve to explain the logic behind many socio-environmental processes occurring within small-scale fishing. Thus the very observations of the informants shaped many of the hypotheses here formulated and much of the theoretical framework which was developed. This study will reflect some of the ideas which appeared repeatedly in the interviews and some which appeared more sporadically but which may point towards certain trends which have not yet fully crystallised within the group as a whole.

It must be stressed that by using this methodology, we are not seeking statistical representativeness (in these sense of having a sample drawn using an established procedure and which could allow certain generalised characteristics to be inferred for that particular population), but rather a representativeness of the different social senses (social imaginary) of the target group. So, the point is not to analyse all of the target population, nor even the most representative part of it; our objective is to represent certain social relationships/significations, those which in each case have been considered pertinent a priori. Representativeness is verified by the saturation of the discourse. We confirm the representativeness of our sample when, after a certain number of interviews, a further interview does not provide relevant new information on the object of study.

In this way, different innovations have been identified in the traditional fishing sector according to the definition given in the second section. Once enumerated, these are analysed individually, paying special attention to the origin of the innovation, as well as its later management and formalization.

4 THREE EXAMPLES OF ECOINNOVATION THROUGH THE CO-MANAGEMENT

The local communities, as such, are the ones who best know the surrounding area and they therefore exert "control" over knowledge of the area based on their experience, residence and collective memory. Such knowledge involves the identification of a space in which to operate: benthic and pelagic routes and sites identified by names, points of reference, resources, seasons, and rates of exploitation; the different species of fish, their behaviour and their environment; the weather, which is related to navigation and the fishing calendar [29].

Such knowledge, considered traditional, has generated an intense debate on whether these traditional systems are truly appropriate for conservation and, if they are, how to further this knowledge. Several authors maintain that the development of conservation starts with the perception of scarcity – in other words, a resource crisis. Others, in contrast, attribute a greater role to traditional ecological knowledge in the use and handling of resources developed over time [30].

Careful reading of the interviews suggests that the two models –the depletion crisis model and the ecological understanding model [31] – are complementary. There is wide awareness of a fishing ground crisis amongst the fishermen and they also consider themselves to be chiefly responsible for the situation. It is not surprising, then, to see that they themselves are trying to seek solutions by using their specific expertise. In fact, in the interviews, the fishermen maintain that many of the practices aimed at establishing sustainability currently enshrined in legislation were originally rules that were established amongst the fishermen through the Association (sometimes they were written down, sometimes not). Over time these were collated and formalised by the regional government.

The personal connections that the fishermen have with the natural surroundings and their daily work provide them with learning opportunities, while also playing an important part in their motivation to protect the environment. They have a particular way of conceiving of nature and this conception could contribute to the development of sustainable resource management practices [32]. This does not mean that biological and environmental conservation is always at the forefront of their minds, especially at times when they are struggling to make a living, but it may be at these times that eco-innovation can bring the two concerns together. Let us now examine three of the eco-innovations identified.

4.1 Discarded bycatch.

Discarded bycatch refers to those specimens of marine species which were not intended to be caught and these are either retained for later sale or are thrown back into the sea, either for legal reasons or for their low value [33]. This practice has a high ecological impact [34].

For a long time, it was thought that the solution to this problem required costly changes of onboard infrastructure or complicated separation, classification and storage protocols that were of little or no benefit to the fishermen [35], which made their successful implementation enormously difficult. However, recent studies have shown that the solution can be achieved via cultural changes rather than using technical instruments or regulation [36].

These cultural changes seem to be gradually becoming part of traditional fishing. Until the 1960s, no importance was given to the bycatch and old fishermen have said that the discards of fish would reach up to their knees. As catches became smaller, action started to be taken to minimise the environmental damage. Fishermen pay particular attention to those species that they know from experience will survive if they are put back into the sea, which include octopus, tellins and clams. They are, however, more critical of the regulations which require them to put dead fish back into the sea.

The case of clams and tellins is worth dwelling on. The Fishermen's Association in Gandía has imposed a two-stage discard process: the first at sea and the second at the fish market. At sea, those fishermen trying to catch tellins filter the catch with *garbells* (sieves) in order to put those species that are not required, or those that are too small, back into the sea. The way in which the technology for this purpose has developed is worth noting. At first, whether because they were already aware of the problem or out of a desire to better classify the catch, the fishermen used the same sieve which is used in rice cultivation and as time has gone on the materials and processes employed have been improved. As regards the discards made at the fish market, the fishermen say that it was the Association itself which prevented specimens below a certain size from being sold and it also the Association which charters and pays for a vessel to go out every day after the auction to dispose of those specimens which are below the minimum size.

From the interviews, it seems clear that for the fishermen the act of discarding is an economic decision and their involvement in the reduction of discards is related to factors such as the price of those bycatch specimens (or in their own words: "the buyer decides which are the discards") and the loss of quality and quantity of the target catch. It is also interesting to note the presence of environmental awareness amongst all of the interviewees and, although they are initially hostile to any type of regulation in this area, they take it on board and learn to adapt for future benefit.

4.2 The minimum size

This is closely related to the previous issue and, along with the close seasons and restricted areas, it is one of the most common stock planning and management measures. The Association takes responsibility for compliance with the existing regulations on this issue, but the fishermen say that there existed a rule on minimum sizes within the Association and that in many cases this was later formalized by the government. For octopus, for example, the Association established a rule that octopuses which weighed less than a kilogramme could not be sold and this is now part of regional legislation.

There is still great hostility towards external regulation and this hostility is higher still when the regulations are more general or originate from further away. The fishermen complain that many regulations are the same for different areas or even seas. They give the example of the minimum size of the tellin, which is based on the Italian tellin, while in this area of the Mediterranean the tellin is smaller.

However, although there is strong criticism in all the interviews of the standardization the law subjects them to, in many cases they complain that the EU regulations are very discriminatory or are too lax, rendering more protectionist local legislation ineffective.

4.3 Fishing quotas

The Association has regulated itself with regard to the number of catches of whichever species it has deemed necessary, both for economic reasons (the saturation of the market leading to a fall in prices) and for environmental ones (reduction in quantity and biological diversity). Just as with the minimum sizes, this internal rule has later formed the basis of regional laws. So, in the case of tellins and clams, the Association decided to establish a quota on daily catches. Although these measures are generally accepted by the fishermen, they also acknowledge that they are frequently ignored, as such catches can be sold "under the counter" and that, although this provides some of them with extra money, it is something that damages their long-term future. They therefore believe that the government should monitor this more closely, since for the Association, sanctions and the monitoring of infractions is one of the most complex issues it faces. The Association has a number of informal social monitoring mechanisms aimed at guaranteeing order within the group and compliance with the regulations, but the effectiveness of this is frequently questioned. The fishermen believe that the government must monitor and punish such fraudulent practices.

5 CONCLUSIONS

The first conclusion of this study is that, despite appearances, traditional fishing is constantly evolving. A series of technological, institutional and process innovations have been taken place within it, which have transformed the way in which fishing takes place [37]. The interviews have revealed a whole series of more or less recent changes which the fishermen have introduced into their way of working, aimed (directly and indirectly) at achieving greater care of the environment, and which could be said to be eco-innovations. As we have shown, these innovations have arisen primarily from internal stimuli, they are based on tacit knowledge and they are managed either by the fishermen themselves or by the *Cofradia*.

We have seen that the fishermen's cofradias play an important role in monitoring the marine environment and for self-supervision of fishing practices. Although the perception that others have is that of environmentally-aware government agencies imposing strict regulations on fishermen, the fishermen themselves perceive it very differently.

It is the fishermen who see that the decreased catches are their main problem and they are aware that overfishing is the cause of this. So, it has been the fishermen themselves who have taken action and innovated on this issue and the government has then collated many of these environmental innovations and incorporated them into law. The fishermen are hostile to the centralised, generalist, top-down fishing policy model. In recent years, the idea that fishing regulations should be established "once the industry has been consulted" has gained strength. Yet this change of attitude seems insufficient and does not correspond to a real co-management process. In traditional fishing in the Spanish Mediterranean, co-management of fishing has been occurring for many years, as the fishermen's associations play a key role in fishery management, making it possible for rules to come from the lower levels and be adopted by the higher ones, rather than seeing the imposition of top-down regulations.

This study has focused on eco-innovation. Eco-innovation is seen as vital by the fishermen. However, many of the policies aimed at imposing eco-innovations fail because of the hostility they induce in the target group. Many fishermen suspect that fishing policies are subordinated to conservationist policies and that the ultimate goal of the regulations is to eradicate fishing. This impression is exacerbated by the perception that the industry is undergoing a crisis. The imposition of a large amount of European regulations has coincided with the breaking-up of hundreds of vessels and the ruin of many fishermen.

The conclusion is that fishing policies, or at least those that are directed at traditional fishing, must take into account the role that these institutions play. In fact, those government agencies which are closest to them have already adapted and formalised many of the innovations which have emerged from the *Cofradia*. Yet if fishing regulations seek to encourage and foster eco-innovation in the fishing industry, it is pointless to impose this externally and from a distance. It makes much more sense to foster innovation from inside the fishing communities, formalising and encouraging co-management models, which in the case of traditional fisheries in the Spanish Mediterranean already exist.

REFERENCE LIST

[1] Pearce, D. W. & Turner, R. (1990). *Economics of Natural Resources and the Environment*, The John Hopkins University Press. Baltimore.

[2] Ostrom, E. (1990). *Governing the commons*, University Press, Cambridge.

[3] Putnam, R. D. (1993). *Making Democracy Work: Civic Traditions in Modern Italy.* Princeton University Press. Princeton.

[4] Grafton, Q. (2005). Social capital and fisheries governance. *Ocean & Coastal Management*, 48, 753-766.

[5] Corley, M., Michie, J. & Oughton, C. (2002). Technology, Growth and Employment. *International Review of Applied Economics*, 16 (3), 265-276.

[6] Crespi, F. & Pianta, M. (2008). Demand and innovation in productivity growth. International. *Review of Applied Economics*, 22, 655-672.

[7] Van Leeuwen, G. & Klomp, L. (2006). On the Contribution of Innovation to Multi-Factor Productivity Growth. *Economics of Innovation and New Technology*, 15, 367- 390.

[8] Huppes, G., Kleijn, R., Huele, R., Ekins, P., Shaw, B., Schaltegger, S. & Esders, M. (2008). *Measuring eco- Innovation: Framework and typology of indicators. Management summary of the final report of the ECODRIVE project.*

[9] Kanerva, M., Arundel, A. & Kemp, R. (2009). *Environmental innovation: Using qualitative models to identify indicator for policy.* United Nations University. Working Papers Series.

[10] Wuppertal Institute (2009). *Eco-innovation : Putting the EU on the path to a resource and energy efficient economy.* Blischwitz, R; Giljun, S; Kuhndt, M; Scmidt-Bleek et al. Bruselas.

[11] Kemp R. & Pearson P. (2008). *Measuring eco-innovation, final report of MEI project for DG Research of the European Commission.* Bruselas.

[12] Calia, R. C., Guerrini, F. M. & Moura, G. L. (2007). Innovation networks: From technological development to business model reconfiguration. *Technovation*, 27, 426-432.

[13] Andersen, B. (2006). If "Intellectual Property Rights" Is The Answer, What Is The Question? Revisiting The Patent Controversies. In ANDERSEN B. *Intellectual Property Rights, Innovation, Governance And The Institutional Environment*, Edward Elgar, Clethenham.

[14] Brunnermeier, S. B. & Cohen, M. A. (2003). Determinants of environmental innovation in US manufacturing industries. *Journal of Environmental Economics and Management*, 45, 278-293.

[15] Carrion-Flores, C. & Inner, R. (2010). Environmental innovation and environmental performance. *Journal of Environmental Economics and Management*, 59, 27-42.

[16] Segarra-Oña, M., Peiró-Signes A., Albors-Garrigós, J. & Miret-Pastor, L. (2011). Impact of Innovative Practices in Environmentally Focused Firms: Moderating Factors. *International Journal of Environment Research*, 5, 425-434.

[17] Montalvo C. (2008). General wisdom concerning the factors affecting the adoption of cleaner technologies: a survey. *Journal of Cleaner Production*, 16, (1), s7-s13.

[18] FAO (2010), *The State of World Fisheries and Aquaculture (SOFIA).* FAO Corporate Document Repository. Roma.

[19] Beise-Zee, M. & Rennings, K. (2005). Lead markets and regulation: a framework for analyzing the international diffusion of environmental innovation. *Ecological Economics,* 52, 5–17.

[20] Rennings, K. (2000). Redefining innovation—eco-innovation research and the contribution from ecological economics. *Ecological Economics,* 32, 319–33.

[21] Chappin, M., Vermeulen, M., Meeus, M. & Hekkert, M. P. (2009). Enhancing our understanding of the role of environmental policy in environmental innovation: adoption explained by the accumulation of policy instruments and agent-based factors. *Environmental Science and Policy*, 12, 934-947.

[22] Jänicke, M. (2005). Trend-Setters in Environmental Policy: The Character and Role of Pioneer Countries. *European Environment*, 15 (2), 129–142.

[23] Hellström, T. (2007). Dimensions of Environmentally Sustainable Innovation: the Structure of Eco-Innovation Concepts. *Sustainable Development*, 15, 148-159.

[24] McConney, P., Pomeroy, R. & Mahon, R. (2003). Guidelines for coastal resource co-management in the Caribbean: communicating the concepts and conditions that favor success. *Caribbean Coastal Co-Management Guidelines Project*. Caribbean Conservation Association.

[25] Nielsen, J.R., Degnbol, P., Viswanathan, K., Ahmed, M., Hara, M. & Raja, N. (2004). Fisheries co-management: an institutional innovation? Lessons from South East Asia and Ostrom, E. (1990). *Governing the commons*, University Press. Cambridge.

[26] Begossi, A. (2006). Temporal stability in fishing spots: conservation and co-management in Brazilian artisanal coastal fisheries. *Ecology and Society*, 11(1).

[27] Gelcich, S., Kaiser M.J., Castilla, J.C. & Edwards, G. (2008). Engagement in co-management of marine benthic resources influences environmental perceptions of artisanal fishers. *Environmental Conservation*, 35 (1), 36–45.

[28] Fanning, L. (2000). The co-management paradigm: examining criteria for meaningful public involvement. In: *Sustainable Marine Resource Management*, ed. E. Mann, A. Chircop, M. McConnell & J. Morgan. University Chicago Press. Chicago.

[29] Féral, F. (2004). *Maritime societies, fisheries law and institutions in the western Mediterranean*. FAO Fisheries Technical Paper, 420. Roma.

[30] Turner, N. & Berkes, F. (2006). Coming to Understanding: Developing Conservation through incremental learning in the Pacific Northwest. *Human Ecology*, 34, (4), 495-513.

[31] Berkes, F. & Turner, N. (2006). Knowledge, Learning and the Evolution of Conservation Practice for Social-Ecological SystemResilience, *Human Ecology*, 34 (4), 479-494.

[32] Berkes, F. (2010). Shifting perspectives on resource management: resilience and the reconceptualization of 'natural resources' and 'management'. MAST, *Maritime Studies*, 9, 11-38.

[33] Harrington, J.M., Myers R.A. & Rosenberg A.A. (2005). Wasted fishery resources: discarded bycatch in the USA. *Fish and Fisheries*, 6, 350–361.

[34] Kelleher, K. (2005). *Discards in the world's marine fisheries. An update*. FAO Fisheries Technical Paper. 470. Rome.

[35] Blanco M., Sotelo, C.G., Chapela M.J. & Pérez-Martín, R.I. (2007). Towards sustainable and efficient use of fishery resources: present and future trends. *Trends in Food Science & Technology*, 18 (1), 29-36.

[36] Johnsen, J.P. & Eliasen, S.Q. (2010). Solving complex fisheries management problems: What the EU can learn from the Nordic experiences of reduction of discards. *Marine Policy*, 35 (2), 130-139.

[37] Christensen, J.L., Dahl, M.S., Nielsen, R.N., Ostergaard, C. R. & Eliasen, S.Q. (2011). Patterns and Collaborators of Innovation in the Primary Sector: A Study of the Danish Agriculture, Forestry and Fishery Industry. *Industry & Innovation*, 18 (2), 203-222.

The necessary cooperation and coordination between the government with different competences on tourism and environment

A.P. DOMÍNGUEZ ALONSO

University of Castilla-la Mancha (Spain), Faculty of Social Sciences of Cuenca, Spain

ABSTRACT

The distribution of competences in the field of tourism and protection of the environment is of a complex and multifaceted. The inevitable concurrence of powers requires the legislature and the executive joint and interventional procedural formulas to harmonize the exercise of their respective competences avoiding displacement or impairment of others. The fulfillment of duty of intergovernmental cooperation involves both a positive dimension to allow articulation of the activity and responsibilities of the various public administrations, as a precautionary measure, to ensure respect for the skills and interests of the other Administrations.

1   INTRODUCTION. MAINSTREAMING AND COMPLEXITY OF RESPONSIBILITIES FOR ENVIRONMENT AND TOURISM.

In relation to tourism, section 148.1, paragraph 18, of the Spanish Constitution of 1978 (CE) attributed to the Autonomous Communities (CCAA) exclusive jurisdiction over "promotion and management of tourism in its territory".

But there are many other state and regional competitions that are directly or indirectly linked to tourism, prominently including those relating to the environment, and also others such as spatial planning, urban development and housing , railways and roads, ports and sport airports, mineral and thermal waters, inland fishing, hunting and river fishing, indoor fairs, handicrafts, heritage monumental attractions of the Autonomous Community; promotion of culture, nationality, immigration, emigration, immigration and asylum; regime customs and tariff, foreign trade, foreign exchange bases and coordination of general planning of economic activity, external health, ports and airports of general interest, traffic and transport, defense of cultural, artistic and monumental Spanish against exportation and spoliation, museums, libraries and archives, and regulation of the conditions for obtaining, issuing and recognition of academic and professional.

This complexity of the allocation and exercise of powers manifested even more strongly on the environment. Article 149.1.23 CE grants the state authority to issue "basic legislation on environmental protection, without prejudice to the powers of the Autonomous Communities to establish additional protection". For the Spanish Constitutional Court (TC), the protection of the environment "is a writ of amparo, support, advocacy and promotion, custody, both preventive and repressive" and can also be characterized as "belligerent activity that attempts to avert the danger and in appropriate, restore the damage and even improve the characteristics of the environment, to ensure your enjoyment for all" (STC 33/2005 , of February 17, FJ6).

In a first approach to the provision, the STC 64/1982 stated that the State is responsible, according to the current general trend, set standards "which necessitate an overall policy framework on environmental matters, given the extent not already national, but international regulation that is the subject and the requirement of the indispensable collective solidarity referred to art. 45.2, but is also attributed to the CCAA own competition not only execution "legal development" of the basic law, and to impose "additional security measures", all of which means that within the framework of global politics of the environment and respect for the principle of solidarity are constitutionally possible a variety of regulations.

Subsequently, the STC 170/1989 went a step further in the delimitation of the powers reserved to the State by Art. 149.1.23 EC in this regard, stating that "the basic legislation has the technical characteristic of minimum standards that allow "additional rules" or an added protection. That is, the basic legislation fails in this case a function of relative uniformity, but rather management using least be respected in all cases, but may allow each of the CCAA with jurisdiction in the matter , establish higher levels of protection would not enter for only that in contradiction with the basic regulations of the State".

The Spanish Constitutional Court has emphasized the complex and multifaceted that present the issues relating to the environment in its decision 102/1995, of June 26. This character is reflected in mainstreaming environmental competence in constitutional setting in that, as the expressed STC 102/1995, the environment impact "on other matters included too, each in its own way, in the scheme constitutional powers (art. 148.1.1, 3, 7, 8, 10 and 11 CE)."

Environmental therefore it is a factor in other sectoral policies with an impact on the various natural resources environmental members (SSTC 102 /1995 FJ 6 and 13/1998, 22 Jan, FJ 7).

Notwithstanding such environmental incardinación than the set of public policies, so that specifically relates to the jurisdictional issues, the TC emphasizes that within the competence of environmental protection have framed solely those activities aimed directly at the preservation, conservation or improvement of natural resources (STC 102/1995), given that these are physical supports a plurality of public and private actions in respect of which the Constitution and Statutes of Autonomy have demarcated different competence titles (for all SSTC 144/1985 , of 25 Oct., 227/1988 , of 29 Nov. , FJ 13 , 243/1993 , of 15 Jul., 102/1995 and 40/1998, of 19 Feb.).

2.- THE DECISIVE IMPORTANCE IN THE SPANISH LAW OF COOPERATION AND COORDINATION BETWEEN THE VARIOUS TERRITORIAL AUTHORITIES WITH RESPONSIBILITY FOR TOURISM AND ENVIRONMENT.

The existence of a general duty of cooperation between the State and the CCAA is clear from the same simple model of territorial organization introduced by the Spanish Constitution of 1978, as noted by the Constitutional Court caselaw (SSTC 80/1985, 18/1982 and 96 /1986, among others, see [1]).

The inter-administrative relations are a manifestation of general interest management from multiple liabilities on various public circles also interests [2].

The constitutional basis of inter-administrative relations can be found in the important article 103.1 of the CE. Indeed, this provision, configurator administrative status of public power as a whole, establishes the principles of efficiency and coordination, undoubtedly claiming the existence of inter-administrative relations. The principles of efficiency and coordination invoke the need for legitimacy of public administration based on its results, its ability to fulfill its purpose of social management instance, cash service to society [3]. There is thus a general interest of the whole society in the coordinated operation of the public administrations, as a global system of government intervention [4].

The Explanatory Memorandum of Law 30/1992 on the Legal Regime of Public Administrations and the Common Administrative Procedure (LRJPAC) rightly points out that the effective performance of the various government makes an active cooperation "not only desirable, but indispensable", configured as a duty not to be justified in specific provisions because "can not be imposed, but remembered, shaped or arranged" [5].

In terms of organization , the LRJPAC formulated a set of principles for the various public administrations act coordinated, respecting its own powers, asistiéndose fairly between them and facilitating the information each needs the other (art. 4) , by notice directly (art. 19). Conferences sectoral cooperation agreements and, where appropriate, partnerships (arts. 5 and ff.) are tools for effective action of all the administrations. Effective administrative organization should be simplified (art. 11.3) and formulas available to expedite the activities of material, technical or service , without altering the ownership and responsibility of the competencies (management parcels with public or private entities, art. LRJPAC 15).

For his part, Law 6/1997 on the Organisation and Functioning of the General State Administration, provides in its Art. 3 as an organizing principle, the principle of economy, sufficiency and adequacy of the means strict institutional purposes (paragraph 1.d) and collects in Art. 3.2 the principles of effectiveness in meeting the objectives (point a) and efficiency in the allocation and use of public resources (point b). As derivations of the principles of effectiveness and efficiency, Law 6/97 points and agility streamlining administrative procedures and materials management activities (art. 3.2.e) effective service to citizens (art. 3.2.f) and cooperation and coordination with other government (art. 3.2.h).

If we translate these principles to complex Spanish scheme of distribution of powers in the fields of tourism and environment, come to the inevitable conclusion that the same leads as indispensable way to close collaboration and intergovernmental cooperation. Indeed, regional powers on tourism and environment have to coexist with those that the state power under Art. 149.1 CE, the exercise can condition, lawfully, the competition marked the CCAA.

3.- THE CASE LAW OF THE CONSTITUTIONAL COURT.

As noted in the STC 149/1991, in all cases in which the distribution of competences is set by reference to a "political" (e. g. Environmental protection, protection of the user, etc). And not for specific sectors of the legal or public activity , such competition can not be understood in terms that the single incardinación objective pursued by the standard (or the specific act) in such policies ignore the competition allows other instances corresponds if the same rule or act are referred from other perspectives. On the other hand, as is also obvious, spatial planning is, in our constitutional system, a title specific competence can not be ignored, reducing it to the simple ability to plan, from the point of view of their impact on the territory, the actions by other titles must perform the entity that holds competition without any consequence arising therefrom whatsoever for the performance of other public bodies in the same territory (STC 149/1991).

STC 40/1998 (FJ 30) notes that this possibility of concurrent competence titles with different legal order, on the same physical space , forcing you to find the formulas in each case allow its concrete articulation and integration, to what should be approached, first, to forms of cooperation, which should be sought with those solutions is achieved optimize the performance of concurrent powers, which you may choose, in each case, the techniques that are most appropriate.

If the principle of partnership between the State and the CCAA implicit in the autonomous system (SSTC 18/1982 and 152/1988, among others) and if "the consolidation and the proper functioning of the autonomous state largely depend of strict adherence to one and other rational formulas of cooperation, consultation, participation, coordination, consultation or agreement provided for in the Constitution and the Statute of Autonomy" (STC 181/1988), this type of formulas are especially necessary in these cases of concurrent competence titles to be sought in those solutions which achieve optimize the performance of both competitions (SSTC 32/1983, 77/1984, 227/1987 and 36/1994) and can chosen, in each case, the techniques that are most appropriate: the mutual exchange of information, the issuance of previous reports in the areas of jurisdiction, creating bodies of mixed composition, etc.

It is possible, however, that these channels result in any case insufficient to resolve conflicts that may arise. For such cases, the TC has stated that "the final decision for the proprietor of competition prevalent" (STC 77/1984) , and that "the state can not be deprived of the exercise of its exclusive jurisdiction by the competition exists, but also is unique, an CCAA" (STC 56/1986). Also, in STC 149/1991 states that the allocation to the regions of the territory ordering function "can not be understood in such absolute terms that removes or destroys the powers that the Constitution reserves to the State , although the use the make them conditional ordination necessarily the territory", being legitimate such conditioning as "the exercise of such other powers remain within their own limits, without using them to proceed under its coverage to planning in which they are to exercised. It must be addressed , therefore, in each case what the competition from the state, and what part of the territory of the Autonomous Community operates , to rule on the legitimacy or illegitimacy of the contested provisions (in the same sense, STC 36/1994) .

In the STC 151/2003, the Court pronounced on the coordinating mechanism established by Article 10 of Law 25/1988 , of July 29, and Article 33.3 of the General Regulations approved by Royal Decree 1812/1994, of September 2, provisions are aimed at resolving the possible conflict between sectoral legislation on state highways (the integrated general interest itineraries or whose role in the transportation system affects more than one region, as to the provisions of art. 4.1 Highways Act), and the determinations of urban planning instruments (prototypically the general planning of the municipalities), while both materials are subjected, respectively, to the exclusive competence of the State the basis of art. 149.1.24 EC, and also exclusive regional competition, ex art. 148.1.3 CE, and given that the performance of both competitions is produced on the same physical space of skills. Well, the STC cited considers the inter-peer cooperative solutions by Road Act and its regulations are respectful of the constitutional and statutory distribution of powers.

As regards the requirements of constitutionally guaranteed local autonomy to municipalities , it is necessary to recall the doctrine contained in STC 159/2001 , in which it was stated that one region is empowered to regulate the activity variously urban, and to give it to the local, and particularly to municipalities [6], greater or lesser presence and participation in the various fields in which it is traditionally divided urban planning (planning, management and discipline plans), provided it respects the minimum core identifiable faculties, powers and functions (at least in terms of performance or urban management) that will make these local bodies are recognizable by the public as an instance of autonomous decision making and individualized.

In short, local autonomy enshrined in Art. 137 CE (with the complement of the arts. 140 and 141 CE) translates into an institutional guarantee of the essential or primary core of local self-government authorities, core must necessarily be respected by the legislature (state or regional general or sectoral) for bringing administrations are recognizable as a self-governing entities endowed [7].

To the extent that the settlor did not predetermine the specific content of local autonomy, the legislature constitutionally empowered to regulate matters of which it is reasonable to say that part of that core unavailable may, indeed, engage in one way or another initial freedom configuration, but can not do so to establish a local autonomy content inconsistent with the general framework outlined in the arts. 137, 140 and 141 CE.

In relation to water law, STC 227/1988 , in FJ 13, pointed out that water is not only a good for which is necessary to establish the legal domain, management and use strictly, but also constitutes the hardware of a plurality of activities, public or private , in connection with which the Constitution and the Statute of Autonomy confer competences to the State and the CCAA: Contracts and administrative concessions, environmental, industrial waste or pollutants, planning, Public Works [8], energy regime, river fishing, protected natural areas [9] and overall planning of economic activity.

Converges on a complex equation waters of concurrent competence titles, State and Regional. This raises to two fundamental problems [10]. The first, of course, is the definition of each of these titles. Although it is very difficult to fix in the abstract these boundaries, you always end up being outlined on the occasion of specific conflicts. The inevitable second and therein challenge the Constitutional Court insists ad nauseum, is the integration and coordination of all of them, so that the operation of the authorities involved as efficient, smooth and seamless as possible X.

As noted in the SSTC 113/1983 and 77/1984, the attribution of jurisdiction over a particular physical environment does not necessarily prevent other powers are exercised in that space, as long as both have different legal subject, and that the exercise of devolved powers do not interfere or disturb the exercise of the state, so often, it will be essential to establish collaborative mechanisms that enable the necessary coordination and cooperation between public administrations involved (in this latter sense, SSTC 149/1991, 13/1992, 36/1994, among many others). In short, the jurisdictional competition can not be solved in terms of exclusion, they must turn to a record of accommodation and integration of competency titles -state and regional- that converge on the same space and, as result, are called to cohonestarse (STC 103/1989).

This criterion of distribution of powers confluent on the same hardware was specifically applied in STC 227/1988 and in STC 149/1991, rearmost reiterating the STC 161/1996, in which FJ 5 is stated that "the most direct way that has the Autonomous Community to influence the interests affected by water management in watersheds that (...) extend beyond its territory, through its participation in the governing bodies of the relevant River Basin , in the terms established by state law (...) respecting the constitutional framework, which includes as an essential principle the principle of collaboration between the State and the Autonomous Communities". Then adding that "the actions that can be performed directly each of the regional governments are merely complement that develop participating in the direction and management of the Hydrographic Confederation itself, and are feasible only to the extent that interfere with the performance of this or disturb" (STC 77/1984 , FJ 2).

Thus, the Constitutional Court has had occasion, for example, to highlight how water is a vital resource, also essential for the realization of many economic activities. For this reason, management of water resources, wherever they are found, can not escape the powers that the State has to exercise to establish the bases and coordination of general planning of economic activity , in accordance in art. 149.1.13 [a] of the Constitution.

The importance of collaboration formulas as described above, should be especially emphasized, because, in many cases, only through joint and coordinated actions, either through formulas procedural intervention, either by integrating instruments sectoral policies such as planning will be possible to exercise regional competition on the river fishing without prejudice to the concurrent jurisdiction of the state and the principle of unity in the planning and management of water in the area of the basin, provided for in art. 4.2 and 16 Water Law, and, as stated in STC 227/1988 (FJ 15) "permits a balanced management of water resources ... in response to all affected interests when Basin extends to the territory of more than one region, are manifestly supracomunitarios".

In its decision 15/1998, of January 22, the Constitutional Court also ruled on the delimitation of competences on water in watersheds supra- and its articulation with the concurrence of other specific areas of competency, as the on freshwater fishing, sectoral impact on the same physical reality.

For the Court, in the case concerned whether the exclusive jurisdiction of the Autonomous Community of Castilla-La Mancha on river fishing, understood as an activity consisting of the capture of different fish species, exhausted by the content described above or, on the contrary, also reaches those other measures aimed at the protection and conservation of fish species that, in many cases inevitably have an impact on the general legal provisions provided for the environment in which they live.

The inevitable competition powers on water basins belonging to the supra-legislator requires both the state and the regional procedural articulation and intervention formulas to harmonize the exercise of their respective competences avoiding displacement or impairment of others [11].

REFERENCE LIST

[1] On the principle of cooperation may be the special issue of the Journal 240 Administrative Documentation (October-December 1994).

[2] Parejo Alfonso , L. (2007), "Notes for a dogmatic construction of inter-administrative relations", RAP 174, p. 161 et seq.

[3] Parejo Alfonso, L. (1983), *Social status and public administration*. Civitas, Madrid, p. 60 et seq .

[4] Ortega Alvarez, L. (1988), *The constitutional system of local competitions*, National Institute of Public Administration, Madrid.

[5] About connecting the principle of cooperation with the principles of administrative efficiency and solidarity, see Sánchez Morón, M. (1990), *Local autonomy. Historical and constitutional significance*, ed. Civitas, Madrid, p. 192.

[6] On inter-administrative relations of the State and the Autonomous Communities with local work see Barberá Climent , J. (1994), "The state and regional cooperation on municipal services" in Muñoz Machado, S. , *Municipal Law Treaty*, Civitas , Madrid , 2nd ed., p. 379 et seq.

[7] Parejo Alfonso, L. (1981), *Institutional and local autonomies Warranty*, Madrid and Embido Irujo, A. (1081), "Municipal Autonomy and Order: approach to the concept and meaning of constitutional declaration of municipal autonomy", REDA 30.

[8] Embid Irujo, A. (2001), stressed the " essential consideration and territorial primarily with water policies that are much more spacious and open than what is deducted from your account as mere water policy " ("Evolution of Law and Water Policy in Spain", XI Water law Conference, Zaragoza) .

[9] In the STC 102/1995 , regarding the declaration and management of protected natural areas where purported to protect the sea shore, rivers, the territorial sea and internal waters and natural resources of the economic zone and the continental shelf , the Court argued that it should be "these public assets in a category may be established ad hoc by its own characteristics and its social significance" with the various figures of protected natural spaces designed in Law 4/1989, on March 7, but in any case the actual ownership title becomes competence from the perspective of environmental protection, subject, of

course, state authority on these goods from their own powers. Consequently , the TC concluded by stating that "the classification of a segment or piece of the maritime zone as part of a natural protectable also corresponds to the Autonomous Community in whose territory (as well as) the management, for the sole effects of environmental protection, without the possibility of mutual interference, a common phenomenon in the exercise of concurrent jurisdiction on the same object for different functions, authorize by absorbing unify for one another" (FJ 20).

[10] Delgado Piqueras, F. (2000), "The general scheme of inland waters and, in particular, mineral and thermal waters in Castilla-La Mancha", *Administrative Law Autonomy of Castilla-La Mancha*, University Castilla - la Mancha, Cuenca, p . 636.

[11] The principles of efficiency and coordination invoke the need for legitimacy of public administration based on its results, its ability to fulfill its purpose of social management instance, cash service to society. There is a general interest of the whole society in the coordinated operation of the public administrations, as a global system of government intervention. See Parejo Alfonso, L. (1983), *Welfare state and public administration*, Civitas, Madrid, p. 60 et seq. and Ortega Alvarez, L. (1988), *The constitutional system of local competitions*, National Institute of Public Administration, Madrid.

Interpretative messages and social networks. New challenges for the strategic communication of protected areas

M. D. TERUEL
Universitat Politècnica de València, Economy and Social Sciences Departament, Spain
M. J. VIÑALS
Universitat Politècnica de València, Cartographic Engineering, Geodesy and Photogrammetry Department, Spain
M. MORANT
Universitat Politècnica de València, Cartographic Engineering, Geodesy and Photogrammetry Department, Spain

ABSTRACT

Interpretative messages are promoted by the administrations responsible for protected areas and are most often aimed at making people aware of this heritage and appreciating it. In the last few years, social networks have become an excellent way for virtual bidirectional communication. This article analyses different factors that intervene in the strategic communication of protected areas in social networks and presents a typology of the different messages referring to the identity and nature of the information. The research results reveal an underuse of social networks, which could be attributed to a lack of ability to manage communication.

1. INTRODUCTION

The virtual bidirectional communications that have been enabled by information and communication technology (ICT) have created challenges for tourist destinations, as ICT is considered an excellent way for such destinations to promote themselves. ICT is considered a particularly great strength for protected areas, especially in regard to the transmission of information, values and experiences between users. The internet is, as we already know, a communications channel that has revolutionised the way in which we promote tourist destinations [1][2]. Studies rarely analyse the potential strength that these destinations could offer [3][4]. Communicative efforts are usually made once visitors are actually present in the protected area where they are presented with interpretative elements, such as signposts, group guides and interpretative activities. These more *traditional* supports are being reinforced by new tools to help achieve different goals of communicative actions, and the way to understand user contact through social networks (and other devices), where the appearance of information, its contents, its audiences, and even its uses have been modified. Those responsible for protected areas are now aware of this; therefore, they have decided to join this new means of communication by making a special effort to achieve communicative goals that modify behaviour and raise awareness about the importance of these spaces.

Social networks are a new type of dynamic communication that challenges the traditional model of unidirectional communication in order to introduce the production and dissemination of messages where answering and participating was not previously considered [5]. The constant actualising and newness of data and content on social networks, the willpower of users to share information and knowledge (*crowdsourcing*) and, most of all, the possibility of interacting with users, have clarified the function of the webpages that are mostly dedicated to presenting information "*in extenso*" from resources. Conversely, the spontaneity of social networks is intended to offer punctual and immediate information that provokes the interest of users in events that are currently happening. Launching messages that emphasise the change of season, a meteorological phenomenon or migratory birds that travel according to the season are revealed in such a way. A protected area's decision to be present on social networks amplifies the audience spectrum, bearing in mind that from the moment the natural area is present on social media, visitors are not only those who resort to the centre of interpretation or who assist in the guided tour; rather, they are also considered to be virtual visitors [6]. Social media is not only considered a good opportunity to reach the greatest number of visitors, but it also requires that messages perform better and be given greater dedication.

The interpretation of heritage is an instrument that enables us to preserve the most fragile areas [7] thanks to the fact that visitors are already informed (before arrival) before acquiring new knowledge. These components of interpretation can be reached or reinforced throughout social networks, as in the *ante-trip*, just as the *post-trip*, without visitors ever being present in the preserved area. Furthermore, the interpretation of heritage aims to achieve knowledge in a voluntary, polite and well-mannered way, which, throughout social networks, sets an example through pictures and texts produced by managers of the natural space. These different elements are then reinforced by the comments of other users (real users, potential users or platonic[14] users). In relation to the interpretation of heritage, social networks reveal the real challenge that exists in adjusting and adapting the emitted messages so that they can reach the goal of the other interpretative traditional "*off-line*" means that, according to Ham [8] or Morales [7], consist in promoting active experiences to visitors and that link them in a sensorial way, emotionally and intellectually. In the particular case of the protected areas, heritage interpretation must be considered as a communicative strategy that offers an approach that is more about explaining than informing, about revealing more than showing, and about awaking and creating curiosity more than satisfying it [9]. This challenge can be achieved in social media, thanks to an open dialogue that is established and that permits users to answer and interact with the community manager. Environmental interpretation is a provocative means of communication, as envisioned by Ham [10], in the sense that it launches messages and questions that have a reinforcing effect through reflection. The prolongation of this effect can be obtained thanks to these social networks.

---

[14] Users are considered platonic if they prove their unconditional support without even visiting the destination.

When strategic communication happens *in situ*, it requires the presence of the tourist guide who, in the traditional communication scheme, corresponds to the emitter of the information. The tourist guide is in charge of adapting the experts' technical language to terms and principles that can be understood, making it more accessible to people. In the special case of social networks, the community manager is the tourist guide or emitter of the information. This is why interpretation via social networks must be administered as if it were a personal means, and why great care of the information that is transmitted must be taken as if it were the guide. The new capacity attributed to the online content manager of a protected area requires the formation and education of the guide to extend not only to the technical contents but also to the communication itself, bearing in mind that the community manager must be responsible for the communication to achieve efficient interpretation through social media. The main goal of this study is to identify and analyse the different messages emitted by the people who are responsible for protected areas that have an active presence in social media. This message can be identified by referring to the identity and nature of these messages in order to know their use. This message analysis will be useful for protected areas to improve their communicative abilities, which in turn improves the efficiency and performance of the messages.

This study centres on identifying and analysing the different factors that intervene in the strategic communication of protected areas in social networks. These factors have been approached from different points of view: studying the intrinsic characteristics of social networks, considering social networks as productive technological tools, studying the factors that enable us to reach intellectual and emotional connections between the users and the *online* content manager, and, finally, presenting the interpretative message and the situation that is reached. Next, we shall proceed to present cases that have been analysed through relevant examples of the previously explained factors.

2. METHODOLOGY

Currently, more and more studies, seminaries and even political agendas consider different social networks as a way to contribute to peace and sustainability (e.g., United Nations and UNESCO). The academic world has also studied this subject and has observed great interest in the tributes generated by this business [5,11,12], such as in the creation of knowledge (creative commons) noted by Libert and Spector [13]. The uses attributed to this are still to be discovered, and it is thought that social networks, as an altruist form of creating shared knowledge, have made a step forward towards influencing users [14], denunciating, creating movements such as the "15M" or the "Arab Spring" and *currents* of thought. They are even thought to influence the way we access knowledge [15], specifically in tourism, for which social networks are seen as a *storage area* for information on destinations [16]. The collection of information has been random, concentrating on protected areas that actually have an active presence on social networks. In a more detailed way, the goal of this study is to analyse ten specific protected areas around the world: the Northern Territory in Australia, Yellowstone National Park and the Everglades National Park in the United States, La Tigra National Park and the archaeological park of Copan Ruinas in Honduras, the Alhambra Palace in Granada, Doñana National Park and Teide National Park in Spain, Parks Canada and the Archaeological Park of Jerash in Jordan. The results of this study focus on the outputs and consequences of these protected spaces' presence on a given social network. For this study, we have chosen Facebook, as it possesses the greatest number of users.

The questions that have guided this analysis attempt to identify the strategic elements of communication, paying special attention to those that could improve the interpretation of heritage through social networks. The investigation that is developed hereafter examines the qualitative aspects of these strategies rather than the quantitative aspects. This study has enabled us to identify the different types of transmitted messages, and we have been able to reach conclusions that shall be presented as a series of recommendations. It is hoped that these conclusions provide new knowledge. Lacome [17] brings forth some fundamental questions that can be adapted to this case of study. They focus on knowing if the idea that is transmitted is relevant to the audience or if the opportunities of connection, both intellectually and emotionally, are organised so that the idea can be adequately developed.

3. GOOD USES OF STRATEGIC COMMUNICATION IN SOCIAL MEDIA AND NETWORKS: KEY FACTORS FOR THE ANALYSIS OF INTERPRETATIVE MESSAGES OF PROTECTED AREAS

The strategic communication emitted by a protected natural area is aimed at offering an efficient interpretation that will be vital in achieving the highest level of quality for the visit and for overall experience. It also aims to prove the possibility of forging a sustainable relationship between tourism in general and the protected spaces [18]. This strategic communication is established on the many strengths that it holds, but there are also several drawbacks. We will examine this matter first of all by studying the actual technological factors (Part 3.1); second, by distinguishing which factors concern the users in highlighting the intentions of online content managers and users as receptacles of messages (Part 3.2); and, finally, we will reveal the factors that actually make up the interpretative message (Part 3.3).

3.1 Social network factors

In this group of factors, we are able to identify intrinsic characteristics, such as communicative productivity or the spontaneous generation of derivative content due to the elevated use of social networks by a high number of users and their willingness to join and participate in social networks. Other extrinsic factors can also be added and are related to *avant-gardism* or the norms that are progressively established. Next, we shall describe some of the identified factors that are related to the interpretative messages; this will enable us to begin thinking about social media and the way protected areas use social networks.

3.1.1 Communicative productivity

The communicative productivity of a message is made up of two fundamental elements: efficiency and effectiveness. Messages emitted in social networks carry out basic functions of communication with a higher level of efficiency that any other type of medium, bearing in mind that the receptor, as well as the user, subscribes voluntarily to the message, as opposed to being forced to submit to commercial communication. The interpretative messages that are emitted from a protected area take advantage of the voluntary aspect of users' subscriptions, which is translated through: (i) a high level of attention and, (ii) a predisposition to receiving positive messages. Another characteristic that increases the performance of communication through social networks is the prolongation of the message that is the result of continual adhesion over time (to the message and to the network). If a user is the *follower* of an institution, he or she remains loyal and receives its information. There exists a special type of loyalty between these two, which is difficult to achieve through other means of communication. As for the phase that precedes the visit to the protected area, social networks act by creating expectations and are considered an important tool that can be used to both reinforce their image and approach the area's attributes and the attractive elements. Many authors have studied the *projected image* that the visitors perceive before they even visit a place. Baloglu and McClearly [19] call this the stimulus factor or image-forming *agents* (concept introduced by Gartner [20]). Andrade [21] calls this the creation of an image of a destination through the internet. Therefore, in this phase of creating expectations, social networks contribute to checking information that is collected by other media, such as websites, blogs, or other digital media either *offline* or *online*.

Another element of communicative productivity is users' contribution to the generation of content. Kaplan and Hanlein [14], Xiang and Gretzel [16] and Munar and Ooi [22] speak of content creation thanks to social network users engaged in spontaneous creation (initiated by the receptor himself or herself), which can be directed (offered by the community manager) around a topic or specific information. In relation to the efficiency of the message, we are able to observe the capacity of the user to actually *prescribe* and recommend the protected area. This characteristic of communicative productivity can be measured due to the tools that are integrated into social networks, such as "Sharing", "Like" on Facebook and the "RT" (retweets) or "+1" on Twitter[15], which can share, approve or report information. This gives users the ability to amplify and fine-tune a message through their comments, converting them into ambassadors for the area and enabling them to recommend and *prescribe the use* of the protected space. In this sense, the intensification of the message is another characteristic that could be measured due to the number of comments that the publication receives in the media. This is what happens on Facebook through different "Comments" or on Twitter with a number of "RT" (retweets) or "Favourites". A comment on a photo or a publication emitted on the natural area is considered to have a high impact and is very important for getting users to adhere to the message and strengthening the message through #hashtags or labels on a specific topic. Comments made by users highlight that they are a valuable source of information that can be used to increase the visibility of the protected area because they multiply the effect of communication and have direct influence on other users (comments are sometimes given more credit than official sources themselves).

The loyal behaviour of users (friends and followers) in social media towards the emitter of information can be observed thanks to comments posted by users. Users often turn out to be loyal to specific destinations even before they visit the protected area. Here again, specific tools are available that give users the opportunity to get free feedback, which the protected area can make use of as a permanent observatory enabling it to assess the impact of the emitted publications and also to manage its *on-line* reputation.

---

[15] Tascon [23] affirms that Retweets (RT) indicate the number of times that a tweet has been shared; Favourites show the number of users that back-up a tweet.

3.1.2 Ubiquity vs technological and digital breach

The use of social networks is not exclusive to the phase that precedes the visit to the protected area; it is maintained throughout and after the visit. The introduction of mobile devices, such as *smartphones* or *tablets*[16] means that users can communicate and be informed during the trip from the moment they conduct research until they actually visit the protected area. Although it is important to know that many protected areas do not have enough technological devices or amenities, these would be necessary to establish a constant connection. Far from being a threat, this could be considered an opportunity to make visitors' experience even more enjoyable. Another element that is considered paradoxical is information that is over-complicated and excessive. It is true that information is necessary, but the excessive quantity of emitted information and the speed at which it is emitted degrades its quality and its efficiency [24], which creates negative impressions due to users' inability to reply to the comments and statements that they receive.

3.1.3 Trends, Enjoyment and Addiction

Attractiveness and the message itself are two characteristics highlighted in Ham's interpretation [8], which can be included in the transmission of information through social networks. As for enjoyment, social networks present themselves in a format that makes entertainment possible; they are a way for users to enjoy themselves because they share space (time and an *area*, as such) with their family and friends. As for the message, it is a fundamental part of the communicative offer and is considered the central *axis* around which the rest of emitted information revolves.

3.1.4 Target group

Tilden [25] first recommends directing the message to a specific public, considering the interests of the target and the different levels of learning. In the case of social networks, it is possible to reach the public after having sorted the different networks into different types, thus creating a typology that sorts them in relation to the audience that the messages target [14]. We can state the case of Tuenti, which is strategically directed to a young audience up to 18 years of age. It is a strategic choice for protected areas to be present in social media, have the ability to transmit their interpretative messages of conservation and make the public more aware from the earliest ages. Other social networks, such as Facebook and Twitter, manage to reach out to people of all ages, from 13 years to 55 years, which means that their target audiences are more mature.

3.2 Factors for users

According to Morales [26], "the interpretation of heritage is a creative process of strategic communication, which produces intellectual and emotional connections between the visitor and the resource that is interpreted, being able to generate its own meaning, for this specific resource, so that it can be appreciated and enjoyed by all". This part of our study is dedicated to users in order to highlight how information is transmitted from the emitter or the community manager and how it is received, or modulated and modified by the receptor. Identification of effective interpretation in representations seeks to obtain intellectual and emotional connections through advice on the correct and positive

---

[16] According to e-Marketer, the number of users of applications for intelligent/smart mobile phones and tablets continues to increase; it is estimated that 21% of the internet users between 35 and 44 years old use tablets in 2012. . https://www.emarketer.com/Coverage/Mobile (acceded 20 February 2013).

interpretation of heritage through social networks. It seems appropriate to ask the following question: how can we adapt social networks to interpretative messages?

3.2.1 Intellectual connections

Ham [27] states that the transmission of information through social networks should be guided towards the production of meaning and the asking of questions that require assessable facts. These high quality, exclusively selected contents must try to go towards the more concrete aspects of the question. The selection and design of themes and of messages are its key elements; they are considered *crucial material* for persuasive communication, which is necessary to connect with users and to highlight the value of protected spaces in social media. The brief amount of time dedicated to reading or watching, and most of all, the time that each user dedicates to each *impact* that internet users receive on social networks, is usually quite brief. Because of this, exposure to content must be done in such a way that it strengthens the impact on the receivers of the message in order to "provoke" [27] users.

Figure 1: Facebook publication of Yellowstone National Park, United States

The intellectual connections are linked to the receptor's inherent "baggage", where the intrinsic elements such as their beliefs, values and prejudices [28] can potentially be a barrier to learning new knowledge, acting as noise and interfering in the communication process. This is why using intangible heritage through stories, anecdotes, sayings and famous expressions about the place increases audiences' interest and promotes a positive image of the structure. It is also possible to use pictures that promote peace, relaxation and wellbeing in order to establish intellectual connections.

In this same way, the interpretative icons that seem familiar, friendly, and easy to understand [29] will enable the park to achieve a positive connection with users. This is the case of Yellowstone National Park, whose Facebook profile shows a picture clearly referencing one of the park's most famous icons: buffalos at the beginning of the spring exodus (fig.1).

The use of social networks to create events and as a tool for launching strategic questions is a way to achieve a cognitive connection with users because it invites them to think about the subject. The following example comes from the Aula Natura Marsh of Gandia

– Valencia (fig.2), which launched an advertising campaign to let people know the sustainable actions that followers usually carry out in the park.

Figure 2: Facebook publication of the Aula Marsh of Gandia (Valencia)

3.2.2 Emotional connections

Emotions can be created and planned thanks to the interpretation and consciousness programme during a visit to the destination. This is how and where the strongest feelings can be produced but also how they can be maintained after the experience a posteriori. It is possible to emulate non-physical stimuli that can persist and be maintained with the help of other visual, textual or audio elements that evoke thoughts and memories, thereby reminding users of emotions generated during the visit.

Saiz et al. [24] speak of positive factors that promote memories in general by distinguishing between the storage of memory in our minds, such as the use of certain music or a strong and famous slogan, which make evoking or recuperating a specific memory much easier. Even visual elements or the repetition of pictures featuring children, sweet animals or puppies serve as factors that enhance the activation of users' attention. Universal concepts, also called "fingerprints of time,"[17] can be used to refer to events in our lives, such as our childhood, adolescence or adult life. These are valid resources that can be used to achieve an emotional connection. Emotional information is subjective and can be stimulated and/or improved through pictures and text that the picture corrects. Social networks such as Instagram or Flickr provide an opportunity to publish and share pictures, and they enable people to share images that evoke positive feelings. Furthermore, music and pictures customise the theme and link it to universal concepts. *Storytelling* techniques through which a story connects with people's emotions are adapted to audio-visual formats for social networks, such as YouTube, to achieve the emotional stimulus that interpretation programmes offer. YouTube is the favoured social network for creating thematic channels on protected areas in an audio-visual format, regardless of whether these spaces are administered by actual managers as official sources or those that, spontaneously or not, are created by specific individuals. Martinez [6] speaks of information and communication technologies (ICT) and interpretation of cultural heritage, which requires use of technology and evolution from a monologue to a dialogue. Social networks allow users to feel good, satisfied, listened to, understood, and

---

[17] Reference to Werner Fuchs writings, in his testimony titled "Neuromarketing Kongress" (2009) http://www.marketingdirecto.com (accessed 22 March 2013)

supported. This characteristic of *out of anonymising,* of personalisation, enables users to be called upon by official sources in order to get their attention and to increase the capacity for creating these emotional connections and boosting users' ability to remember.

3.3 Factors of the interpretative message

Assuming that the natural protected spaces are also present in social networks and that they are dedicated to launching messages, the question that now arises is: what type of messages do they emit and what is their purpose?

As we stated previously, the finality of interpretative messages is to provoke changes in individuals' attitude and for them to participate actively in conserving natural, cultural and historic resources. In this way, the goal of interpretation is to communicate a message that expresses the harmony that must exist between the human being and the environment [7]. The factors that intervene in the structure of an efficient message through social networks will be studied in this part. This is when we can think about the formal concepts that must be contained in the message for the strategic communication and offer a few recommendations. We are therefore able to offer a typology of messages, distinguishing between conservationists' attitudes or behaviour, as well as institutional and descriptive information about the resources.

3.3.1 Presentation of the message

In social media, it is difficult to establish a logical sequence for presenting contents as they would happen at the moment of the visit during an exhibition or of a centre of interpretation. The immediateness of the emitted messages generally causes them to be presented in an isolated manner. These messages sometimes rely on important and relevant events, such as what could be considered universal commemoration days, e.g., the Day of Water or the Day of Marshes. This can be used as a reason to make people think about this subject. In the same way, the use of short stories that have a great amount of information and real life testimonials of people who are involved in managing a protected space are an interesting way to present an interpretative message.

When *designing* strategic communication, the interpretative messages require the most important aspects in first and final terms because according to investigations on learning and memory [29], the retention level of messages is higher than if the messages are emitted through an intermediary. The capacity to influence the cognitive level of users will be higher inside a process of behavioural modification. It is convenient for the speech to be well organised in order to achieve explicit conclusions that are easy to understand and increase the efficiency in regard to influencing users' attitudes. It is important not to forget that there are other types of methodologies for analysing interpretative messages [18] and, as we commented previously, that the effectiveness of the message depends on the objectivity of the public, the type of theme and the surrounding in which the user *receives* the message. It is convenient to consider that the influence on users is limited and that it is not always possible to obtain significant results. In the physical space, stimulants are stronger and more present in the area, and the audience is more attentive to comments that the interpreter or guide makes. Certain situations can distract the attention of users. In social networks, the behaviour of internet surfers is not lineal, and we are able to observe different types of attention *spikes* and deviations of their attention due to other types of information and instant messaging channels that all link-up. As we commented previously, users possess other types of intrinsic filters, such as their beliefs, values or prejudices [28] that constitute obstacles for natural access to information. Meanwhile, if the communicative impact is brief but manages to persuade users during a future visit, or entice pro-environmental behaviour [31], the effect can be considered successful.

3.3.2   Unique interpretative scheme

This concept has been used in other disciplines, such as advertising, and it refers to the sale of a product using a unique means of selling (unique selling scheme). When this concept is applied to thematic interpretation, it refers to the development of a unique sales *pitch* or a theme that contains a unique concept to transmit to reach visitors' sensitivity by creating an intellectual or an emotional connection. This effect in social networks is obtained by directly demanding critical aspects and bringing forth thoughts on the subject owing to important questions that create interest and awareness around the main topic. The extensive use of data *dilutes* the main theme and causes it to lose effectiveness. This is why the transmitted information must be relevant in order to increase the capacity of retaining the message.

3.3.3   Anchoring the text and the image

The visual elements that accompany the text help *anchor* the message and attribute its literal content; this increases the efficiency that an isolated picture or image alone would not have. It is a fact that the literal component does not leave much room for imagination, but in the meantime, when verbal information is accompanied by powerful imagination, pictures and images will offer the possibility of immediately recalling the natural area. It is possible to present an idyllic landscape, but if we do not know what part of the world the landscape belongs to, or where it can be found, the efficiency that is reached will be quite low. The use of other means to back up the message, such as graphics, notes, illustrations and even cartoons, will be useful in order to amplify the action of the non-verbal messages.

3.3.4   Yin Yang communication

This concept refers to the emission of opposite messages that have contrary components, in a way that the audience can get to know the attributes, strengths and benefits but also the negative aspects of the subject. This is why we use *auto references* that make the audience the protagonists and that make them, through interiorising, reach the goal of the communication. Other resources that are used are the questions that make a person think about the determined preservationist aspects.

3.3.5   Types of messages

The revision of the emitted messages by the protected spaces that were selected for this study took us into anterior investigations [4] that then drove us to identify four types of messages:

- Conservationist messages that transmit the identity, values and appreciation of a specific place and are opposed to stereotypes (exotic values). Most of the identified messages attempt to highlight the importance of heritage owing to messages that call out to their own attractiveness.
- Messages of attitude and behaviour that express the fears and preoccupations for conservation and preserving a place by revealing its fragility. These messages usually include an ethical behaviour code. Its aim is to influence the attitude of

visitors, but this does not mean that they are always achieved in the long term. It would be considered a great success if it was achieved at short term.

- Institutional messages that are aimed at highlighting the management and investments in the place.
- Descriptive information on the heritage but that lacks messages including a big amount of data and information about natural and/or cultural heritage, without concentrating the dialogue on any specific aspects.

4. DATA ANALYSIS

Concerning the qualitative aspects, we can observe the presentation of a message through names or references to the seasons of the year, or to specific meteorological phenomena. This is the central theme of many messages that are launched, e.g., Teide National Park (also in Spain), which informed us on the intense rainfall that occurred. The change of season is also a basis for creating messages, and we shall mention here the case of the Everglades that recently published a photography of a palm tree with an explosion of seeds, or Doñana National Park, which made a reference to the pictures of migratory birds flying over marshlands.

Other news is also frequently mentioned, such as the organisation of parks in relation to managing public use by opening a new pathway or closing off a road due to forest fires, which is what Everglades National Park did. There are reminders of special events, such as the announcement of courses for guides and interpreters at Teide National Park, or the organisation of thematic open *"days"*. Facebook allows users to be invited to a particular event and even to request confirmation of their assistance in the event. In this same way, the celebration of universal days is a reason for natural areas to communicate through social networks. An example is the information provided by the Aula of Natura Marsh of Gandia to celebrate the Worldwide Day of the Marshlands, or a publication by Teide National Park for the day in which respect is paid to the scientist who founded the centre. The celebration of meetings or reunions of veterans and park volunteers are also transmitted and communicated in this way by creating an important sentimental and emotional link, which the Everglades National Park managed to do.

Another resource that is frequently used is testimonials; the Everglades uses videos that feature park employees, i.e., rangers who share information on a given subject through *conservationist messages*. In this way, La Tigra National Park shows one of the guards' chores, for example alerting people to the high risk of forest fires. Telling stories about a specific species or a type of plant easily captivates the attention of readers, which creates an emotional and intellectual connection that reinforces the capacity to remember the experience. The Archaeological Park of Jerash (Jordan) used this technique to talk about a type of plant that flourishes in springtime by creating a *story* about the use of this plant at wedding ceremonies in this country and its symbolism.

As we have previously mentioned, excessive information can provoke *noise* and interferences and can reduce the efficiency of communication. The consequence of this is that communication is weakened. The use of pictures to attract the users' attention towards flora and fauna can be identified or observed in every single communication channel that is used. Now, in order to make direct use of the topic, some text must accompany the pictures to have an *anchoring* result. Teide National Park uses this visual resource extensively by launching thoughts and reflections that feature short texts to illustrate a picture, which are useful for grasping the attention of a specific theme or topic to bring forth new knowledge. On the other hand, the Everglades clearly exploits this opportunity, using small paragraphs of text that offer information on the published picture. If the picture is not referenced, or does not indicate the type of flora or fauna, the interpretative effect will therefore be diluted and weakened.

In relation to the different types of messages, which shall be commented hereafter, most of the identified messages give information about a park's management aspects in relation to its public use. To look back on what we described earlier, Teide National Park classifies descriptive information on different types of flora throughout its monthly publications. Yellowstone National Park publishes a daily question, "Tuesday Trivia," to talk about a theme or give information on specific resources that can be found in the park. Other protected areas emit messages related to attitude and behaviour, as in the case of La Tigra, which explains actions such as the gathering residues or examples of users' incorrect use of the natural protected area. Institutional messages can remind users of other events, such as the opening of a new walkway or the most common types of investments that are made in the park, e.g., the Alhambra Palace of Granada or Parks Canada. Lastly, we shall add that the messages that are clearly identified as having a conservationist vocation, (for instance the case of La Tigra) are also quite common; this increases the necessity of working on the physical elements present in the park that favour the transmission of values and culture taking place *in situ*, the point of which is to boost their diffusion.

5. CONCLUSIONS AND FINAL RECOMMENDATIONS

Social networks are currently at an early stage, rapidly and continuously evolving. This provides an opportunity for us to create and develop new practices with the goal of offering new ways to understand the different uses that can be achieved thanks to this type of media (social networks) and the advantages that it includes when planning the strategic communication of protected areas. Social networks have countless advantages confirming the high potential that they possess given the voluntary union of users. The manager of a protected area must make use of these *adherences* as a platform in order to send out messages that will help achieve the transmission of values, knowledge, respect and safeguarding of the park. Throughout our study, we have detected some good examples, which confirms our initial idea that constituted the foundation of this study. Nonetheless, we have also detected some examples in which it does not always turn out so well, which is due to information to be transmitted in a disorganized way and without a clear interpretative message.

One of the other advantages is the users' contribution to comments as a tool for measuring the quality of a protected space. This potential, for the manager of the area, constitutes an important source of *retro-feedback*. New social networks appear on a daily basis, and although we think that subscription to them is free, in the end it is not, given that being present on this type of media means dedicating a certain amount of funds and resources, an online content manager or *community manager* who can properly attend to internet users' needs, and, most of all, activating and stimulating the social network and giving it interesting content. The emitter of information, in our case the conserved area, must consider planning these *ways* of communication such that users' presence and the general activity on these networks reaches the communicative productivity that was intended. The manager of online content could be compared to an interpreter or tour guide; the responsibility that is given to them is very high because they (the content managers) are converted into a virtual *cicerone* of the preserved area. The competence that is attributed to the online content manager requires that a tourist guide training programme be developed and improved with technical content but also with communication techniques that are necessary in order to reach the communicative productivity of interpretation through these social networks.

Finally, we shall say that the general study of social networks, and the specific study that this report has conducted, is focused on strategic communication in particular, as it recollects information from different disciplines in order to integrate synergies and present a holistic vision. In this sense, we have taken a great number of factors into account: the advertisement aspect in the analysis of rhetorical figures and tropes that are used because of the character and nature of the messages, the necessary psychology in order to detect and identify the intellectual and emotional connections that users perceive, and the marketing that is focused on the consumers' behaviour and the promotion of the protected spaces. Thanks to this study, we have been able to supply new knowledge of social media networks in the realms of conception, design and diffusion of the interpretative messages in preserved spaces. This makes it possible to contribute to the *educational environmental* objectives that these fragile areas are trying to accomplish. These goals are supposed to be the perfect balance between preservation and enjoyment of nature.

REFERENCE LIST

[1] Di Placido, A., (2010). Interactividad usuario-usuario y redes sociales online en el sector turístico. *Turitec*, 2010.

[2] Shin, L.,& Yoo, E.E., (2012). TripAdvisor.com vs NYCGO.com: Evaluation of functional components of generalist and specialist tourism websites. *Information and communication Technologies in Tourism* 2012, 121-131.

[3] Diaz Luque, P., Guevara Plaza, A. J. & Anton Clave, S. (2006). La presencia en Internet de los municipios turísticos de sol y playa Mediterráneo y Canarias. *Turitec*.

[4] Teruel, M.D. & Viñals, M.J. (2010). Internet application for strategic communication, tourism and local communities in relation to heritage. UNESCO. *World Heritage Papers.* 31, 55-60.

[5] Celaya, J. (2008). La empresa en la Web 2.0. Barcelona. Ediciones Gestión 2000.

[6] Martinez Sanz, R. (2012). Nuevos retos comunicativos para los museos y centros de arte. El valor del portal web. *Boletín de Interpretación* nº26. Mayo 2012

[7] Morales, J (2000). Técnicas para la interpretación del patrimonio. Caracas. UPEL-IIPC.

[8] Ham, S. H. (1992). Interpretación Ambiental, Una Guía Práctica. *North American Press, Colorado.*

[9] Aranguren, J., Diaz, E., Moncada, J., Pellegrini, N. & Diez de Trancredi (2000). La interpretación ambiental, camino hacia la conservación. *Revista de Investigación.* 46, 11-44

[10] Ham, S.H. & Morales, J. (2008). ¿A qué interpretación nos referimos? *Boletín de Interpretación* número 19.4-7.

[11] Dans, E. (2010).Lo que la presencia en Facebook dice de tu empresa. [blog] < http://www.enriquedans.com/2010/07/ (accessed 21st march 2013)

[12] Castelló, A. (2010). Estrategias empresariales en la Web 2.0.) Editorial Club Universitario. San Vicente (Alicante)

[13] Libert, B. & Spector, J (2008). Nosotros es más inteligente que yo. Desate el poder de sus colaboradores. Editorial Gestión 2000. Barcelona.

[14] Kaplan, A.M. and Haenlein, M. (2010). Users of the world, unite! The challenges and opportunities of Social Media. *Business Horizons* nº 53, 59-68

[15] Santamaria Gonzalez, F. (2008).Redes sociales y comunidades educativas *TELOS. Cuadernos de Comunicación e Innovación* | Nº 76

[16] Xiang, Z. & Gretzel, U., (2010).Role of social media in online travel information research. *Tourism Management*, 31, 179-189

[17] Lacome, B. (2008). ¡Analice esto¡ Analizar y medir la efectividad interpretativa. *Boletín de Interpretación.* Nº 19.

[18] Moscardo, G., (1996). Mindfuld Visitors: Heritage and Tourism. *Annals of Tourism Research,* 23 (2), 376-397.

[19] Baloglu, S. & Mcclearly, K.W. (1999). A model of destination image formation. *Annals of Tourism Research*, nº 26 (4), 868-897.

[20] Gartner, W.C. (1993). Image formation process. *Journal of Travel and Tourism Marketing*, nº2 (2-3). 191-215

[21] Andrade Suarez, M.J. (2012). El uso de Internet como fuente de información turística; propuesta metodológica para el análisis de la imagen del destino. *Papers de Turisme,* 52, 44-62.

[22] Munar, A.M., & Ooi, Can-Seng, 2012. What social media tell us about the heritage experience?. *Copenhagen Business School center for Leisure and Culture Services.*

[23] Tascon, M., (2012).Twitter en Escribir en Internet. Fundeu BBVA. Galaxia Gutenberg : Círculo de Lectores. Madrid.

[24] Saiz, D., Baques, J. & Saiz, M. (1999). Factores que pueden mejora la codificación de los mensajes publicitaros. ¿una cuestión de memoria implícita o de memoria explicita?. *Psicothema*, 11 nº 4, 891-900

[25] Tilden, F. (1977). Intepreting Our Heritage (3rd Edition). Chapel Hill. University of North Carolina Press.

[26] Morales, J. (2008). La interpretación del patrimonio tiene que ver con significados". http://www.ilam.org (accessed 23 march 2013)

[27] Ham, S.H. (2011). La interpretación es persuasiva cuando el tema es convincente". *Boletín de interpretación.* 25, 18-20.

[28] Garcia-Lago, V. (2002). ¿Educamos En Prejuicios O Educamos En Valores?. *Educación y futuro: revista de investigación aplicada y experiencias educativas.*7

[29] Viñals, M.J., Morant, M, Teruel, M.D. (2013). Confort psicológico y experiencia turística. Casos de estudio de espacios naturales protegidos de la Comunidad Valencia (España). Inédito

[30] Aguado-Aguilar, I., (2001). Aprendizaje y Memoria. Congreso Virtual de Neuropsicología. *Revista de Neurología*, 32 (4). 373-381

[31] Ham, S.H. (2006). La psicología cognitiva y la interpretación: síntesis y aplicación". *Boletín de Interpretación número.* 15, 14-21.

Analysis of the supply of accommodation at an inland tourist destination in the context of a general recession

E. PÉREZ-CALDERÓN
University of Extremadura, Faculty of Business and Tourism Studies. Spain
F. J. ORTEGA ROSSELL
University of Extremadura, Faculty of Business and Tourism Studies. Spain
P. MILANÉS-MONTERO
University of Extremadura, Faculty of Economics. Spain

ABSTRACT

Given the current crisis situation, tourism development in Extremadura has been stagnant. In comparison with the most tourist cities in Spain, the competitiveness of this region is based on more significant price adjustments. There is a cultural and natural heritage in its main cities enough to increase its tourist attraction. At the same time, these cities could let the visitors discover other resources which have been unknown until this time. As a consequence of that, the average stay of the visits and the revenues could be increased.

1. INTRODUCTION

One of the characteristics of tourism today is that it increasingly not only gives travellers the opportunity for leisure and rest but is also a source of sensations, of experience for enrichment both on the personal and cultural levels. Tourism today is much more than travelling and spending more than three days away, whether for work or leisure reasons [1].

The historical, cultural, natural and gastronomic attractions found at the destination together with the complementary offer that goes with them makes a whole, allowing both travellers and tourists to experience local traditions, residents' customs, lifestyles and food and drink, and this whole constituting the main reason for choosing one particular destination rather than another, because these factors are decisive when it comes to deciding on or programming our leisure time.

Extremadura is a Spanish region located in the southwest of the Iberian Peninsula. It comprises the two largest provinces in Spain: Cáceres in the north and Badajoz in the south, where gastronomic, natural and cultural resources abound, nature having been generous in both provinces, giving it spectacular natural spaces, especially in the north and south west of the region, the biosphere reserve of the Villuercas-Ibores-Jara, where there are excellent conditions for observation of the animals which spend the winter in the region, and the Tagus International Natural Park being outstanding for their grandeur.

This region is a unique tourism setting, which has been helped by its secular isolation from industrialised production systems, and the development of an economy traditionally based on primary sector activities, which has allowed not only its wilderness but also its regional traditions and identities to be conserved. It is mainly its towns, such as Badajoz, Cáceres, Trujillo, Plasencia and Mérida (the Target Cities), where the most interesting gastronomic initiatives and developments based on the quality of its basic materials and variety of the traditional cuisine of Extremadura are encouraged and concentrated.

It is precisely f this group of Target Cities which also concentrates the highest number of attractions of a historical, artistic and cultural nature and which have the greatest possibilities for the design and introduction of "food routes" promoting the excellence of the gastronomic raw materials from smaller places nearby. In addition, they can be entrance points through which both to access countryside and scenery and for observation of the fauna existing there and around [1].

Extremadura's inland tourism offer has the necessary characteristics to be able to compete within Spain as a gastronomic tourism destination, having ideal resources in sufficient quantity to attract and satisfy travellers and tourists wanting authentic experiences as well as an infrastructure, the technical and human resource capable of supporting and sustaining a genuine leisure offer.

Its gastronomic heritage is famous and of recognised prestige because of the quality of its wine and ham, more present in the province of Badajoz than in the Cáceres, especially outstanding being Monesterio ham, the cheese from Casar de Cáceres and la Serena, and the wine of Ribera del Guadiana. The region's cultural heritage is extraordinary, this being more important in the province of Cáceres than in Badajoz, especially what is called the "world heritage triangle" consisting of the UNESCO-listed towns of Cáceres, Guadalupe and Mérida.

Extremadura is a region with a large cultural heritage concentrated in its urban centres, which have increased their supply of hotel accommodation as the presence of tourists at the different destinations has risen. In addition, the area's lavish, splendidly conserved nature is perfect for rural and natural tourism, propitiating the opening of numerous camps and rural lodgings, mainly concentrated in the north of the province of Cáceres and in the south of the province of Badajoz.

2. THE HOTEL ACCOMMODATION SUPPLY IN EXTREMADURA

The development of tourism in Extremadura over the last 30 years can be divided into two important stages, the first taking place over the last two decades of the 20[th]century, during which a progressive increase took place in the number of lodgings and hotel beds in the main cities and now consolidated tourist destinations, at the end of which, in 1997, the number of existing establishments was 405, providing 13,600 beds, hotel staff being very small in general with certain exceptions.

In the second stage, in the first decade of the 21st century, not only has a great increase in the number of beds occurred (33,000 units), but there has also been dispersion over the entire region as a result of the change occurring in the estimation in which tourists hold the region, Extremadura having changed from being a tourist area of transit between the north and south of Spain, i.e., a stopping-off point on journeys towards other final destinations, and become a final destination in itself, these tourists being attracted by the rich and various tourist attractions of the region, both cultural and natural, as described above, combined with their economic development and promotional campaigns carried out (See Figure 1).

Description and analysis of the present hotel industry in Extremadura through its recent development in the five most touristic cities in the region, the Target Cities, is essential to be able to decide how to adapt to the existing infrastructures in the region to the needs inherent to a destination basically orientated towards cultural and nature tourism.

Extremadura is a huge region with countless tourist resources capable of attracting the attention and curiosity of travellers and even motivating them to visit it as a destination, because of their excellent quality and conservation and because it has the necessary services to be able to compete with other destinations located in Spain's interior.

The evolution and characteristics of the hotel infrastructures decisive in evaluating one destination's capacity for success compared with similar ones, so we have analysed hotel size range, occupation rate, seasonal variations, quality and capacity for creating employment and wealth and compared them with other tourist destinations to determine the position the tourist cities of Extremadura have in relation to other Spanish cities classified as inland destinations, up to a total of 33 tourist cities in Spain (Reference Cities), including the great tourist destinations of Seville, Granada, Santiago de Compostela, Saragossa or Salamanca [2].

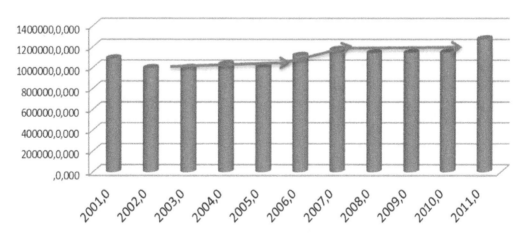

Figure 1: Travelers hosted in Extremadura: 2001-2011

In order to achieve our goals we have basically used the official data from 2008 to 2011 provided by the EOH (hotel occupation survey) carried out by the INE (national statistics institute), together with data and reports prepared by the Spanish tourism institute and others provided by the government of Extremadura[3-5].

2.1. Present hotel range

By in-depth analysis of the size and growth of the hotel range in the five Extremadura cities studied in this research, after carrying out classification of them, we have observed an important relationship between the size of hotel establishments and quality levels.

According to the figures published by the EOH at the end of 2011, the hotel range of the Target Cities included 116 establishments and 8,300 beds. Tourist accommodation has grown by +14.86% since 2008, a figure which corresponds to a total of 15 new establishments (See Figure 2).

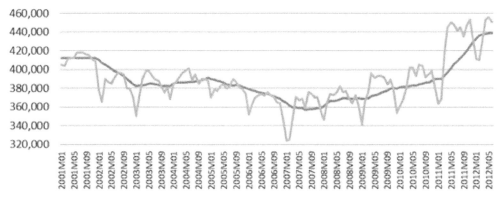

Figure 2: Hotel establishments (2001-2012)

The figure shows san increasing trend in hotel size in the Target Cities, however this must be considered small compared with the hotel sizes in the Reference Cities. In 2011, the average size for the Target Cities was lower than the average of 54 hotel establishments in the Reference Cities showing the great difference in variation separating the Extremaduran destinations from the main Spanish tourism destinations like Seville, Granada or Salamanca.

Analysis of a longer length of time in our study showed that the investment effort made continuously from 2008 on in Cáceres, Trujillo, Mérida and Badajoz was much greater than that made in the other destinations. These cities of Extremadura increased their hotel range in relative terms between 5% and 7%, above the growth rates of other tourist destinations with a larger hotel range.

The opening of new hotel establishments has increased the number of beds available. In the period from 2008 to 2011, the total increased by 926 beds, which corresponds to an annual growth rate of +2.91%. The study carried out has shown that the size of hotel establishments not only improves productivity, but also their rating, i.e., the larger the establishment, the higher the category.

Aggregating the data for each province shows that, in 2011, while the number of new high-end hotel establishments was fifty-six in the province of Badajoz, the number of establishments of that type opening in the province of Cáceres was thirty, this classification including hotels of more than three stars. Apart from this high end offer, and there are a hundred and sixty-one hotels and apart hotels in the intermediate range of three stars and below. Finally, the total of lower rating establishments is two hundred and seventy-nine, this category including hostels and pensions.

The data analysis carried out shows that the changes occurring in the hotel range in the Target Cities in the last four years have contributed towards better rating of the offer in both provinces, although it should be pointed out that the change has been more intense in the province of Cáceres. However, the size of high rating hotels in the province of Badajoz is greater than the size of hotels in the same range in the province of Cáceres. Finally, in this respect, at the end of 2011 the greatest number of hotel beds offered in the group of Target Cities, the most touristic towns in Extremadura, is provided by high-end establishments, which are providing and maintaining high quality levels for both travellers and tourists.

2.2 Length of stay and consumer preference

The average length of stay characterising the tourist cities of Extremadura shows that the number of nights spent there is lower compared with the average for the other inland made continuously tourist destinations in Spain. In fact, the average stay in the latter is 1.75 days compared with 1.5 days in Extremadura.

The trend is for average length of stay at inland destinations to decrease. Within that trend, a larger drop is recorded for Extremadura, with a negative rate of -0.9% compared with the -0.6% of the other inland tourist destinations.

Length of stay is not homogeneous for the target city group, for example, the longest stays are had in the towns of Plasencia and Badajoz with an average length of 1.75 days per visitor. The length of stay in Cáceres and Trujillo is 1.5 days and Mérida has stays below that. Simple reflection on the average length of stay of visitors to a particular destination allows it to be said that length of stay is in itself an efficient indicator for evaluation of consumer preferences for certain cities over others.

In accordance with this, assuming that average stay is a figure which shows the success of a tourist city and the appreciation of its accommodation offer, it is concluded that the tourist industry of Extremadura is not competitive, because, by having short stays, travellers announce lower preference compared with other inland destinations.

This lack of competitiveness, shown by over 4 percentage points compared with the data related with the preference for other inland destinations, confirms the need to promote the group of touristic cities in Extremadura on the tourist market with a differentiating product and an attractive, innovative, proposal, promoting as well as its well-known cultural heritage in its urban centres new gastronomic initiatives, which should include the "food routes" associated with high quality food products such as Iberian ham and sheep's and goat's cheese as a first class competitive opportunity, stressing the uniqueness of these areas and their identifying elements.

Analysis of the data collected related with preference for the Target Cities based on length of stay, clearly shows a falling trend for Mérida and Cáceres, Mérida being the "least favourite" of the Reference Cities group. On the other hand, the trend for Badajoz and Plasencia is rising, while Trujillo is stabilised. This behaviour would be related with the greater preference and average length of stay in the destinations of Badajoz and Plasencia because of the innovativeness of their proposals and greater presence on regional and national tourist circuits. On the other hand, Mérida, Cáceres and Trujillo, being more consolidated and perhaps more mature destinations, are suffering a certain stagnation largely caused by the economic crisis undermining the presence of tourists from the region of Madrid and Andalucía [2, 6].

The study carried out of the occupation rate, the average price and the revenue per room (Revpar) shows that the occupation level of the Target Cities has been considerably lower in comparison with the of the inland destinations especially with those located on the Atlantic coast (See Figure 3). In spite of its low opposition on the Spanish ranking at the regional level all the destinations in Extremadura except Badajoz increased their occupation level. The flow of travellers who visited Extremadura in the four years studied underwent an increase quantifiable as 50% compared with 2008. The increase undergone by the Target Cities has changed the relative weight of travellers who visit them out of the total tourism in 2008 by 2 percentage points, arising from 4% to 6%.

According to the EOH (INE, 2011), the international tourists visiting Extremadura are approximately 15%, most of them coming from Europe, although extra-European visitors had over 40,000 overnight stays in 2011.

The most important foreign markets for Extremadura are the Portuguese and French markets, followed by the German market. The latter is largely attracted by the reached varied natural and cultural heritage characterising the main tourist cities of the region, as well as the good weather and gastronomy. The affluence and presence of Belgian and Dutch tourists in Mérida is frequent, with a total of 6,606 and 5,101 of the night stays respectively, distributed over the target city group.

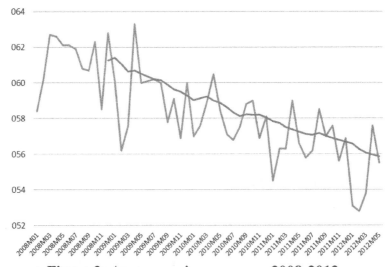

Figure 3: Average price per room 2008-2012

It is highly significant that tourism from outside the European Union, American and Japanese, is very low, not to reaching consistent shares of the Extremaduran market, although on the other hand a continuous slight increase of 2.4% a year, is observed, showing that it would be desirable to make greater efforts in promotion and communication in these foreign markets taking advantage of the region's huge potential.

Employment in the tourist industry is connected with the productivity of the local accommodation system. The figures analysed the related with employment generated by tourism in the Target Cities show that over the last four years the level of employment generated has fluctuated negatively by -0.18%, compared with -0.41% for the group of Reference Cities, 0.32% in inland destinations.

The seasonal nature of Extremaduran destinations does not affect employment, which indicates that tourism is a very stable sector in the economy and society. Cáceres is the city which employs the highest number of people in the hotel industry with a proportion of 33% of the total of jobs in the city. The other Extremaduran tourist centres have lower figures, Plasencia and Trujillo being in last place with unemployment rate close to 14%.

3. CONCLUSIONS

The tourist sector plays an important stimulating role in the economy and society because of its ability to create employment; in Extremadura, the development of tourism has provided various social and economic benefits, complementing farming revenues in rural areas, keeping the population in the area, as well as improving residents' quality of life.

The opening of new establishments in the Extremaduran cities has caused some adjustment of staff levels, reducing their average size which is in general still small, with an average of 11-12 employees in Mérida, Cáceres and Plasencia and 9-10 in Badajoz, Trujillo being the destination with the smallest average staff with seven employees.

Analysis of the data shows that the tourist accommodation industry in Extremadura, although small compared with other groups of destinations with which it has been compared, maintains levels of efficiency and profitability from the point of view of the employment generation. It can be concluded therefore that the tourist sector is not only strategic in the region but also has great potential to exercise more weight in the regional economy and is deserving of greater attention, effort and dedication from all economic agents, especially groups of interest to tourism activities of a priority nature, with the aim of improving and competitiveness with other inland destinations, increasing the amount of activity and the level of employment using the huge potential offered by the efficient management of the rich cultural heritage, nature and gastronomy existing in the region of Extremadura.

REFERENCE LIST

[1] Ortega-Rosell, F. J., Sánchez-Martín, J. M. & Hernández-Mogollón, J. M. (2012). *La gastronomía de alta gama, de lujo o de calidad como eje potenciador del turismo cultural y de sensaciones en Extremadura*. Ed. Fundacion Caja Extremadura, Cáceres.
[2] Guisan, M.C. & Neira, I. (2001).Un análisis econométrico del turismo hotelero y extra hotelero en las regiones y provincias españolas. *Estudios Económicos Regionales y Sectoriales*. 1, 2-18.

[3] Instituto Nacional Estadistica, INE (2011). *Encuesta Ocupación Hotelera (EOH).* Available on: http://www.ine.es/inebmenu/mnu_hosteleria.htm. Visited 07.06.13.

[4] Instituto de Estudios Turisticos, ITE (2011). Survey *of cross-border tourist movements (Frontur).* Secretary of State for Tourism, Ministry of Industry, Trade and Tourism. Annual Report, Madrid. <http://unef.es/2011/07/informe-anual-2011/> Visited 10.07.12.

[5] Government of Extremadura, Gobex (2010). *Strategic plan for tourism in Extremadura 2010-2015.* < http://extremadoriiturismo.blogspot.com.es> Visited 10.12.12.

[6] Lopez, J. & Lopez, L. (2006). La concentración estacional en las regiones españolas desde una perspectiva de la oferta turística. *Revista de Estudios Regionales.* 77, 77-104.

Pensions and employment in Spain: An alternative view

E. FEBRERO
University of Castilla-La Mancha. Department of Economics and Finance. Spain.
F. BERMEJO
University of Castilla-La Mancha. Department of Economics and Finance. Spain.

ABSTRACT

This chapter focuses on the analysis of the employment required to produce the consumption basket that retired people can purchase with their state pension. First, using input-output techniques, we calculate the labour requirements for 22 industries in Spain during the period 1995-2005. Next, we present some scenarios to estimate how many jobs would depend on pensions in 2030, when the viability of the Spanish pension system is under threat. We consider the payment of pensions not as a burden on a given full employment economic system, but as a source of job creation when an economy operates below full employment.

1 INTRODUCTION

Longer life expectancy and lower fertility rates will lead to an ageing population in almost all countries over the world [1]. This is quite a complex phenomenon which, apparently, should be welcomed because it will stabilize the world population, providing some additional benefits at the individual and household level (e.g. lower child mortality and a better quality of life for ageing people). Nevertheless, these benefits will come at the expense of a negative shock on labour markets, a rising bill for long-term care and medical assistance for the ageing population and a growing financial imbalance of pension systems.

In this chapter, we focus on an alternative angle of the ageing process. We aim at quantifying the total amount of labour that is required, directly and indirectly, to produce the basket of goods and services purchased by old age pensioners (OAP from now on) since it is expected that there will be more beneficiaries in the near future.

We shall focus on the Spanish economy because it is, after Japan, the one with the largest life expectancy and the lowest fertility rates (together with Italy and Germany) in the whole world, and also because this economy suffers from a secular problem of massive involuntary unemployment. We proceed in two stages. Firstly, we measure the labour requirements to attend OAP's demands in 1995, 2000 and 2005, using input-output techniques. With this analysis, we estimate not only the total amount of employment created by pensions but also its disaggregated distribution at 22 industries. In the second stage, we build up some scenarios in order to estimate how many jobs will depend on pensions in 2030 in Spain, when the viability of the Spanish PAYG -acronym for Pay-As-You-Go– pension system is under threat, as baby boomers begin to retire.

The novelty of our research rests on the fact that we consider the payment of pensions (in a defined benefit, PAYG scheme) as a source of job creation when an economy operates below full employment, and not as a burden on an economy operating around a full employment position. This allows us to consider the viability of a PAYG scheme from a radically different perspective. Obviously, we implicitly adopt a Keynesian theoretical standpoint, where the amount of employment and economic activity is governed by aggregate demand, employment does not constrain economic growth and the endogeneity of money makes it possible to spend first, and then create the resources to pay back this debt. It is from that perspective that we consider that pension spending shall play a relevant role in the allocation of the labour endowment in the near future.

Notwithstanding, it should be clear to the reader from the very beginning that we are simply considering scenarios. This is not the same as considering a pension-led economy for example. We are aware that the financial viability of pension schemes is complex, and we only deal with a particular aspect of the issue at stake in this investigation.

The structure of this chapter is as follows. In the second section, we justify our theoretical viewpoint. In the third section, the model used to measure total labour requirements is described. The fourth section contains the projection of different scenarios. In section five we give a summary of the main empirical results. Section six concludes.

2 PENSIONS IN A DB-PAYG SCHEME: A BURDEN FOR THE SYSTEM OR LARGER AGGREGATE DEMAND?

Most societies all over the world are ageing. Table 1 shows that this is a rather generalized phenomenon. Ageing is a source of concern in countries like Japan, Korea, Spain or even Germany; a little less worrying in France or the UK, and is less relevant, though important in relative terms, for countries like China, Brazil, Mexico or the USA.

Defined benefit, pay-as-you-go pension schemes (DB-PAYG onwards) are the most generalized pension systems across market economies[18].These schemes have been subject to criticism for a long time. In the 1970s (e.g. Feldstein [2]) it was argued that funded systems could contribute to a larger rate of accumulation and a larger level of output. In essence, the argument was that DB-PAYG systems lead to lower saving rates and, additionally, to a lower labour supply, because agents consume more and work less in the

---

[18]It is common knowledge that the term PAYG means that current contributions fund the payment of current pensions. In other words, it is a non funded pension scheme. And the term defined benefit, DB, means that the stream of pensions received by an OAP, once the first pension is determined according to past earnings, is not constrained by the amount of contributions made by this agent during the working life.

present if they know that they will get a pension from the government when they retire (a moral hazard problem).

Table 1. Old age dependency rate: Population aged above 64 over population aged between 20 and 64. Source: Statistics OECD

	Germany	Brazil	Korea	China	Spain	France	Japan	Mexico	UK	USA
1995	22.66	7.96	8.33	9.07	22.47	23.22	20.95	7.29	24.50	19.38
2005	28.37	9.31	12.65	10.74	24.36	25.23	30.51	8.19	24.22	18.58
2015	32.29	11.59	17.64	13.21	27.90	29.32	43.98	10.05	27.99	21.96
2025	39.90	16.26	29.10	19.49	34.06	35.74	51.23	14.27	32.47	28.68
2035	52.98	22.93	46.80	29.60	46.66	41.92	59.20	21.46	38.50	32.77
2050	55.79	35.90	72.05	37.99	67.54	45.60	76.36	34.30	40.52	33.30

From the early 1990s onwards, the main criticism shifted towards the financial unsustainability of unfunded systems, due to demographic shocks: falling fertility rates and a longer life expectancy would lead to an extremely ageing population, where young workers would be urged to make unbearable contributions in order to run a balanced social security system. Otherwise, public debt should cover the social security deficit, far beyond any bearable limit (see, for instance, Feldstein [3]).

Table 2. Gross public pension expenditure (%GDP). Source: European Commission, 2012. Table 2.5, p. 101 [4]

	Germany	Spain	France	Italy	UK	Norway	Austria
2010	10.8	10.1	14.6	15.3	7.7	9.3	14.1
2020	10.9	10.6	14.4	14.5	7	11.6	15.1
2040	21.7	12.3	15.2	15.6	8.2	13.7	16.5
2060	13.4	13.7	15.1	14.4	9.2	14.2	16.1

Proposals for reforming pension systems have evolved from asking for a radical shift towards funded systems (for instance, Feldstein [1]), to parametric reforms on existing DB-PAYG (delaying the retirement age, reducing benefits, etc.), combining the already existing unfunded pension schemes with capitalized systems, funded with voluntary and mandatory contributions and privately managed [5].[19]

A theoretical element underlying both the criticisms to DB-PAYG and the reform proposals mentioned above, is the assumption that economic systems naturally gravitate around a full employment position and that the level of activity is ruled by the endowment of resources –and their distribution–, a given set of inter-temporal preferences and a set of production techniques (i.e. the *Say's Law* holds). Consequently, a DB-PAYG is viewed as a burden which distorts the *normal* outcome which, presumably, should be attained

---

[19] In some countries (e.g. Italy, Sweden amongst others), notional defined contribution accounts have been introduced since the 1990s. This is an unfunded pension scheme which takes into account financial-actuarial adjustment systems (see, for instance, Vidal-Meliá *et al* [7], or Gronchi and Nisticò [8]), in order to make PAYG systems financially sustainable.

according to the conventional neoclassical general equilibrium approach (a good reference for this can be found in Goodfriend [6]).

However, from a Keynesian position which, as everyone knows, holds that advanced market economies are constrained by the demand side (see Keynes [9]), pensions in a DB-PAYG are not a burden but a source of additional demand (see Cesaratto [10]). Indeed, pensioners' spending on consumer goods can put in motion productive resources which, otherwise, would have remained idle. For this strand of thought, the limit to the sustainability of a pension system rests on the full employment clause.

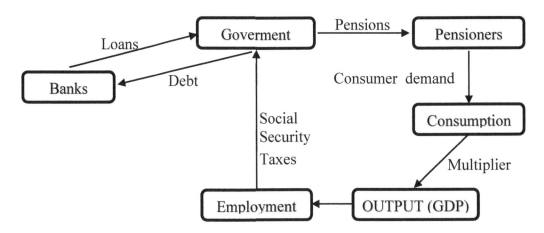

Figure 1. Keynesian view of a DB-PAYG scheme

This figure encapsulates, at a rather simplified level, the (post-)Keynesian view of the working of a DB-PAYG pension scheme [11], especially chapter 4 for further details).

According to the (post-)Keynesian strand, banks create money *ex nihilo* when they make loans (the endogenous money view: Moore [12]) to fund the government payment of pensions; next, these pensions are spent on consumer goods. This is additional aggregate demand which, according to the Keynesian principle of effective demand, will lead, through the multiplier, to a larger level of output. This growing output requires more employment which, in turn, pays taxes and social security contributions which go back to the government as revenue so that it can cancel its initial debt to banks.

We are aware that the Neoclassical and the Keynesian strands of thought hold opposing views and cannot be reconciled. The former stresses the burden of pensions, whilst the latter gives prominence to their role within aggregate demand. Without dismissing the fact that ageing poses a serious challenge to modern societies, we believe that measuring the labour required to attend pensioners' demands in the future will contribute to a better understanding of the problem. The Keynesian approach, we believe, provides a better ground for the analysis that we carry out in this investigation, because it links employment to pensions with a causality running from the latter to the former.

Table provides an estimation of the expected rate of unemployment for some European countries in 2060. We see that, for instance, in the Spanish or French cases, employment could be higher simply by increasing the employment rate or, else, by reducing the unemployment rate expected in the very long term (NAIRU).

Table 3. Long-term projections. Employment and unemployment. Source: European Commission, 2012, Table 1.7, p. 85 [4]

	Employment rate (16-64)		Unemployment rate (16-64)	
	2010	2060	2010	2060
Germany	71.2	74.0	7.2	4.8
Spain	58.6	71.8	20.2	7.3
France	63.8	69.2	9.4	7.3
Italy	56.9	61.7	8.5	7.3
UK	69.4	72.4	8.0	5.6

To sum up, there is no magic wand which we can wave to solve social security problems. The ageing of the population will lead to a burden on the whole society but it also will create new markets. As pointed out in the introduction, and we hope this will become clearer in the next section, we estimate the total amount of labour required to produce the goods that cover the demand by pensioners in the present and also for the next 20 years, setting aside the problem of the funding of social security. The reader should not think that we are dismissing the question of the funding of the system. Here we just consider "only one side of the coin" as we believe that both questions, funding and pensioners' spending can be singled out. We think that this is an interesting exercise as it provides us with quantitative information about one of the aspects of ageing and the economy.

3 MEASURING EMPLOYMENT TO COVER THE PENSIONER'S DEMAND OF CONSUMER GOODS

In this section we describe how we compute the total amount of domestic labour required to produce the goods and services which can be funded with OAP's pensions. It should be clear that we are not computing the labour required to produce *all* goods and services demanded by retired people (they may fund part of their consumption demand with past savings, for instance), neither do we assume that the rate of savings on pensions is nil, nor the total amount of labour required to produce a given basket of commodities. What we intend measuring is total domestic labour embodied in the consumption basket corresponding to the mass of OAP's pensions.

This empirical exercise requires three groups of data, two of them provided by symmetric input-output tables -the total domestic output required to produce the basket of goods and services corresponding to pensions, and the labour required to produce such a basket – and the third one –the basket of consumer goods demanded by workers and OAPs– provided by the Household budget survey.

Input-output tables are based on the condition that total supply equals total demand. It is common knowledge, in formal terms that:

$$[3.1] \quad X + M = A^d \cdot X + Y^d + A^m \cdot X + Y^m$$

Where X is a (row) vector of total output domestically produced and M is also a vector, now of total imports; on the other side of the equality sign, we have intermediate inputs domestically produced, final demand covered with domestic output (final demand includes final private and public consumption, investment and exports), imported intermediate inputs and final demand covered with imports. A^d and A^m account for matrices of technical coefficients.

We are interested in the domestically produced total output, needed to match pensioners' demands, which we shall call X^p:

[3.2] $\quad X^p = A^d \cdot X^p + d^d \cdot a_n \cdot X^p + c$

In the expression above, d^d is the (column) vector accounting for the consumption basket of domestically produced goods and services which can be purchased with the average monetary wage corresponding to one unit of labour; a_n is the (row) vector of direct labour requirements, and c is the (row) vector of the consumer goods which pensions can buy.

Expression [3.2] above can be arranged to yield:

[3.2.*bis*] $X^p = \left[I - \left(A^d + d^d \cdot a_n\right)\right]^{-1} \cdot c$

Finally, the vector of total labour embodied in the mass of pensions is given by the expression:

[3.3] $\quad l_T = a_n \cdot < X^p > = a_n \cdot [I - A^*]^{-1} \cdot < c >$

Where the symbols $<>$ denote a diagonal matrix and $A^* = A^d + d^d \cdot a_n$. The detailed meaning of the terms in the expression above is as follows:

a_n is a (1 x 22) vector of labour requirements, directly required to produce one million euros of sectoral output. In formal terms, this is defined in the literature as:

[3.4] $\quad a_n = a_{nf} < p >^{-1} = l < X >^{-1} < p >^{-1}$

Here, a_{nf} is the vector of direct labour requirements per unit of output in physical terms, l is a (row) vector of direct sectoral employment (number of people employed in each industry), X accounts for a vector of total sectoral output, and p is the set of commodity prices. By and large, we do not have separate information on prices and quantities of output, but of millions of euros of sectoral output. Therefore, a_n measures the labour directly required to produce one million euros of output for each industrial branch.

$[I - A^*]^{-1}$ is the usual Leontief inverse, where I is the identity matrix and A^* is a socio-technical matrix which has been described above.

Obviously, the wage per unit of labour *w* can be divided into consumption plus saving:

[3.5] $\quad w = p \left(d_f^d + d_f^m\right) + s$

Where *w* is the money wage of a unit of labour, p is a (row) vector of prices, d_f^d is a (column) vector which accounts for the physical quantities of domestically produced consumer goods in the wage basket, d_f^m is a (column) vector of imported physical consumer goods in the wage basket, and s is the part of the money wage which is saved.

Hence, we can define the second matrix, in physical terms, as:

[3.6] $A_f^c = d_f^d \cdot a_{nf}$

And in monetary terms:

[3.7] $A^c = <p> A_f^c <p>^{-1}$

Then, in monetary terms:

[3.8] $A^* = A^d + A^c$

And in physical terms:

[3.9] $A_f^* = A_f^d + A_f^c$

Again, we do not have separate information on prices, on the one hand, and quantities, on the other hand. What we really have is:

[3.10] $A^* = <p> A_f^* <p>^{-1}$

Hence, when taking into account prices and quantities separately, the Leontief inverse is:

[3.11] $[I - <p> A_f^* <p>^{-1}]^{-1} = <p> [I - A_f^*]^{-1} <p>^{-1}$

Finally, the diagonal matrix $<c>$ stands for the consumption of OAPs (measured in monetary terms), which is funded exclusively with their pensions, under the assumptions that the rate of savings on pensions is nil and all consumer goods in the OAP's consumption basket are produced domestically. In formal terms:

[3.12] $<c> = <p> \cdot <c_f> \cdot R$

[3.13] $b = p \cdot c_f$

With $<c_f>$ being the basket of consumer goods, in physical terms, which one pension can purchase, R is the number of OAPs and b is the average (yearly) pension per pensioner (a scalar).

Expression [3.3] can be written as:

[3.3.*bis*] $l_T = a_{nf} <p>^{-1} <p> [I - A_f^*]^{-1} <p>^{-1} <p> <c_f> \cdot R$

This expression makes clear for the reader that, although we do not know how many physical units are consumed by OAPs, because we do not have separate information on prices and quantities, the vector of total labour required to produce these consumer goods is independent from the set of prices. Therefore, we can make comparisons between the labour requirements in two different periods of time without deflating.

4 PROJECTING SCENARIOS. LABOUR REQUIRED TO DEAL WITH PENSIONERS' DEMANDS IN 2030

Our purpose in this section is to take into consideration what *could* happen in 2030, regarding the amount of employment required to cover pensioners' demands. We are aware that 20 years is a very long period of time. Hence, we build up some scenarios in order to quantify how much employment, and in which industries, would be required to attend the demand of consumption by pensioners in 20 years time, when baby boomers begin to retire, under different circumstances. This exercise requires a lot of assumptions, and it would be rather *naïve* to believe that we are predicting what is going to happen in the distant future with a high degree of accuracy. Therefore, it should be clear that we do not aim at estimating how much employment will actually depend on pensions in the future, nor do we take for granted that the social security system will remain the same, despite the expected demographic shocks.

We believe that this exercise is useful because it can shed some light on the impact of changes on the structure of the Spanish economy, caused by demographic changes.

Briefly, the assumptions are the following. Firstly, the vector of vertically integrated labour coefficients is assumed to change according to this pattern:

$$[4.1] \quad v_i(t) = v_i(0) \cdot (1 + g_{v(i)})^t$$

Where $g_{v(i)}$ is the yearly average rate of the fall in the vertically integrated labour in sector i.

Secondly, we consider three scenarios, regarding the evolution of the pension benefit per pensioner:

- In the first scenario, the pension per OAP remains constant.

- In the second one, the pension per OAP increases 20%, but its composition remains the same as in 2005.

- In the third one, the pension per OAP increases 10% on average, and its composition changes according to the pattern of change shown between 1995 and 2005:

$$[4.2] \quad c_i(t) = (1 + 0.1) \cdot \theta_i \cdot c(0) \cdot (1 + g_{c(i)})^t$$

Where θ_i stands for the relative weight of commodity i in the basket of consumer goods of a pensioner in the base year.

And thirdly, we consider two scenarios with respect to the number of pension beneficiaries:

- In the first one, the number of future beneficiaries will be given by the percentage of OAPs out of the total amount of people aged 65 or above in the base year, multiplied by the number of aged people in 2030.

- In the second scenario, we increase the percentage used above by 10%.

We justify these scenarios because of the following reasons:

- In 2030 the number of pensioners who had previously worked in the agriculture or retail trade industries will decline. In these industries, the contribution to social security has been traditionally lower than the average and, therefore, the pension due has been lower. Consequently, the average pension is expected to increase in the future.

- The viability of a pension system can be under threat for, at least, two reasons: (i) the number of OAPs increases beyond a threshold, relative to young people, and (ii) the rate of unemployment outstrips a certain level, leading to insufficient contributions to the balance the payment of pensions. In the present analysis, we just focus on the first problem, so that we shall assume a system gravitating around a full employment position. This assumption entails more people contributing during a longer period of time and, therefore, higher pensions (in Spain there is a defined benefit pension scheme).

5 MAIN EMPIRICAL RESULTS

We began this section by describing how vector c of OAP consumption, presented in expression (3.2) above has been obtained. First, we extract the information related to the consumption of pensioners from the consumption of the total number of households included in the Input-Output Table. Then we get these data by defining specific filters related to age, main activity and earnings over the sample of roughly 24.000 households of the Household Budget Survey provided by the INE.A similar procedure is applied to obtain the consumption of the workers that produce the goods and serviced demanded by the pensioners.

This calculation of the consumption has been performed taking into account two important requirements: (i) the deduction of VAT, since we have to know the expenditure of pensioners in basic prices to make it compatible with the Input-Output Table data and (ii) the discounting of the imputed rents included in the values of housing and real estate, since the nature of this expenditure would distort the labour input linked to this activity. The left hand side column of every year in Table 4 shows the monetary value of OAP's consumption referenced to 1995.

Table 4. Monetary value of pensioners' consumption (in prices of 1995).
Source: Authors' calculations

	C_{ret} (€)		
	1995	**2000**	**2005**
Agriculture and Fishing	132,43	194,64	168,72
Mining and Quarrying	2,90	0,77	4,21
Gas and other fuels for households	101,56	177,13	217,32
Electricity	132,85	119,97	142,35
Water supply	31,17	42,62	51,26
Food, Beverages and Tobacco	647,67	726,46	752,54
Clothing and Footwear	160,98	163,01	183,37
Chemicals and Intermediate Products	137,84	49,59	118,53
Machinery and Tools	78,74	73,64	124,30
Furnishings, Equipment and Services for Maintenance	93,28	91,65	71,47
Housing and Real Estate activities	77,03	81,78	139,24
Purchase and Maintenance of vehicles and fuels	110,87	140,74	153,82
Wholesale and retail trade	920,81	1.202,49	1.159,17
Restaurants and Hotels	904,92	1.109,37	1.014,62
Transport and Communication	314,94	363,37	260,78
Insurance and Financial Services	232,63	357,70	407,29
Business Services	56,29	86,01	121,96
Public administration	25,63	35,10	40,45
Education	33,19	26,41	31,64
Health and Social Work	201,14	258,00	416,98
Recreation and Cultural Services	303,73	481,48	577,80
Private households with employed persons	168,49	187,08	229,67
Total	**4.869,07**	**5.969,01**	**6.387,49**

Broadly speaking, although the OAP basket reflects a fairly balanced composition during the observation period, the expenditure increases considerably in most of the activities, which is consistent with the ageing process that is taking place in Spain. As a result of this demographic change, the number of pensioners raised by 10.38% from 1995 to 2000 and by 3.07% from 2000 to 2005 and, consequently, the economic activity related to the consumption of the elderly also expanded at a similar pace.

Once we know OAP and workers' consumption, we proceed to estimate the total amount of labour required to produce such a basket of goods and services, as stated in equation [3.3]. Table 5 includes the total labour required to produce the pensioners' consumption basket and its percentage over the labour linked to the total output.

Table 5. Employment associated to pensioners' consumption.
Source: Authors' calculations

	1995		2000		2005	
	L_{ret}	% L_{ret} s/tot	L_{ret}	% L_{ret} s/tot	L_{ret}	% L_{ret} s/tot
Agriculture and Fishing	93.072	8,93%	86.443	9,09%	81.295	9,20%
Mining and Quarrying	2.599	5,27%	1.631	3,93%	1.251	3,37%
Gas and other fuels for households	1.081	7,72%	969	7,18%	999	7,46%
Electricity	4.033	8,35%	3.040	8,08%	2.112	7,82%
Water supply	2.747	10,03%	3.511	10,77%	4.108	10,84%
Food, Beverages and Tobacco	42.880	10,66%	45.802	11,10%	46.733	11,11%
Clothing and Footwear	23.863	7,33%	24.516	6,93%	20.913	7,79%
Chemicals and Intermediate Products	35.047	3,47%	33.703	2,69%	35.318	2,78%
Machinery and Tools	8.191	2,14%	8.723	1,79%	7.422	1,72%
Furnishings, Equipment and Services for Maintenance	10.479	6,59%	13.585	5,97%	11.622	5,23%
Housing and Real Estate activities	27.451	2,15%	38.896	2,08%	57.126	2,18%
Purchase and Maintenance of vehicles and fuels	30.949	8,21%	28.785	8,02%	28.385	7,64%
Wholesale and retail trade	160.479	9,70%	211.985	9,98%	228.995	9,04%
Restaurants and Hotels	84.985	11,17%	122.786	12,33%	141.119	11,69%
Transport and Communication	57.035	7,16%	56.683	6,66%	58.035	6,10%
Insurance and Financial Services	41.960	12,09%	32.272	9,04%	32.342	8,82%
Business Services	33.225	4,68%	50.586	4,56%	70.014	4,46%
Public administration	5.116	0,42%	8.855	0,68%	9.272	0,74%
Education	15.623	2,25%	19.947	2,39%	20.831	2,20%
Health and Social Work	28.002	3,60%	36.630	4,18%	47.906	4,31%
Recreation and Cultural Services	46.236	8,80%	64.985	8,33%	76.419	8,09%
Private households with employed persons	66.077	15,77%	67.782	16,73%	90.450	19,04%
Total	**821.131**	**6,30%**	**962.114**	**6,14%**	**1.072.669**	**5,97%**
Pensions paid to N>65 / GDP		**3,95%**		**4,65%**		**4,24%**

Finally, Table 6 presents the results of the employment projections for 2030, where the three columns on the far right hand side account for three hypothetical scenarios, which are briefly described as follows.

Table 6. Labour requirements projections for 2030. Source: Authors' calculations

	L_{2005}	L_{2030}		
		S1	S2	S3
Agriculture and Fishing	81.295	38.304	50.561	46.351
Mining and Quarrying	1.251	145	191	177
Gas and other fuels for households	999	60	79	77
Electricity	2.112	322	425	383
Water supply	4.108	1.986	2.622	2.465
Food, Beverages and Tobacco	46.733	31.983	42.217	38.348
Clothing and Footwear	20.913	9.050	11.946	10.830
Chemicals and Intermediate Products	35.318	43.800	57.817	50.960
Machinery and Tools	7.422	1.463	1.931	1.808
Furnishings, Equipment and Services for Maintenance	11.622	33.717	44.507	38.778
Housing and Real Estate activities	57.126	67.478	89.071	84.562
Purchase and Maintenance of vehicles and fuels	28.385	7.084	9.351	8.646
Wholesale and retail trade	228.995	245.323	323.826	296.509
Restaurants and Hotels	141.119	318.788	420.800	380.867
Transport and Communication	58.035	60.736	80.171	70.396
Insurance and Financial Services	32.342	2.256	2.977	2.818
Business Services	70.014	26.776	35.345	34.169
Public administration	9.272	4.319	5.702	5.340
Education	20.831	47.564	62.785	55.912
Health and Social Work	47.906	14.310	18.889	18.180
Recreation and Cultural Services	76.419	26.749	35.309	33.694
Private households with employed persons	90.450	63.159	83.370	76.946
Total (Average)	**1.072.669**	**1.045.374**	**1.379.893**	**1.258.217**

Scenario 1 assumes no changes in the consumer basket nor in the ratio between pension beneficiaries and people aged 65 or older in 2005. Only the number of pensioners changes *pari passu* with the number of people aged over 64.

Scenario 2 gives information about the number of workers required to produce a pensioners' consumption basket with the same composition as in 2005, though 20% more expensive and a ratio between pension beneficiaries over the population older than 64 which increases by 10% with respect to 2005.

Scenario 3 accounts for changes in the composition of the pensioner's consumption basket according to the trend estimated between 1995 and 2005, as well as a 20% increase in the *size* of the pensioners' consumer basket and a 10% increase in the ratio between pension beneficiaries and population older than 64 with respect to 2005. Under the assumptions of Scenario 3, labour increases a little less than in Scenario 2. Labour figures are relevant in Restaurants and hotels, Wholesale and retail trade and, to a lesser extent, Private households with employed persons.

6 CONCLUSIONS

OAP spending accounts for a relevant percentage of total aggregate demand. Although total pension spending over GDP stands above 8% between 1995 and 2005, the ratio between OAP benefits and GDP is roughly one half of the above figure, the rest being pensions paid to people aged below 65, orphans, widows or disabled people. The total labour required to produce the OAP consumer basket is nearly 6% of total employment in that period of time. In 2030, the total amount of labour linked to OAP spending may increase to roughly 1.3 million people, depending on different assumptions on the generosity and eligibility of the pension system. We find particularly relevant increases in wholesale and retail trade, restaurants and hotels, and private households with employed persons.

REFERENCE LIST

[1]   United Nations (2012). Population facts, 2012/2 April, Department of Economic and Social Affairs, Population Division. Available at: http://www.un.org/esa/population/publications/popfacts/popfacts__2012-2.pdf (last accessed 20-05-2013).

[2]   Feldstein, M. (1974). Social security, induced retirement, and aggregate capital accumulation, *Journal of Political Economy*, vol. 82, 905-926.

[3]   Feldstein, M. (2006). The effects of the ageing European population on economic growth and budgets: Implications for immigration and other policies, NBER Working paper series. Working paper 12736.

[4]   European Commission (2012). The 2012 Ageing Report, Directorate-General for Economic   and   Financial   Affairs,   Luxemburg.   Available   at: http://ec.europa.eu/economy_finance/publications/european_economy/2012/pdf/ee-2012-2_en.pdf (last accessed 20-05-2013).

[5]   World Bank (1994). Averting the old age crisis: policies to protect the old and promote growth, Washington, D.C.: Oxford University Press.

[6]   Goodfriend, M. (2002). Monetary Policy in the New Neoclassical Synthesis: A Primer, *International Finance*, vol 5 (2), 165-191.

[7]   Vidal Meliá, C., Devesa Carpio, J. & Lejárraga García, A. (2002). Cuentas nocionales de aportación definida: fundamentos actuariales y aspectos aplicados. *Anales del Instituto de Actuarios de España* (Tercera época), vol. 8, 137-186.

[8]   Gronchi, S. & Nisticò, S. (2008). Theoretical Foundations Of Pay-As-You-Go Defined-Contribution Pension Schemes. *Metroeconomica* vol. 59(2), 131-159.

[9]   Keynes, J.M. (1936). The General Theory of Employment, Interest and Money. New York: Harcourt & Brace.

[10]   Cesaratto, S. (2002). The economics of pensions: a non-conventional approach. *Review of Political Economy*, vol. 14, 149-177.

[11]   Lavoie, M. (1992). Foundations of Post Keynesian Economic Analysis. Aldershot: Edward Elgar.

[12]   Moore, B. (1998). Horizontalists and Verticalists: the Macroeconomics of Credit Money, Cambridge. Cambridge University Press.

Ecotourism in Latin America, latest trends

C CARRASCOSA-LOPEZ
Universitat Politècnica, Management Department, Valencia, Spain
M SEGARRA-OÑA
Universitat Politècnica, Management Department, Valencia, Spain
A PEIRÓ-SIGNES
Universitat Politècnica, Management Department, Valencia, Spain
M. DE-MIGUEL-MOLINA
Universitat Politècnica, Management Department, Valencia, Spain

ABSTRACT

Ecotourism is the tourism based on nature protection. This sector has made a great progress in recent years and its rise is linked to the increasing environmental awareness at all levels. Latin America has a wonderful natural heritage and an incredibly rich biodiversity, its protection and conservation is certainly worth. It is intended in this article to review the recent literature in ecotourism. The purpose is to find out which the latest trends in eco-tourism are in different countries of Latin America, which problems are observed and what aspects can be improved.

1.- INTRODUCTION

Tourism is becoming one of the economic activities with greater development. Its importance is great for all economies, but it is especially so for developing countries because it is responsible for most of their international flight arrivals [1]. Competition in Latin America has increased in the tourism sector, due to the emergence of new destinations and the arrival of international tour operators as a result of the globalization process among other reasons. That is why is so interesting to analyze the factors that may influence its competitiveness [1].

There have been found different definitions of ecotourism in the academic literature, for example, ecotourism can be defined as tourism based on the protection of natural areas. It can be an alternative that allows profits basing on the preservation of the natural environment [2]. According to Sánchez & Ramírez [3], ecotourism is considered as the tourism whose principal purpose to travel is the contemplation of nature. Furthermore ecotourism can be defined as the environmentally responsible form of tourism, consisting in visiting natural areas for the purpose of appreciate, enjoy and explore the landscape, flora or fauna. It is distinguished from mere nature tourism by its emphasis on education and environmental conservation [4, 5]. This type of tourism is known by various names, such as bio tourism, environmental tourism, green, academic, ethno tourism, depending on to the aspect on which it focuses. Ecotourism still represents a small share of world tourism, although its importance is growing in recent years, and its growth rate exceeds that of conventional tourism [6]. Particularly in Latin America its development potential is great because of its richness and biodiversity [7].

Many authors see clear evidence of the relationship between the best nature conservation where ecotourism occurs, especially in protected areas, which is where this fact most frequently occurs [8]. It is also clear the relationship between environmental education and the existence of protected areas, it is important to create projects that help preserve the environment and lead to improvements in living conditions at the same time [9]. Ecotourism promotes environmental education and ecological values that help to improve the relationship of people with the environment [10]. This clearly shows the unequivocal relationship between ecotourism and environmental education [8].

The most common places where ecotourism takes place are rural settlements near protected areas. These areas attract tourists for their particular characteristics [3]. Ecotourism near protected areas increases employment opportunities for people living in their surroundings [11].

Ecotourism is recognized increasingly as a tool that simultaneously promotes conservation of nature and is capable of contributing to the local rural development as well [4, 7, 11]. Other authors recognize this as community based tourism, this type of tourism is responsible for strengthening the positive impact of tourism with nature, this improves the living standards of rural regions by developing the countries involving local people and allowing them to share the positive economic impact of it [11, 12].

It is also true that some dissenting opinions have been found, they question to some extent the results of certain ecotourism projects, especially in terms of improving conditions of the natural areas [8]. An example of this discrepancy would be the reductions that have suffered certain protected areas [4]. There have also been found studies about the effects of ecotourism in the Galapagos Islands, famous for hosting very attractive endemic animal species. According to them it is demonstrated that even well aware people disturb, the mere presence of humans causes direct reactions in the behavior of other species that may affect biodiversity [13].

The positive aspects of ecotourism are many, evidently it is worthwhile and interesting its promotion. Although its benefits are well received, it is also very interesting to know what are the improvement areas. It is for this reason interesting and advisable to look into environmental change associated with ecotourism, to assess its actual impact [4].

There are in recent years many initiatives focused towards ecotourism in many countries in Latin America. Let us study some of them to analyze their effects, observe its benefits and its possibilities of improvement.

The main objective of this study is this, a deeper understanding of ecotourism through the analysis of several ecotourism projects that have recently been carried out in different parts of Latin America. A better understanding helps better decision making to maximize the potential of ecotourism as a valid tool that promotes the conservation of nature in conjunction with the improvement of living conditions in the areas where it is practiced [7], although it is valuable not to forget to minimize those aspects with place for improvement.

2.- METHODOLOGY

The methodology used to prepare this article is the review of recent academic literature on ecotourism in Latin America. This study tries to find out what the current status of ecotourism in Latin American countries is. It compares the results of various ecotourism projects that we have been able to observe, and analyzes the possibilities for improvement. The comparison among them helps to find similarities and differences between them, but above all the most interesting is that it allows the development of ideas for improvement that can be very useful.

3.- COSTA RICA

Costa Rica is an eminently touristic country; the tourism industry is the most important source of wealth of its economy. Costa Rica is a pioneer in the development of ecotourism; its beginnings were in the 90s, though Costa Rica was demonstrating concerns of conservation of its natural wealth before. The exotic beauty of its natural environment makes Costa Rica one of the most sought paradises in Latin America, despite its small size has more variety of fauna and flora that United States and Canada together [4].

Although not all of its tourism is ecological, as there is a lot of sun and beach tourism, ecotourism is used as a differentiator value and the whole country is grouped with a natural destination image [4]. Costa Rica is considered as a leader in the development of ecotourism worldwide [14].

Costa Rica has a lot of natural attractions; this has allowed the development of a very wide range of ecotourism, from visiting a national park, the walk through the different types of forests, bird watching, alligators and exotic animal observing. The tourist can visit both coasts in the Caribbean an in the Pacific Ocean, where he can enjoy diving and observing reefs, dolphins, sharks, different types of fish, the turtle nesting. Tourists can walk among lush vegetation trails, visit waterfalls, cross rivers, climb volcanoes.
It is recommended to visit and stay in rural communities where people can participate in their daily activities. With regard to ethno, native villages can be visited to appreciate their customs and traditions, such as the observation of the culture and art of ethnic or Guamí Bribri in Puntarenas [14].

These activities in rural communities are generally promoted by different associations. Costa Rica´s government is aware if its benefits and supports the creation of local groups that support the sector such as cooperatives, women´s groups, conservation support groups and other different kinds of local development associations. Some examples of these associations is the Talamanca Association for Ecotourism and Conservation (ATEC) formed for the promotion of ecotourism in the protected area of Cahuita National

Park, Indian reservation CZK Koldi and Life Refuge wild Chamomile [10]. More examples can be given: ASEPALECO, Paquera divers, farmers settlement in Drake Plans, organized groups of Playa Grande or association of ecotourism ladies in Chira Island. These associations have been created to develop different environmental activities [14]. The existence of these associations and the interaction between them can facilitate the development of their skills and improve the utilization of their environment more efficiently [14]. These associations exist throughout the country, and it is observed that through them local population get benefits and simultaneously the negative impact of tourism is reduced [15]. An example of this is located in La Fortuna, where local products are promoted to improve increasing competition between them, thereby their quality is increased and therefore the local economy can grow in quality and quantity [15]. Another feature of these associations is that local people retain ownership of the land, even many residents maintain their agricultural activities alongside its tourist activity thus diversifying their income [15].

However, Costa Rican local communities do not always get the expected benefits of ecotourism [12], this fact causes opposition and rejection reactions by not being equally included in the distribution of benefits.

Government support to ecotourism is also great, there are several institutions responsible for monitoring environmental issues in conjunction with ecotourism: The Costa Rican Tourism Institute (ICT), the Ministry of Environment (MINAE), the National System of Conservation Areas, the Environmental Court, the National Environmental Technical Secretariat and the Environmental Court [4].

In Costa Rica does exist the degree in Ecotourism based in the University of Guanacaste. It is pioneer in Latin America, it began in 1991 with the aim of creating specialists in this field [1]. Its fundamental task is to contribute to the local ecotourism development in the country; its main objective is the promotion of the research in Ecotourism in order to identify the efficiency of the tourist farms trying at the same time to prevent the alteration of the environment. It is also involve in some exchange programs with the Polytechnic School of Chimborazo (Ecuador), the University of Guadalajara (Mexico) and the University of Bremen (Germany). Recently it has been created the Sustainable Tourism Observatory Guanacaste, responsible for supporting the creation of new projects.

However, in Costa Rica there are some studies that demonstrate the contradiction between the theoretical and the actual ecotourism, one clear example is the fact that some protected areas are losing ground, endangering biodiversity [4].

Precisely because the Costa Rican economy depends directly on tourism, authorities try to attract more and more visitors. International hotel chains recently settled in the country are promoting tourism of sun and beach, with a profile of visitors that generates more waste with a greater environmental impact that threating certain species, such as the Sapo Dorado of Monteverde, for instance [14]. This should be taken into account and properly assessed, the image of Costa Rica as a paradise could be damaged and the consequences of losing this status could be irreversible.

Another remarkable point is that the focus of ecotourism is mostly addressed to foreign tourists with high purchasing power, paradoxically Costa Ricans are often out of the ecotourism experience [4]. This should be evaluated and corrected, because it is a paradox that the inhabitants of a country do not benefit equally from their own bounties of nature.

4.- PERU

Peru receives about 1 million visitors a year, its archaeological wealth and its biodiversity are the main reasons [7]. The Historic Sanctuary of Machu Picchu is the main attraction, but it is noteworthy to highlight that approximately 70% of visitors travel at least to a natural reserve; the main ones are Manu, Paracas and Tambopata Nature Reserve [7]. It is also noteworthy Titicaca Lake, the highest navigable lake in the world, where unique varieties of fish and amphibians can be found.

Peru's positioning in the international context is clear, provides the historical sanctuary of Machu Picchu as a major international tourist attraction, its control is in the hands of international tour operators [11]. However, it is observed that Peru has ideal characteristics for the development of community tourism initiatives; it is recommendable the promotion of local communities participating in ecotourism projects [11]

There are different community ecotourism projects as Posada Amazonas, Refugio Amazonas, and Tambopata Research Center. Its benefits are obvious according to several authors, it increases the GDP, it is a tool to combat poverty, it preserves natural and rural areas and ethnic identity [11]. The case of Posada Amazonas is very interesting as an example of collaborations between indigenous community and tour operators. Both parts signed an agreement to work together and to share profits in a positive way [12].

However, there are various community ecotourism studies showing the great difficulties encountered by natives to manage this ecotourism projects [7], these same studies suggest the union in Joint ventures between local communities and specialist tour companies as the best option for management [7].

It is also recommended ecotourism development to be complementary and not a substitute of traditional agricultural activities [11]. Although these ecotourism projects have the potential to improve local living conditions should not be confused as a panacea that can solve all regional problems, as its capacity is limited [7].

The main criticism of existing ecotourism projects is the need to size them better, [7], for example visitors excess Machu Picchu needs revision because it is over-exploited [11].

There is also literature that criticizes how ethno-tourism is introduced, tourism related to indigenous populations. In the Lima Declaration, indigenous people are encouraged to become involved in ecotourism because it helps sustainable development of their communities. However, in the international Indigenous Tourism Forum, the Indians refuse to be the subject of tourism development, since they do not feel respected [16].

5.- ECUADOR

Ecuador has lots of ecosystems and many options for ecotourism. The most emblematic places are tropical Cuyabeno Fauna Reserve, protected in 1979, the national park Llanganates, and runner-Sangay Llanganates with a variety of flora and fauna, nominated as the first ecological corridor in Ecuador. The National Park El Cajas and in coastal Machalilla National Park[20] (See figure 1), which includes terrestrial and marine attractions. It should be noted that the first seeds started in the 70s in the Galapagos Islands when excursions to the islands were initiated with the aim of promoting knowledge and protection. Subsequently there have been developed several projects in the Amazon region.

Figure 1 Image of Machalilla National Park

A successful experience managed by indigenous is the one the Cofans manage in the northern jungle in Ecuador, its project is based on the supply of the environment to the visitors. It is managed by the Cofan members and the profits are used to fund the local organization to help them preserve their land [17].

There can be found examples of successful ecotourism projects managed by joint ventures, for example the Achuar community is running the project nearly on its own after a private company provided capital for building the lodge. This partnership worked very well for 10 years until the indigenous community got it transferred, when they got enough management skills [18].

However is noticed a lack of development and government support, and the creation of organizations to promote ecotourism. On the other hand internal stresses appear contrary to ecotourism, for example by the International Indigenous Tourism Forum, whereby indigenous reject tourism development because they feel invaded and not respected [2]. For example the case is being reviewed in the Galapagos Islands, famous for its flora and fauna virtually unique, and its numerous endemic species because the overhead of visitors is causing reactions in the environment [13].

---

[20] http://www.machalillanationalpark.com/machalilla_national_park.shtml

6.- COLOMBIA

In Colombia ecotourism is fairly recent, as well as awareness of the wealth of natural protected areas. Colombia is exceptional in biodiversity. This makes that ecotourism is considered as one of the main products to be developed in the coming years. The government is interested in developing ecotourism, because it can provide new economic opportunities associating the environment protection with the improvement of local population standard of life [5]. Therefore the government established the Unit of the System of Natural National Parks (UAESPNN) to help with the development of ecotourism [19] and also a web site with all the information[21] (See figure 2).

Nevertheless, the fact that a lot of territory is occupied by the FARC makes this development more difficult. The government doesn´t have the control over important areas of the country where ecotourism could take place.

There is no clear statement of the potential of ecotourism in Colombia as a consequence of the conflict, and the development of ecotourism will remain limited while the conflict is not solved [19]. The relationship between war an ecotourism in the national parks in Colombia has been deeply studied [20, 21].

Signing a peace agreement with the FARC will probably be the first step to be done in order to increase the government´s territorial control over important areas where Ecotourism could be developed.

Despite the conflict, there are some existing projects in free conflict areas, run by both government entities and private concessions and the results are positive. Although there are oppositions to its development because there are doubts how benefits are shared [5].

---

[21]http://www.parquesnacionales.gov.co/PNN/portel/libreria/php/decide.php?patron=02.0202

Figure 2 Website of National Parks of Colombia

7.- CONCLUSIONS

In Latin America there are many protected natural areas of exceptional richness, however there has been identified some place for improvement to achieve a better sustainable economic development of them.

The ecotourist profile has changed in recent years, now they demand better conditions of life in their stay, while enjoying its beginnings to the place of destination through rough roads [4], this has pushed infrastructure construction that can produce an irreversible habitat degradation.

The potential benefits of ecotourism in protected areas depends on the strategy to be applied, an essential factor to consider is to achieve awareness and local participation. Many of these farms are given to foreign concessions, it would be recommended the connection between the native communities and specialized tourism companies that can provide themselves with the knowledge, experience and awareness in order to better develop ecotourism projects

It would be necessary to discuss which tourism development model is most suitable from the point of view of its social and environmental impact, and assess what is best for the development of the local economy. In this debate all members involved should be represented, from public authorities to the private sector and the local population in general [14], combining local expertise along with tourism businesses contributes to a better distribution of wealth. [15]

Then it would be advisable to draw up an action plan articulated by the competitive advantages of the territory and its inhabitants. The goal would be the development of an ecotourism cluster to build on the local attractions, encouraging its conservation and enabling and encouraging a favorable competitive development, always bearing in mind which is the main differentiating factor, nature, based on maintaining its fundamental essence. The awareness of the nature which attracts tourism should be maintained [15], and any doubts should be avoided at all costs. In this sense several ecotourism farms should be resized to ensure their sustainability [7, 13]. The reinforcement of regulations to ensure that ecotourism development do not damage the environment is important [12].

A key element in promotion of Ecotourism values should be the university. The example of Costa Rica with the degree in Ecotourism based in the University of Guanacaste should be followed by other countries were this degree still doesn´t exist. With the involvement of university the creation of specialists in this field would be easier.

Another remarkable point is that the focus of ecotourism is mostly addressed to foreign tourists with high purchasing power, paradoxically Latin Americans are often out of the ecotourism experience [4]. Therefore is so vital to include as much as possible local people. More promotion of ecotourism values internally in education programs would be necessary.

The main conclusion that appears is that ecotourism should retain its essence, which is a model of sustainability, preserving ecosystems and satisfying local people improving their living conditions [5].

AKNOWLEDGEMENTS

The authors would like to thank the Spanish Economy and Competitiveness Ministry for its support through the research project ECO2011-27369.

REFERENCE LIST

[1] Arrieta Murillo, G., & Rivera Hernández, G. (2011) La Carrera de Turismo Ecológico de la Sede Guanacaste y el desarrollo del ecoturismo en La universidad de Costa Rica. *Intersedes*, 7, 41-53.
[2] Smith, R. (2010). *Manual de ecoturismo para la Amazonia ecuatoriana. Imágenes para un Nuevo Mundo*. Ediciones Abya-Yala. Sangolquí, Ecuador, 3rd Ed.
[3] Sánchez, V. B. & Ramírez, E. M. (2011). Desarrollo regional por medio de un cluster ecoturístico en la huasteca norte potosina. *Revista da Micro e Pequeña Empresa*, 2, 13-27.
[4] Alvarado, B. (2010). *Ecoturismo en Costa Rica: mito o realidad, la verdad.* Thesis, Master of Arts in Hispanic Language and Literature, Stony Brook University, The Graduate School, Stony Brook, NY (USA).
[5] Molina, C. D. M. (2011). Ecoturismo en Colombia: una respuesta a nuestra invaluable riqueza natural. *TURyDES. Revista de Investigación y desarrollo local,* 4, 1-6.
[6] Schulte, S. (2003). Guía conceptual y metodológica para el desarrollo y la planificación del sector turismo (Vol. 25). United Nations Publications. http://www.eclac.cl/cgi-bin/getProd.asp?xml=/publicaciones/xml/2/13092/P13092.xml&xsl=/ilpes/tpl/p9f.xsl

[7] Torres-Sovero, C., González, J. A., Martín-López, B., & Kirkby, C. A. (2011). Social–ecological factors influencing tourist satisfaction in three ecotourism lodges in the southeastern Peruvian Amazon. *Tourism Management*, 33, 545-552.

[8] Álvarez, Á. P., Segura, M. D. G. & Campos, H. G. (2012). Ecoturismo y educación ambiental para la sustentabilidad en la reserva de la biosfera de Los Tuxtlas (México). *Turismo y Desarrollo Local*, 5, 1-24.

[9] Reyes Ruiz, F.J. & Castro Rosales, E.A. (2008). Educación para la sustentabilidad en áreas protegidas [online]. Available at: http://www.comie.org.mx/congreso/memoria/v10/pdf/area_tematica_03/ponencias/1043 -F.pdf> [Accessed 7 June 2010].

[10] Lee, W.H. & Moscardo, G. (2005). Understanding the impact of ecotourism resort experiences on tourists' environmental attitudes and behavioural intentions. *Journal of Sustainable Tourism*, 13, 546-565.

[11] Casas Jurado, A. C., Soler Domingo, A., & Jaime Pastor, V. (2012). El turismo comunitario como instrumento de erradicación de la pobreza: potencialidades para su desarrollo en Cuzco (Perú). *Cuadernos de Turismo*, 30, 91-108.

[12] Coria, J. & Calfucura, E. (2012). Ecotourism and the development of indigenous communities: The good, the bad, and the ugly. *Ecological Economics*, 73, 47-55.

[13] González-Pérez, F. & Cubero-Pardo, P. (2010). Efecto de actividades turísticas sobre el comportamiento de fauna representativa de las Islas Galápagos, Ecuador. *Latin American Journal of Aquatic Research*, 38, 493-500.

[14] Chen Mok, S. & García Cousin, K. (2009). Puntarenas y el turismo: ¿Qué ha pasado con la "Perla del Pacífico"? *Inter Sedes,* 8, 109-131.

[15] Matarrita-Cascante, D., Brennan, M.A. & Luloff, A.E, (2010). Community agency and sustainable tourism development: the case of La Fortuna, Costa Rica. *Journal of Sustainable Tourism*, 18, 735–756

[16] Dachary, A. C., & Arnaiz Burne, S. M. (2009). Pueblos originarios y turismo en América Latina: La conquista continúa. *Estudios y perspectivas en turismo*, 18, 69-91.

[17] Borman, R. (2008). Ecotourism and conservation: the Cofan experience. *CAB International*, 6, 21-29.

[18] Stronza, A. & Gordillo, J. (2008). Community views of ecotourism. *Annals of Tourism Research*, 35, 448-468.

[19] Ospina, G. (2006). War and ecotourism in the National Parks of Colombia: Some reflections on the public risk and adventure. *International Journal of Tourism Research*, 8, 241-246.

[20] Ojeda, D. (2011). Whose Paradise? Conservation, tourism and land grabbing in Tayrona Natural Park, Colombia. In *International Conference Global Land Grabbing Conference Proceedings*, 6-8.

[21] Weaver, D. B. & Lawton, L. J. (2007). Twenty years on: The state of contemporary ecotourism research. *Tourism Management*, 28, 1168-1179.

The current Spanish feed-in tariff system. An economic and financial analysis of solar photovoltaic plants installed in Extremadura

P. MILANÉS-MONTERO
University of Extremadura, Faculty of Economics. Spain
A. ARROYO-FARRONA
University of Extremadura, Faculty of Economics. Spain
E. PÉREZ-CALDERÓN
University of Extremadura, Faculty of Business and Tourism Studies Spain
F.J. ORTEGA-ROSSELL
University of Extremadura, Faculty of Business and Tourism Studies Spain

ABSTRACT

Unpredictable changes in macroeconomic variables have made investors who installed photovoltaic power plants in Spain to look for the way of maintaining the desirable level of profitability with lower prices of sale, higher taxes and financial costs, etc. It would be necessary for solar photovoltaic systems to achieve grid parity or become cost-competitive with conventional electric energy prices. The objectives of this paper are the following: first of all, to elaborate a map of photovoltaic plants which have been installed in Extremadura, at least, since 2007 and to classify them by location, technology, installed power capacity, type of solar cells, climate zone and regulation; secondly, to analyze the economic and financial performance of a sample of this plants during the period 2007-2011 taking into consideration the evolution of rules and regulations regarding the economic incentives to this industry.

1. INTRODUCTION

Numerous initiatives have been taken in recent years on a domestic, European and international level to promote energy saving and to invest in renewable energy sources such as photovoltaic (PV) energy. A series of measures have been put forward in all these proposals with a view to encouraging investment in renewable energies, on the other hand, to putting into practice actions that increase energy saving not only by the production sectors themselves, but also by the general public. This paper focuses on grid solar PV connected systems, in which energy is produced as a direct result of the conversion of the energy of the solar ray, using the so-called PV effect [1].

Concerning the Solar PV energy in the world, the information provided by the European Photovoltaic Industry Association (EPIA) in 2012 show that China was the top non-European PV market in 2011, with 2.2GW installed, followed by USA, with 1.9GW. Nevertheless, in terms of global cumulative installed capacity, Europe still leads the way with more than 51GW installed. This represents about 75% of the world's total PV cumulative capacity. Next in the ranking are Japan (5GW) and the USA (4.4GW), followed by China (3.1GW) which reached its first GW in 2011. Many of the markets outside Europe, in particular China, the USA and Japan, but also Australia (1.3GW) and India (0.46GW), have addressed only a very small part of their enormous potential; several countries from large sunbelt regions like Africa, the Middle East, South East Asia and Latin America are on the brink of starting their development. Even so, the cumulative installed capacity outside Europe almost doubled between 2010 and 2011, demonstrating the ongoing rebalancing between Europe and the rest of the world and reflecting more closely the patterns in electricity consumption. Europe has dominated the global PV market for years but the rest of the world clearly has the biggest potential for growth. Driven by local and global energy demand, the fastest PV growth is expected to continue in China and India, followed by Southeast Asia, Latin America and the Middle East and North African countries. China took first place among these countries with 2.2GW, followed by the USA with 1.9GW and Japan with 1.3GW [2].

International Energy Agency (IAE) analyzes the market trends and projections to 2017 with reference to the renewable energies in its report from 2012 and find that in a range of countries, with China, India and Brazil emerging as leaders in deployment, the Global renewable electricity production is increasing. In this report it is recognized that much of the renewable energy success has stemmed from economic incentives and significant policy effort by countries, particularly those in The Organisation for Economic Co-operation and Development (OECD). Massive investment has taken place on a global scale, with costs for most technologies falling steadily. As a result, renewable energy technologies are becoming more economically attractive in those countries [3].

A steady increase in hydropower and the rapid expansion of wind and solar power has cemented the position of renewables as an indispensable part of the global energy mix; by 2035, renewables account for almost one-third of total electricity output. Solar grows more rapidly than any other renewable technology. Renewables become the world's second-largest source of power generation by 2015 (roughly half that of coal) and, by 2035, they approach coal as the primary source of global electricity [4].

With reference to the current situation of Spanish solar PV industry, since 1998 Spanish PV generators can get a fix tariff. The rest of electricity coming from renewable energy technologies can be sold in the electricity spot market getting an additional premium or can opt for a fixed-FIT [5]. Others authors [6], estate that it is difficult to conclude whether government support using Feed-in-Tariff (FITs) is expensive or not. The authors distinguishes two different interpretations of the cost of the system: One of them might well be the additional costs paid by consumers for renewable compared to conventional electricity and the share of these renewable energy sources promotion costs in their electricity bill; other interpretations would be if the social cost of renewable energy sources promotion are worth paying, given its social, economic and environmental benefits.

Regarding the Spanish region of Extremadura, the exploitation of solar PV energy has undergone major development since the Renewable Energies Plan (REP) 2005-2010 was implemented [7]. However, all of this has been made possible by extremely high incentives that encouraged investment and that, after achieving the aims of the REP, were cut back by both the Ministry and the National Energy Commission.

If activity in the sector is to remain high after the abolition of the incentives and the subsidies, it is essential to control and to reduce production costs, to enable not only the small facilities but also the major power plants in the zone to be competitive, bringing the sale price into line with that of conventional energies; if this is done, it will be possible to achieve ongoing growth for the sector, with all the advantages that this entails for the economy in these regions, in terms of creating employment and wealth.

In this scenario, our main goal is to examine whether in solar PV plants installed in the Spanish region of Extremadura have been a drop of their return on investment since 2007 to 2011, given the evolution of governmental incentives available. To achieve this objective, we construct a database with the main characteristics of these plants (location, technology, installed power capacity, climate zone, types of solar cells, and regulation), based on different information sources, and elaborate a map with the software MapPpoint. In addition, we analyze the economic and financial structure of these firms and the evolution of the main economic and financial and ratios.

With this purpose, the article starts with a theoretical background in which it is revised the situation of solar PV energy in Extremadura, in Spain and in the world, and it is justified the importance of analyzing the current economic and financial situation of the installations, taking into consideration the unpredictable regulatory framework. We focused on grid connected PV systems on-floor. Secondly, we present the used method by means of the definition of the sample, the variables, and the research methodology and we show the obtained results. Finally, we show the main conclusions of the study and future researches.

2. BACKGROUND

2.1 Solar PV energy in Spain. The region of Extremadura

Focusing on Spain, due to the fact that this country gests a large number of hours of sunshine, it is one of the more important producers of solar PV energy in the world. Nevertheless, this capacity is not growing so much since 2008 because of the reduction in subsidies from the government which, as we are going to analyze in the next epigraph, were finally removed in 2012 [8].

With reference to the solar PV energy production in Spain, after the sharp increase in solar PV energy in 2007, a gradual slowing down affected the sector throughout 2009, not only as a result of the regulatory standards that applied to these activities, but also as a consequence of the world economic crisis, a downturn in the United States economy, an increase in the price of oil products, commodities & raw materials, and the appreciation of the Euro.

The latest data that it has been possible to obtain from the Renewable Energies Plan 2011-2020 concerning the situation in Spain, brings to light the fact that Spain comes second to Germany in the world ranking where installed power is concerned [9]. The total accumulated power in 2010 was 3.787MW.

In the case of Extremadura, the Extremadura Energy Agency [10], states that in 2008, around 90% of the total power available until then was put into operation in that Region. To be specific, in 2008 an electricity production of 347GWh in Extremadura, all of this coming from PV facilities connected to the grid in special regime.

In 2009, this energy production stood at 880GWh. Furthermore, according to the Annual Report issued by the Photovoltaic Industry Association [11], with respect to covering the demand for electricity, the situation in Extremadura repeated itself once again in 2011, catering for nearly 16% of the demand.

Figure 1 show how the cumulative installed power developed in the Autonomous Region of Extremadura in the period 2006-2010. At the end of 2010, there were PV facilities in Extremadura connected to the grid, with a total power of 470MW.

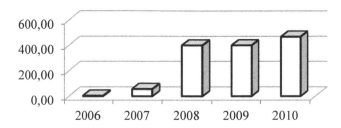

Figure 1. Installed capacity (MW) [10]

However, a payment cut of more than 30% that has affected the PV industry in Spain has enhanced the struggle that the Spanish Photovoltaic Union (UNEF) has been involved in as it endeavours to prevent cutbacks in the bonuses and tax increases. These activities that are being carried out by the Government to try to reduce the rate deficit are having an adverse effect on the profitability of the sector, as will be seen in the descriptive empirical study shown below.

What is a reality is the fact that the rapid increase in renewable energy is underpinned by falling technology cost, rising fossil-fuel prices and carbon pricing, but mainly by continued subsides. Subsidy measures to support new renewable energy projects need to be adjusted over time as capacity increases and as the costs of renewable technologies fall, to avoid excessive burdens on governments and consumers [8].

In the next epigraph we are going to analyze the evolution of the regulatory framework, what is going to support our empirical analysis.

2.2 Feed –in tariffs in Spain. Evolution of the regulatory framework

Regarding public support for PV, we can evaluate the annual cost of public support for PV from an extensive policy review [12]. This cost is divided into different measure categories: investment subsidies and loans and market incentives, feed-in tariffs and subsidies for R&D, and was considered against installed capacities. No country can be said to have a perfect policy since each one is a particular case (different electricity mixes, different energy dependences, different electricity prices, different involvement of the Governments, etc.). Indeed, despite the participation of the government in the initial phase of renewable energies is necessary for securing their development and protecting them from direct competition from conventional technologies, there is not a consensus about which mechanism is the most efficient [13].

Nevertheless, focusing on feed-in tariff, it has proven to be the most effective government incentive program for renewable technologies [14]. The feed-in-tariff guarantees a competitive price for the producers of renewable energies electricity over a long period of time thus reducing risks with revenues. Other support measures include tax incentives, investment subsidies, low interest loans, etc. [04]. This author point out the necessity of long-term policies and strong commercialization strategies to bring the new energy technologies to breakeven point. He recognizes the complexity of assessing the true cost of making new energy technologies fully competitive.

What is a cause of considerable concern for the time being is to delimit the amount of public support to renewable energies. In regard to it, some authors suggest that the amount of subsidies to the utility companies, in the form of tax exemptions, tariff-in schemes, etc., could be planned according to the predicted evolution of concentration solar power (CSP) electricity costs [15]. Studies on the CSP electricity cost evolution can be of great significance from the point of view of energy policy planning, since the International Energy Agency (IEA) roadmaps and others elaborated by prestigious institutions, forecast that by 2050 about 10% of the electricity will be produced by CSP systems. However, policymakers must recognize that dropping costs in solar technology will not automatically resolve the energy problems [15].

With reference to the success of countries using feed-in tariffs, it has several reasons [16]:

- FiT offers long-term security for investors through guaranteed and fixed tariffs for long periods on a relative high level (high price per kilowatt hour).
- The existence of well-built financial subsidy programs.
- Regional investments towards economic and social welfare.
- Technology-specific and location dependent differentiation.
- Stable governmental regulations

In this regard, some authors analyze the success factors of the mechanism that promote renewable energy in the two European countries that are leaders in terms of installed power and production capacity in renewable energy in EU. They find that, in both cases, the development of the renewable energy entails [13]:

a) an element of environmental protection (by means of the reduction of pollutant emission;
b) a considerable increase of employment;
c) a positive contribution to GDP;

d) the development research, investment and innovation with the consequent creation of important industrial fabrication sector. Therefore, the establishment of a feed-in tariff system allows for the development of these production technologies (especially wind and PV solar energy).

Regarding Spanish support for PV, in 1998 Royal Decree 2818/1998, dated 23rd December, regulated, for the very first time, the implementation of an incentive system for the facilities based upon renewable energies and waste. The aim is to enable renewable energies to increase their contribution to the energy demand in Spain.

In our opinion it is very important to know how public support measures and cost reduction can operate. Regarding this topic, Avril et al. [12] establish that PV costs are intended to decrease since this technology is rather young compared to the competitive ones like coal, gas or nuclear power plants.

Therefore, on the basis of the ideas developed above, and taking into consideration the main pieces of regulation since 1998 and during the period of studio of Spanish PV plants located in Extremadura, further research about the economic consequences of those rules and regulations is especially important taking into account, mainly, Technology and Solar Irradiance Zone.

3. METHODOLOGY

3.1 Population and sample

We are in agree with Lesourd [1] with respect to the fact that it is somewhat difficult to obtain reliable historical data for PV systems. There are many sources, which are only roughly in agreement with each other; earlier data are somewhat approximate, because for a long time, the PV industry had not reached mass production until at least the mid-1980s. Even now, we are still finding difficulty in obtaining actual data about these Plants.

Given this fact, our population, which has been selected from Iberian Balance-sheets Analysis System (SABI) and Mercantile Register, consists of 62 grid connected PV systems on floor installed in Extremadura from 2007. Most of the population, 61,29% consist of PV plants located in the province of Badajoz and covered in Royal Decree 661/2007. The 25,81% is integrated by plants from Badajoz and covered in Royal Decree 1578/2008. The plants of the population located in the province of Cáceres are only around a 13% of the whole population, the 6,45 covered in Royal Decree 661/2007 and the other 6,45% covered in Royal Decree 1578/2008.

The composition of the final sample, integrated by 44 PV plants, those whose managers answered the questionnaire design to obtain data about the main characteristics of PV plants from Extremadura. As we can see, both compositions are similar, taking into consideration the province (Caceres and Badajoz) and the regulation (Royal Decree 661/2007 and Royal Decree 1578/2008).

3.2 Variables definition

Given the influence of the Solar Irradiance Zones and the Technology on the regulation, these are two of the variables used to describe the characteristics of our sample. In regard to the Location variable, Dusonchet & Telaretti [17] perform an economic analysis of the main support mechanism that are implemented in eastern European Union (EU) countries based on the calculation of the cash flow, the Net Present value and the Internal Rate of Return indices and find that in particular, the value of the solar irradiation, which is very different from different points of the same country, can influence the conclusions.

Moreover, we use the variables Regulation, Types of Solar Cells, Power Installed Capacity and Province. Table 1 shows the values of these variables, which have been obtained from several sources like SABI, Mercantile Register from Cáceres and Badajoz, and a telephone survey.

Regarding the Solar Irradiance Zone variable, Figure 2 shows the five solar zones in Spain taking into consideration the average daily solar irradiation in units of kWh/m^2 per day. As we can see, Extremadura is located in Zones V and IV. Therefore, it is one of the regions of Spain with more hours of sunshine.

With respect to the technology used, we distinguee among fixed PV installations, single axis trackers and dual axis trackers. The trackers are used to minimize the angle of incidence between the incoming sunlight and a PV panel and, therefore, to increase the amount of energy produced.

Concerning the Types of Solar Cells, the three most common types of them are distinguished by the type of silicon used in them: monocrystalline, polycrystalline and amorphous (amorfo thin film solar PV module). Monocrystalline cells produce the most electricity per unit area and amorphous cells the least. Polycrystalline cells contain many crystals than monocrystalline and, therefore, they have a less perfect surface (they absorb slightly less solar energy and produce slightly less electricity per square metre, although these cells are generally cheaper). In order to maximize solar electricity generation for a given area, the best option is to select the most efficient monocrystalline PV panels you can afford. On the other hand, to cover a given area at the lowest cost, then the best option is to install amorphous panels. If you are concerned with maximizing your solar electricity generation for the lowest cost, then it is best to look at the cost-effectiveness of a panel regardless of its technology by examining its cost per rated production [18]:

PV panel cost (€) / Rated PV panel output (watts)

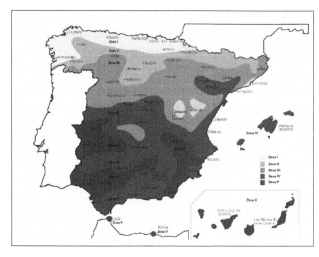

Zona I: H < 3,8
Zona II: 3,8 ≤ H < 4,2
Zona III: 4,2 ≤ H < 4,6
Zona IV: 4,6 ≤ H < 5,0
Zona V: H ≥ 5,0

H (kWh/m²·día) es la Radiación Media Diaria

Fuente: INM. Radiación Media Diaria. Generado a partir de isolíneas de radiación solar global anual sobre superficie horizontal.

Figure 2. Solar radiation map of Spain

Finally, with reference to the Power Installed Capacity variable, its values have been fixed taking into consideration the installed capacity established in Royal Decree 661/2007 due to the fact that the tariff depends on that capacity.

Table 1. Variables definition of the PV plants

Variable	Values
Solar Irradiance Zones	-Zone I: $H<3,8$ -Zone II: $3,8 \leq H \leq 4,2$ -Zone III: $4,2 \leq H \leq 4,6$ -Zone IV: $4,6 \leq H \leq 5,0$ -Zone V: $H \geq 5,0$
Technology	-Fixed PV panels -Single axis trackers -Dual axis trackers
Regulation	-Royal Decree 661/2007 -Royal Decree 1578/2008
Types of solar cells	-Monocrystalline -Polycrystalline -Amorphous
Power installed capacity	-P<100kW -100kW<P<10MW -10MW<P<50MW
Province	-Cáceres -Badajoz

Regarding the variables used to analyze economic and financial structure of solar PV plants installed in Extremadura and to observe the evolution of the return on investment from 2008 to 2011, taking into consideration the evolution of rules and regulations concerning the government incentives, Table 2 shows their definitions. Their values have been obtained from SABI.

Table 2. Variables definition to analyze economic and financial structure

Variable	Definition
NCA/TA	Non-current Assets / Total Assets
CF/CA	Cash-Flow / Current Assets
FC/R	Financial Costs / Revenue

LEVER	Leverage = Debt / Equity
ROI	Return on investment = Profit Before Interest and Tax / Total Investment

4. RESULTS

4.1 Map of PV plants included in the sample and their technical characteristics

Based on the information about the defined variables provided by the sources described above, we elaborate a map of PV plants installed in floor in Extremadura by means of MapPoint Software and a contingency table, using SPSS program, in which we classify the sample in regard to the main characteristics of the plants. Figures 3 and 4 show the concentration of most of the solar PV systems on floor in the South of the Spanish region of Extremadura.

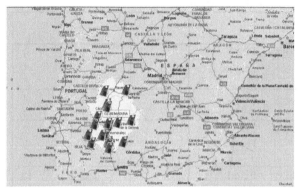 

Figure 3. Sample concentration in Spain   **Figure 4. Sample in Extremadura**

With reference to the main characteristics of the sample, Figure 5 show that most of the grid connected PV plants were installed with the purpose of getting the incentives regulated in Royal Decree 661/2007, and Figures 3 and 4 reveals that Badajoz, in the South of Extremadura, is the place of the region where most of the plants were installed.

This fact can also be observed in the table above (Table 3), which, in addition, shows the distribution of the sample by Climate Zone, Types of solar cells, and Technology. As we can see, only a tiny minority of the plants is located in Zone IV, and the vast majority of them belongs to Zone V. This circumstance is very important because Royal Decree-Low 14/2010 limits the operating time eligible for premium of grid connected PV plants taking into account the solar zone, being Zone 5 the zone with the greater number of hours eligible for premium.

Moreover, the Royal Decree-Low 14/2010, also limits the operating time eligible for premium taking into consideration the Technology, being the dual axis trackers structures the technology with the largest number of hours eligible for premium and fixed structures the technology with the fewest number of hours with premium.

In our sample, around 65% of the plants are fixed PV installations and around 35% has dual axis trackers. These last ones are the most benefited by the regulation and, apart from that, the amount of energy that they produce is higher.

Nevertheless, investors from Extremadura decided to install fixed structures, which is cheaper than trackers ones. Other advantages of this technology are the mechanical simplicity and, therefore, the lower installation and maintenance costs. However, fixed structures are not as efficient as trackers ones so it is required a large number of panels to increase the efficiency. This is not a problem in Extremadura because it is one of the largest regions of Spain.

Regarding the types of solar cells, despite in 2007 most of the plants were installed with cells of monocrystalline silicon, in 2008 all of them used polycrystalline silicon. This circumstance might have been due to the fact that Royal Decree 1578/2008 regulate lower premium than Royal Decree 661/2007, therefore, investors might have decided to installed cheaper type of cells, despite its lower production.

Table 3. Sample distribution by climate zone, rules and regulations, types of solar cells, and technology

ROYAL_DECREE Types of solar cells				ZONE		
				IV	V	Total
1578/2008		Technology	Fixed	2	2	4
			Dual axis	0	1	1
		Total		2	3	5
	Polycrystalline silicon	Technology	Fixed	3	1	4
		Total		3	1	4
661/2007		Technology	Fixed	1	1	2
			Dual axis	2	7	9
		Total		3	8	11
	Monocrystallyne silicon	Technology	Fixed		18	18
		Total			18	18
	Silicon Monocrystalline and Polycrystalline	Technology	Dual axis		4	4
		Total			4	4
	Polycrystalline silicon	Technology	Fixed		1	1
			Dual axis		1	1
		Total			2	2

Finally, Table 4 shows the power installed capacity, being it, in almost all the cases, lower that 10 MW. This fact let the investors to get the higher premiums regulated in Royal Decree 661/2007.

What is unquestionable, on the basis of the analysis developed above, is that investors who decided to install grid solar PV connected systems in Extremadura with the objective of getting the government premiums, selected a specific technology, solar cells, solar zone and power installed capacity taking into consideration rules and regulation approved by the Government.

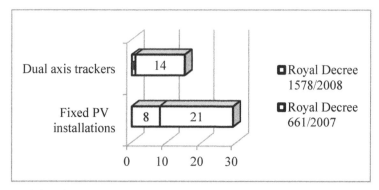

Figure 5. Distribution of the sample by Royal Decree and Technology

Table 4. Sample distribution by power installed capacity, taking into consideration rules, regulations, and technology

Royal Decree			Power installed capacity			
			Power <100 kW	100 kW < Power < 10 MW	10 MW < Power < 50 MW	Total
1578/2008	Technology	Fixed	2	5	1	8
		Dual axis	0	1	0	1
	Total		2	6	1	9
661/2007	Technology	Fixed	18	3		21
		Dual axis	2	12		14
	Total		20	15		35

Nevertheless, by the time being, those rules and regulations are not the same ones than six years ago. Therefore, this situation has become a cause of considerable concern to the investors who have the desire of maintaining the return of their investment and don't know how to achieve this objective.

4.2 Economic and financial analysis

Given the circumstance explained above, and with the purpose of analyzing the economic and financial structure of solar PV plants in the sample, firstly, we develop a vertical and horizontal analysis of their balance Sheets and Profit and Loose Accounts. We use descriptive statistics (means, standard deviation, minimum, and maximum) for numeric variables in our set of data, described above.

Table 5 shows that the economic structure of these plants reveals that most of the total assets are noncurrent assets, and that the ratio "noncurrent assets/total assets" is increasing year by year since 2008. Therefore, capital costs are the most important costs that these plants have to assume.

With this respect, Ayompe et al. [19] state that significant decreases in capital costs might occur, therefore, if many buyers and sellers entered the market and information were more freely available. In our opinion, this is the main problem of Spanish electric system.

The indirect approach given to the cost control problem proved ineffective in preventing the economic impact of the production capacity growth occurred in 2009. This mechanism increase the cost of the electricity system and, together with the tariff deficit, led to the adoption of aggressive and retroactive actions which severely questioned the trustability of future investments in the Spanish renewable energy sector. The main issue is shown to be the management of the cost problem generated within the previous legal framework [20].

Regarding the composition of the current assets, Table 5 shows that there has been a dramatic increase in the percentage of cash-flow that belongs to current assets. The reason of it is that there has been a decrease in the Leverage and, because of it, in the financial costs. Apart from that, these firms don't have existences due to the fact that the energy generated doesn't is stored and, in addition, the financial assets have also experimented a drop. All these circumstances have made cash have more weight in the current assets.

After this vertical and horizontal analysis of the balance Sheets and Profit and Loose Accounts of the PV plants that belong to the sample, we analyze the evolution of the Return on Investment Ratio.

Table 5. Evolution of the economic and financial structure

	N	Minimum	Maximum	Mean	S. deviation
NCA/TA_08	15	35	84	73.67	14.387
NCA/TA_09	19	40.85	91.28	83.4666	16.01269
NCA/TA_10	20	42.38	98.07	84.8619	15.14160
NCA/TA_11	17	48.97	95.25	87.1730	14.78139
N valid	14				
	N	Minimum	Maximum	Mean	S. deviation
CF/CA_08	15	-1	65	11.93	15.324
CF/CA_09	18	-9.77	91.36	48.9116	21.09388
CF/CA_10	19	-88.20	229.60	57.4161	58.25886
CF/CA_11	16	-1.67	106.82	71.5227	28.89164
N valid	14				
	N	Minimum	Maximum	Mean	S. deviation
FC/R_08	14	0	85	67.53	28.657
FC/R_09	16	0	57	45.39	21.094
FC/R_10	17	.00	78.48	40.2936	18.88370
FC/R_11	14	1	40	32.80	11.687
N valid	13				
	N	Minimum	Maximum	Mean	S. deviation
LEVER_08	14	1	219	124.79	84.995
LEVER_09	16	-106	184	93.04	85.853
LEVER_10	16	-52	162	68.61	66.600
LEVER_11	15	1	257	73.88	67.593
N valid	14				

Bernal-Agustín & Dufo-López [21] developed and economical analysis whose results shown that with the prices available in that moment, investment in a grid connected PV systems was generally profitability. However, the high Pay-Back Time (not less than 9 years) could dissuade investors. A slight reduction in the available incentives (a reduction in the reference or average tariff available then) could result in the investment never being recuperated.

Table 6. Return on Investment (ROI) evolution

	N	Minimum	Maximum	Mean	S. Deviation
ROI_08	14	0	11	3.02	2.542
ROI_09	17	-6.07	8.07	5.3422	3.37818
ROI_10	18	-3.06	8.49	4.9182	2.56792
ROI_11	15	-.48	12.58	4.3994	2.58920
N valid	13				

With reference to our sample, as Table 6 shows, there has been a decrease in the ROI since 2010, which might have been due to the limitation of equivalent hours by the Royal Decree-Law 14/2010.

In this regard, we can think that limiting the operating time of new GCPVS (RDL14/2010) may discourage from increasing energy production and/or improving efficiency [20]. In any case, we are in agreement with these authors regarding the idea that relaxing this constraint should be accompanied by further control measures aimed at preventing the opportunistic repowering of existing.

5. CONCLUSIONS AND FUTURE WORK

In this paper it has been proved the idea defended by Chi-Jen [15] about the fact that the rapid growth in PV deployment in recent years is largely policy-driven and such rapid growth would not be sustainable unless governments continue to expand financial incentives and policy mandates, as well as address regulatory and market barriers.

Nevertheless, in Spain, in the last years, the variable and uncertainty Spanish support scheme has been being a cause of considerable concern for the investors instead of providing him high levels of security by guaranteeing revenue stability to high initial capital investments.

With this respect, we think that this certainty may particularly apply to the short or medium terms as in the long run fixed feed-in-tariffs may be unsustainable either because of high cost-inefficiencies involved or because they are not compatible with a liberalised, competitive market and a system of harmonized, renewable energy policies within the EU. Apart from that, one of the negative aspects of the system is that costs are almost entirely paid by only one type of actor, consumers, reducing their economic surplus without general knowledge on this [06].

On the basis of these ideas, we have elaborated, firstly, a map of solar PV installations from Extremadura with information about their main technical characteristics, their solar zone and the rules and regulations that determine their revenues based on a telephone survey. Secondly, we have analyzed their return on investment ratio during the period 2008-2011 to check the influence of the dramatic drop in incentives on this ratio.

The found results are consistent with the comparative financial analysis developed by Muhammad-Sukki et al. [22], who illustrates that the ROI in other countries are exceptionally higher than the one in the UK (between 6% and 11%). The authors suggest that the UK Government should consider opting for a higher generation tariff than the proposed one, (e.g. between 25p and 35p per kWh produced, depending on the band) to ensure growth in the UK solar PV industry.

Our main recommendation as future work in this regard is the necessity of further research into the generation process in solar PV plants in Extremadura, the cost involved and the way in which consumption takes place, thereby allowing for ongoing improvement, while at the same time making them more competitive and increasing their profit margins by adapting them to the market economy system conditions that will gradually be removing protective measures in the sector, such as the sale price bonus that, up until the present time, has provided most of the profit obtained. Nevertheless, the most important limitation found in this work and in future ones, is the difficult to obtain reliable data or PV plants.

REFERENCES LIST

[1] Lesourd, J.B. (2001). Solar photovoltaic systems: the economics of a renewable energy resource. *Environmental Modeling & Software.* 16, 147-156.

[2] European Photovoltaic Industry Association, EPIA (2012). *Global Market Outlook for Photovoltaics until 2016.* Available on: http://www.epia.org/news/ publications/. Visited 15.10.2012.

[3] International Energy Agency (IEA), 2012b. *Medium-Term Renewable Energy Market Report,* 2012. Available on: http://www.iea.org/textbase/npsum/ mtrenew2012Sum.pdf> Visited 17.12.12.

[4] Lund, P.H. (2011). Boosting new renewable technologies towards grid parity-Economic and policy aspects. *Renewable Energy.* 36, 2776-2784.

[5] Challenberg-Rodriguez, J., & Haas, R. (2012). Fixed feed-in tariff versus premium: A review of the current Spanish system. *Renewable and Sustainable Energy Reviews.* 16(1), 293-305.

[6] Del Río, P., & Gual, M.A. (2007). An integrated assessment of the feed-in-tariff system in Spain. *Energy Policy.* 35, 994-1012.

[7] Institute for Diversification and Saving of Energy, IDAE (2005). *Renewable Energies Plan 2005-2010.* Available on: http://www.idae.es/index.php/mod.pags/ mem.detalle-/id.14/relmenu.12. Visited 15.10.12.

[8] International Energy Agency (IEA), 2012a. *World Energy Outlook, 2012. Executive Summary.* Available on: http://www.iea.org/publications/ freepublications/publication/English.pdf. Visited 17.12.12.

[9] Institute for Diversification and Saving of Energy, IDAE (2009). *Renewable Energies Plan 2011-2020.* Available on: http://www.idae.es/index.php/id.670/ relmenu.303/mod.pags-/mem.detalle. Visited 15.10.12.

[10] Extremadura Energy Agency, AGENEX (2011). *Energía solar fotovoltaica. Situación en Extremadura.* Available on: http://mail.agenex.org/es/dptos/ departamento-de-energias-renovables/67 -energia-solar-fotovoltaica.html. Visited 03.12.12.

[11] Photovoltaic Industry Association, PIA (2011). *Informe anual 2011. Hacia el crecimiento sostenido de la fotovoltaica en España.* Available on: http://unef.es/2011/07/informe-anual-2011/. Visited 10.12.12.

[12] Avril, S., Mansilla, C., Busson, M., & Lemaire, T. (2012). Photovoltaic energy policy: Financial estimation and performance comparison of the public support in five representative countries. *Energy Policy.* 51, 244-258.

[13] García-Álvarez, R.M., & Mariz-Pérez, M.T. (2012). Analysis of the success of feed-in tariff for renewable energy promotion mechanism in the EU: lessons from Germany and Spain. *Procedia-Social and Behavioral Sciences.* 65, 52-57.

[14] Wiginton, L.K., Nguyen, H.T., & Pearce, J.M. (2010). Quantifying rooftop solar photovoltaic potential for regional renewable energy policy. *Computers, Environment and Urban Systems.* 34, 345-357.

[15] Chi-Jen, Y. (2010). Reconsidering solar grid parity. *Energy Policy.* 38 (7), 3270–3273.

[16] Ayoub, N., & Naka Yuji, N. (2012). Governmental intervention approaches to promote renewable energies. Special emphasis on Japanese feed-in tariff. *Energy Policy.* 43, 191-201.

[17] Dusonchet, L., & Telaretti, E. (2010). Economic analysis of different supporting policies for the production of electrical energy by solar photovoltaic in eastern European Union countries. *Energy Policy.* 38, 4011-4020.

[18] Canada Mortgage and Housing Corporation (CMHC). *Photovoltaic Systems* Available on: http://www.cmhc-schl.gc.ca/en/co/maho/enefcosa/enefcosa_003.cfm. Visited 05.05.13.

[19] Ayompe, L.M., Duffy, A., McCormack, S.J., & Conlon, M. (2010). Projected costs of a grid-connected domestic PV system under different scenarios in Ireland, using measured data from a trial installation. *Energy Policy.* 38, 3731-3743.

[20] De la Hoz, J., Martín, H., Ballart, J. Córcoles, & F., Graells, M. (2013). Evaluating the new control structure for the promotion of grid connected photovoltaic systems in Spain: Performance analysis of the period 2008-2010. *Renewable and Sustainable Energy Reviews.* 19, 541-554.

[21] Bernal-Agustín, J.L. & Dufo-López, R. (2006). Economical and environmental analysis of grid connected photovoltaic systems in Spain. *Renewable Energy.* 31(8), 1107-1128.

[22] Muhammad-Sukki, F., Ramirez-Iniguez, R., Bakar-Munir, A., Mohd-Yasin, S.H., Abu-Bakar, S.H., McMeekin, S.G., & Stewart, B.G. (2013). Revised feed-in tariff for solar photovoltaic in the United Kingdom: A cloudy future ahead. *Energy Policy.* 52 (January), 832-838

Lightning Source UK Ltd.
Milton Keynes UK
UKOW06f1030020315

247091UK00005B/89/P